PUBLISHERS ON PUBLISHING

Inside India's Book Business

In this book, 65 insiders—all from within India's enduring publishing establishments, emerging niches and the surrounding ecosystem—share views, trends and stories on Indian publishing.

In interviews and short essays, key themes and issues facing India's vibrant book business across various genre and languages, are discussed. Local and regional publishers, independents, MNCs and family-run concerns—all sit within its covers, alongside burgeoning self-publishing and app-based publishing startups. In the process there is some navel gazing as well as blue sky thinking by the contributors.

Publishers on Publishing is lucid and informative, with emphasis on individual and organizational journeys and views. The Editor's Preface and Introduction provide the context and frame to view and review India's vast and varied publishing landscape.

Authors, editors, publishers and bibliophiles, will find in it much to know, debate and share.

NITASHA DEVASAR has spent 24 years in academic publishing and is Managing Director, Taylor & Francis India. She is Vice President, Association of Publishers in India (API) and sits on the FICCI Publishing Committee. Nitasha is Advisor to the Women Leadership Forum of Asia (WLFA) and was featured as one of Asia's Women of Substance 2017 by Channel News Asia (CNA).

PUBLISHERS ON PUBLISHING

Inside India's Book Business

edited by

NITASHA DEVASAR

ALL ABOUT BOOK PUBLISHING

First published 2018
by All About Book Publishing
406, Sant Nagar, East of Kailash,
New Delhi 110065, India

ISBN: 978-81-936594-0-3

Typeset in Bembo 9.75/14
by 3P Solutions, New Delhi
Printed and bound by Avantika Printers Private Limited

CONTENTS

PREFACE

Books on India's publishing industry are few and far between. Ironic for an industry considered both vibrant and with growth potential, in a country that sees its future as a knowledge economy.

This one is both experiential and experimental. It evolved from a continual engagement, within the community, on the need for a volume on Indian publishing, and an increasing realization of the lack of a wider understanding of the role of publishing in today's information overloaded, digital world. This got me thinking of all that I, as a publisher, would want to showcase in a book on publishing in India and once I had that down, the book just took on a life of its own. On top of the list, were insider views and the representation of a wide spectrum of publishing voices that were usually separated by time and space. The idea was to get individual views and experiences and not a macro sweep of the industry; to cover old ground anew as well as current and emerging trends; and get as many different sorts of publishing and allied activities within its ambit, as possible. The challenge was not just how to do this quickly, accessibly, and in a non-partisan manner but also a more fundamental one to be found in how we publishers view ourselves.

The Indian market for publishing is quite fragmented and that has over the last 70 years created both challenges and opportunities. As a result, many publishing universes coexist and rarely come together. English language publishers see themselves as distinct from those in Indian Languages and the latter return the favour. Within the English universe too, local players and multinational ones are separated by size, scale and often perspective. There are niche players, independents, family businesses, and more recently the tech. innovators and disruptors, challenging traditional publishing in varying ways. The allied industries, printing and publishing services, the professional editors and designers, literary agencies and fairs and festivals, all tend to stay in separate yet overlapping cocoons.

As any insider knows, there is rarely one or even a few views on the industry and publishers are yet to find a cohesive voice on the external challenges that impact publishing. How then could we coherently capture the diverse insights and divergent views, that have kept the industry growing at a healthy 20 per cent yearly, in spite of adverse external conditions?

The last few years have been tough ones for publishers of all hues. The bulk, 94 per cent according to the Nielsen Report*, of India's publishing (at least in English) is educational and hence dependent on government policies and on funding of education, both school and higher education and research. In a youthful and aspirational nation like ours, access to education is politically charged and hence susceptible to changing political climates and fortunes. Add to this the digital revolution, the proliferation of mobile connectivity and fading reading habits and you get an industry struggling to sustain itself. Coming together to face common challenges, lobbying government agencies and advocating the importance of the industry for education, entertainment, well-being and nation building is more important today than ever before.

As outreach is vital, I hit on the conversation format as a way to get individuals from the industry to share their journeys and views. Contributors could either answer a bunch of questions on a topic, based on their experience or expertise or write a short piece. However, we needed professionals from the media to conduct these interviews and transcribe them effectively. Speed was also of the essence, for meeting a variety of deadlines, so publishing via conventional means was ruled out. As a result, the partnership with *All About Book Publishing* came about.

*All references to the Nielsen Report in the book refer to: *The India Book Market: Understanding the India Book Market,* Nielsen BookScan, 2015

The response was overwhelming and almost all we asked gave generously. In a few months, we had interviews and essays from 65 publishing professionals with formidable collective experience. In the process we captured a multiplicity of views and perspectives. There were both overlaps and contradictions which have been maintained, based as they are on the experiences of people who are insiders in this industry, by either profession or birth or both.

As with all such works, some contributors didn't stick to topics or formats asked; some chose to deviate from word counts, others gave alternate topics or did extensive re-writes and a couple sent us a bunch of their existing interviews to sift through. In most cases we went with the flow and tried to fill the resulting gaps and pave over the overlaps alongside. A few pieces found their way into *All About Book Publishing* acting as teasers for the book. My role as editor has therefore been one of encompassing and then continually restructuring and reorganizing, rather than gate keeper and style police. Still, the end product is quite close to what I envisioned at the start.

The volume is by no means comprehensive and was not intended to be so. My own experience is with English language publishing and that shows in the overwhelming focus of the volume and the way in which Indian Language publishing has been approached. Educational publishing, especially school, is well represented and there is a strong coverage of enduring and newer trends and challenges in Indian publishing. Several topics not conventionally clubbed with publishing, like publishing services and supply chains, teaching of publishing and publisher associations, literary festivals and library movements, literary agents, self-publishing and digital innovations, government policies and India in the global context, all can be found within these covers.

There were some issues on which we had multiple feeds and others that contributors were reluctant to cover. This is perhaps a sign of the times we live in more than anything intrinsic to Indian publishing. What is interesting is that the gaps tell their own story.

Adding a select bibliography on publishing to the book was a difficult but necessary task. This one is based more on my personal collection and word-of-mouth, than on Amazon searches.

This book is about publishers talking to their own fraternity and to their readers, authors and communities, at a time when the industry faces more challenges and disruptions than ever before but remains optimistic and buoyant nevertheless. It brings together various pieces of the Indian publishing puzzle to create a picture, admittedly partial, of the what, why and how of India's book business. In the process it raises questions, highlights yawning gaps and calls out for more action both by publishers themselves as also by other partners in the knowledge ecosystem that publishing is part of.

Nitasha Devasar
January 2018

INTRODUCTION

Indian Publishing: An Insider's Perspective

Nitasha Devasar

The Indian publishing industry has grown and evolved over time and in 2017 was estimated at US $6.7 billion. With a growing youthful population and the fourth largest higher education systems in the world, India is well placed to become a leading knowledge economy. A key requirement to achieve this goal is enhancement in the quality of our educational and research output and its outreach globally. This is virtually impossible without the services and support of the publishing industry. There is also the larger societal influence that publishing output brings at all levels and if you add Indian language publishing to that in English, the impact can be immense.

According to the 2015 Nielsen Report, Indian is the second largest English language, print book market in the world, with over 9,000 publishers producing 90,000 books annually and a CAGR of over 20 per cent over the last few years. These publishers directly employ 40,000 people and indirectly provide thousands of jobs in allied industries. Additionally, according to some estimates, 94 per cent of global content passes through India at some publishing stage, generating yet more employment.

For an industry that is larger than Bollywood and can have such a profound impact on future generation of Indians, some pretty fundamental questions have dogged publishers in recent times.

First, in the era of self-publishing and infinite free content (often called knowledge), what is it that publishers actually do? Underlying this is the view: why should we pay for books, when it is all out there for free?

A related query, given the immense role technology has played in this free information boom, is: is the (print) book dead?

There is now sufficient data to disprove the imminent death of print, at least in the immediate future. Flipkart stopped offering e-books for download in December 2015, announcing that 'The Indian book market is overwhelmingly dominated by physical books.' Worldwide, e-books sales have declined and plateaued out in recent years.

The first, more fundamental question, however, not only persists but has steadily gained ground. This may be one of the reasons why the impact of publishing on society is less recognized and issues such as copyright protection and the importance of preserving intellectual property do not get their due.

India is one of the few countries in the world where books are relatively inexpensive, cheaper than even many countries of Africa. Most multinational publishers across the spectrum price to market in India, providing special pricing on offerings that are relevant to users locally. This is true for locally published books as well. Yet, piracy is rampant and re-export of these low-priced editions to first world markets creates problems for the industry globally.

So, what is it that publishers do?*

At a time when there is a problem of plenty in research, knowledge and information (50 million articles are published globally every year and research output is doubling every 20 years), and with self-publishing proliferating, publishers:

- Filter to curate the best, i.e., the most reliable and relevant.
- Frame, setting the format and in case of e-books, the technology. They provide the branding and the casing or covering. All this to:
- Amplify, marketing and selling, driving discoverability and visibility, digitally.

Additionally, in the age of plenty, they provide:

* See Michael Bhaskar, *The Content Machine: Towards a Theory of Publishing from the Printing Press to the Digital Network,* Anthem Press, 2013

- Services for authors and other customers, to support their unmet needs, at levels and prices that are accessible.

It is these services, rather than the book itself, that are the arena of maximum creative activity currently. These could take the form of test prep or evaluation tools and teaching aids at the basic level to audio/video feeds, specialist networks and communities to support different categories of readers. In case of paid services, most publishers offer special pricing to categories of customers, like students or researchers, located in India. Increasingly, local language options are also emerging, with startups like Pratilipi and Matrubharti as well Indian language publishing by mainstream English language publishers, both in the academic and the general books space.

One of our contributors, Karthika V.K. of Westland, puts across the value proposition of publishing beautifully, 'Publishing is about contributing, generating readership and engaging with ideas that matter. For example, Rujuta Diwekar's books have transformed the way people eat in India.'

In an industry where you have no 100 per cent formula for converting ideas into profit, successful books are a hit-or-miss affair. In spite of the hearty macro numbers, the economics of survival is a continuing challenge in a low price market with a why-buy-if-you-can-get-for-free mentality. As Ravi Singh of Speaking Tiger, eloquently puts it, 'every day is a bit of a battle.. .' Yet, there is a wider perception of publishers as rapacious rent seekers at the cost of authors and readers. We explore the author-publisher relationship as well as the wealth of publishing innovations and self-publishing options on offer, to seek out the enduring value proposition of publishing in these changing times.

How has technology impacted publishing?

Technology has transformed the publishing industry both inside and out. The first wave was in typesetting and printing, making these processes faster, easier and eventually cheaper. This arguably allows books to never go out of print and saved warehousing costs alongside. Next came the use of technology for dissemination and outreach: email got added to snail mail and now social media outreach is taking this further. For researchers and pop authors alike, visibility and discoverability in the maze of free information is key and technology plays a vital role in connecting them to their audience. The seductive convenience of online selling closed the circle effectively. Books account for 15 per cent of e-commerce in the country, pegging growth at 20 per cent annually.

Increasingly now, a plethora of additional technology-led, value-added services including, assessment and outcomes, teaching aids, learning across time, space and platforms is on offer by mainstream publishers. A series of interactions with both general books and academic publishers showcases these myriad trends and the variety of ways they play out, contributing substantively to the question of the relevance of publishers in the digital age. As Vikas Gupta of Wiley, wryly points out in his conversation with us, 'It's all about getting noticed and getting paid!'

However, in the segmented Indian market, the traditional channels of distribution and collections sit alongside social media marketing and e-solutions. Talking to industry veterans in this space shows that the vast network of distribution with its roots in Daryaganj remains virtually unchanged and the traditional problems of slow collections, squeezed margins and spotty outreach have endured.

Yet there is some movement here too. 'Distribution channels have become more efficient and easier with technology,' says Ramesh Chandra Jain from Manohar Publishers & Distributors.

Who reads books now?

Another issue facing publishing is the decline in reading as books compete for screen time with other forms of education and entertainment. Educational publishing, which is purposeful and subsidized, forms the bulk of Indian publishing, has been the most stable historically, with general books publishing seeing much more volatility. Dependent as it is on government funding and policies that are in flux, uncertainties have grown in the educational space as well.

However, a silent parallel revolution of reading movements and revival of libraries (not always defined in the traditional sense of dedicated physical spaces housing books) is unfolding. The mobile libraries of the Delhi Public Library (DPL), National Book Trust's (NBT) mobile sales vans and the Walking Book Fairs, have taken libraries to non-metros and remote areas. The initiatives by Katha and Pratham are not new, but their expanding reach and working collectively with mainstream publishers and other agencies to grow reading and readers is. Rightly, supporting reading for children is a focus and publishers like Penguin Random House, Pearson and Scholastic see this as part of their role and objective. This is also a space where innovations are being seen every day. Says Himanshu Giri of Pratham, 'Reading is a habit and introducing children to engaging, well-illustrated storybooks at an early age works.'

Book fairs and literary festivals are not just here to stay but are growing and proliferating with the current number standing at 70. Each year the crowds at the World Book Fair in Delhi surprise industry veterans and as our conversations with the founders of some of the earliest festivals, reveal, are growing and thriving. As Namita Gokhale of the Jaipur Literary Festival says, 'the audience [at festivals] is more flexible and listening to one another…because of literary festivals, a literary community has emerged.'

Alongside we have more budding writers than ever before. It is no surprise that self-publishing is growing, book fairs multiplying and literary agencies proliferating. The growing professionalism is evident as is the discernment of writers as the catch ups with the literary agents and self-publishing companies, reveal. These were some of the quickest sections of the book to get written up and are amongst the most buoyant and upbeat.

These are positive developments for mainstream publishing as festival organizers need publishers to showcase their books and authors and self-published books often find their way to mainstream publishers, Amish Tripathi, being the most famous recent example. Big general books publishers no longer wade through their 'slush piles' relying on literary agents to bring them elusive bestsellers or do they? As always in India, multiple forces are at play. Says Thomas Abraham of Hachette, 'whether offered by a literary agent, or picked from the slush pile, or commissioned a bestseller is first an idea approved in-house…That is backed by the sales and marketing teams supporting the book and doing what it takes to build the first tailwind.'

Is there a future for publishers?

In spite of challenges Indian publishing lives in interesting times. Independent publishers rub shoulders with multinationals and robust local publishing business have their say alongside Indian language publishers. Translations are finally getting their day in the sun and have emerged as a bridge between the smaller and big players and between IL and E publishing. 'In translations lie our histories, identities and belonging', says Mini Krishnan of Oxford University Press.

Tie-ups and collaborations between niche players and those with global networks are also growing. The creativity and fierce independence of the small and the scale and commerce of the bigger players come together, probably for the first time, to share their journeys and experiences and some of the creative tensions that underlie this universe seeps through.

India is one of the few markets in the world where print book sales continue to sustain alongside burgeoning e-book sales and both traditional and new forms of publishing live alongside each other, at least for the foreseeable future.

Innovations are growing as new players come up to bridge obvious gaps and existing players explore newer avenues: twitter reads, mobile apps for tutorials and tests, using AI in illustrated books and digital comics and games. Veterans and innovators tell us about these developments and more.

In recent years, industry associations have come of age and are making individual and collective efforts to build consensus on key industry issues, lobby for policy changes and grow advocacy around copyright and role of publishers in building the knowledge economy, externally. Perhaps reflecting the hurdles and difficulties we face, this was one of the toughest parts of the book to put together.

Enduring gaps in copyright awareness and publishing ethics are hurting the industry and denting its credibility in the global publishing arena which otherwise views India's growing youthful population, higher education spending and the use of English as the language of learning and research, as a promising and steady market for multinational publishers. These aspects are covered in articles by professionals in the thick of advocacy and action, globally.

There is much for us to do as an industry collectively to impact any or all of the challenges that face us. Whether it is specific issues, like the GST (Goods and Services Tax) on author royalties and e-content or widespread ones, like piracy, freedom to publish and quality of educational books, it is clear that we need to come together and work with fellow stakeholders, like parents, teachers, researchers, students and, most of all, our authors, consistently and persistently, to bring positive change.

In the words of Asoke Ghosh of PHI, a veteran publisher with over 50 years of experience, 'The future of publishing looks promising...If you are in it, put your mind to do better, make more money, produce more books, find more readership, maximize your sales, and get more results.'

There is clearly much to be done and as the 65 voices in this book eloquently showcase, publishing and publishers are here for the long haul and are growing, innovating and creating, for a larger common good.

PART

1

The Sector Today

PART I • THE SECTOR TODAY

THE SECTOR TODAY

Publishing in India is at once traditional, caught up in the bylanes of Ansari Road, the Old Delhi books street, and digitally aspirational, in its plush offices in the NCR (National Capital Region). The contributors in this section have weathered many publishing storms and their conversations reveal the inherent contradictions in Indian publishing where old problems and new opportunities can, and often do, coexist. Competition and collaboration between existing and new forces and entities are more visible that ever before. Local publishers are facing the heat and need to catch up with the rapid technological changes in publishing, while multinational publishers look to marry content and technology to move up the value chain.

Yet all agree that the long-standing problems of poor quality content, deep discounting and long collection cycles, piracy and re-export of low-priced editions, are challenges faced by the entire community. The distribution channels of the book trade have endured over the past 70 years with e-commerce offering complementary channels to improve visibility and outreach of books but also, unfortunately, as conduits for piracy.

Publishing services in India are used globally for their cost and quality effectiveness and this sector needs to get its due place in mainstream publishing for its contributions to local employment and to global publishing needs.

1

ENDURING ISSUES FOR INDIAN PUBLISHING

"Publishers have the role of an educator"

Asoke Ghosh

Q: Where is the Indian publishing industry placed today? How does it compare with other emerging markets?

AG: When we visit any book fair like New Delhi World Book Fair or Frankfurt Book Fair, we get to know and can make up our mind as to how publishing is doing. It is heartwarming to see so many publishers participating with thousands of books on different subjects, especially in areas that we have never learned about or studied before. This hugely encourages me to remain in publishing and work cohesively for its prosperity. I am happy to see so many people from all over the world engaged in publishing today.

According to *The India Book Market: Understanding the India Book Market* report by Nielsen, there are 9,000 publishers in India, with over 21,000 retailers, publishing in 22 official languages and if we include regional dialects, the total is about 1,600. Literacy, in India, is rising rapidly; it surged from 65 per cent in 2001 to 74 per cent in 2011 and is predicted to reach 90 per cent by 2020. With such impressive figures, the industry has a long way to go.

Q: What are the landmarks or milestones in the Indian publishing industry?

AG: In my opinion, publication of a large number of books and addition of more and more new players in publishing is the milestone of the industry in India. Most encouraging is the fact that a lot of publishers from abroad are leading Indian publishing now. Due to their involvement in the publishing industry, publishers in India, though facing stiff competition, are also gaining new heights in business with partnerships and collaborations.

Also, in the last 10 years, we have seen an increase in the number of Indian authors, which I consider another milestone in the Indian publishing industry, because many of them are quite popular today for their contribution.

Q: To what extent have the changes in technology, both in production and in marketing, affected the working of Indian publishing?
AG: I think the impact of technology is quite high. It has affected every sphere of publishing, including production and marketing. The internet, print-on-demand, digital publishing and e-books are the main drivers of this change. Technology has opened up significant opportunities for self-publishing, wherein the author can publish and promote their work, and also interact with the readers. Everybody in India, from a publisher or printer to retailer, are striving towards automating their mechanism, right from pre-press to press, and from inventory management and control to the marketing of books online. Technology has given a way to Indian publishers to market their books worldwide but, at the same time, it has stolen the beauty of bookshelves, both of living room and academic libraries. Still, no doubt, the technology has changed the publishing scenario in India, of course favourably, I feel.

Q: Local Indian publishing is mostly family-run businesses. What are the changes, if any, seen in these businesses in the last decade or so?
AG: In many family businesses, professional management has been brought in to compete with others. Whereas, a few publishing houses are still reluctant to give away the control to professionals as they want to have full supervision over the company. Fortunately, in most of the family-run businesses, the younger generation—the innovative minds, who are well-qualified and trained in modern technologies—is helping the company in making it technically proficient and reaching out to the readers worldwide by having tie-ups with online marketing giants.

Q: What are the enduring challenges of Indian publishing?

AG: If you ask me, there are many challenges in publishing such as distribution, substandard content, cost of production, pricing a book at an affordable rate and so on. But, of course, piracy and re-export are few among the other enduring challenges in India. However, we are trying to fight this evil; prevalent in India. Since it is a herculean task which, more than money, involves time, it is difficult to have a complete check on piracy. This brings us to a big question–should we engage ourselves in publishing or pursuing?

Another challenge that I feel is the problem of cut-paste, low quality content. However, with plagiarism software, we can overcome this problem up to certain extent, and decline publication of such content. In India, sometimes people do it unknowingly, due to ignorance, as they believe that anything on the internet is copyright free and is available in public domain, which is not true. So, with the help of our various associations like FIP, API we organize workshops on copyright awareness, which is helping us a lot. Publishers should be aware that publishing of a plagiarized content is the violation of copyright norms, and they may have to face legal action or difficulty in selling their books online.

Another challenge that a publisher is facing today is the long collection cycles and problems related to overdue payments. This is the weakest link in the Indian publishing industry. One sells a book to a distributor and you are really lucky if you get payment within six months; the credit periods have now gone up to one year. In these circumstances, one may find it difficult to startup a new publishing company in India, particularly in the present situation of credit in the market.

Q: Would you agree that use of technology has enhanced these issues?

AG: No, I feel that the use of technology has addressed some of these issues. The best part is that if you sell majority of your product (books) online, you get returns so quickly. But, it would have been really good if we could maintain conventional supply chain. I fully understand that people in retail are also suffering today as they too have to invest a lot.

But breaking off this supply chain will further kill the industry in spite of high potential and future scope of publishing.

Q: What is your take on e-books and other digital platforms? Why do you think local publishers have not taken to these technologies? Does the Indian publishing industry still feel threatened by these trends?

AG: Technology goes hand-in-hand with publishing. Wherever there are printed books, there will be e-books too. Each and every book of mine is available in both the versions. Many a time, a person likes to have both versions of the same book, to make his reading comfortable and enjoyable while sitting at home and, at the same time, he/she can carry the device (mobile or kindle) to continue reading the book when travelling. E-books are the future of publishing. It is quite convenient to market and supply them, and one does not even need to maintain a large inventory. Online publishing is also same; it can be done quickly, in no time.

In my view, these technologies are here to aid the publishers and do not cause any hindrance in their way. Real publishers will certainly like to embrace the technological advances and will use them for their benefit. Also, cost is not a major concern for the publishers in our country, as producing an e-book is highly cost effective; it is not at all a costly affair. If you ask me, whether I would like to print 1,000 copies or produce an e-book, immediately my answer would be the e-book!

But, the e-reader is little expensive for a common man in India. In fact, the infrastructure is not yet truly compatible for digital India. Anyway, things are changing now and people are buying e-readers for their children to make them go with the fast-paced digital age.

Q: How about online selling? Is this popular with local publishers? How is it used?

AG: Online selling is quite popular these days. If we wish to buy something, we immediately go online and buy the item of our choice. It is so easy!

But, the same is not prevalent in case of books, especially for textbooks. If a student is prescribed a book by his/her teacher or institute, he/she still depends fully on the local bookstore for purchase. In digital India, when people prefer online shopping for most of the items, from clothes to all households, then why not for textbooks. I repeat, it is so easy and convenient!

Q: What are your views on the 'glamourization' of publishing with a profusion of lit fests, book fairs, reading events, etc.? Do they at all benefit the publishing industry?

AG: Of course, in today's world the 'glamourization' of any business or industry is must, and so is for publishing, though book fairs are getting less popular now; one of the major reasons of this being online availability of the books. People get to see a book of their choice on publisher's website and other e-marketing portals in this era of technology. They can even browse content of the book sitting leisurely at home. But still I would say book fairs are a great place to connect with all publishers, and moreover, every company cannot afford to place their books online, especially the small players. Also, if a reader does not have any information about the publication, the author, or the publisher of the book, it will be hard for him/her to browse through to find a book online . . . here comes the role and significance of book fairs. There are many more benefits of such events.

Like book fairs, literature festivals also bring the authors and the publishing world to the reading public. It helps publishers to acquire new manuscripts, and even the reader get chance to meet and interact with their favourite authors face-to-face; the author-publisher and author-reader interaction is a delight at these fests. New ideas take birth at such fests . . . I am always in favour of literature festivals. I strongly believe, these events will continue receiving people's support and will certainly continue to exist.

Q: Another important trend is bigwigs like Amazon coming into publishing. How is it affecting publishers?

AG: Amazon is like a monopoly. They want to do everything themselves. But, we are in a trade where we always propagate freedom of speech, freedom of expression and freedom to publish . . . where the small and the big–all should exist. Imagine a country where only three or four publishers dominate, then if somebody writes a book, unless the author strongly pursues with the publisher, his/her work will not get to see the light of the day. A publisher plays a role of an educator and one must recall that we are contributing to the growth of education in our country. And do remember, it is a noble profession.

Q: In recent times because of government policies, funding issues, etc., the industry has been beset with problems. Are there enough platforms where publishers can voice their opinions or issues and get a solution? Are publishing associations and industry bodies able to rally to make an impact/ raise their voices?

AG: It all depends on the government. As far as the publishers are concerned, we are operating for more than 50 years. In the last 50 years, we have been in regular contact with the government whether in the centre or the state. There are many problems which we are facing and have been discussing with the government from time to time. Sometimes we get a relief but, at times, our suggestions are not accepted.

In my view, the government should create a body to address policy issues related to book publishing because publishing and selling books is a highly specialized business. We are a capital-intensive industry but with low returns. Whether it is a bookseller or a publisher, one is into publishing business because of his/her personal interest in books; of course, with an expectation of better rate of returns. After all, we give employment to a huge mass of population and to run this industry we expect significant gains. A few bureaucrats in the ministries are aware of our contribution and are helpful too.

Q: What in your view are the key issues with various bodies coming together?

AG: All the associations should work together with a common agenda to solve the issues that I have mentioned before. Book writing in itself is not a big money making profession, unless you are a bestselling author like Chetan Bhagat or Amish Tripathi. Everybody is not making money, so some kind of encouragement should be given to the authors so that they come forward and translate their ideas and thoughts into writing. This is more than a necessity for academic books. India is a huge country with 700 universities and 35,000 plus colleges, and to cater to these institutions one has to face tough competition, and in turn, the share of copies sold per publisher is so less that one cannot do justice with the authors.

Another important concern is the availability of funds and the payment issues. Most importantly, the plagiarism issue, which I have mentioned earlier. So, we all should come together to resolve these common issues, and to make the present infrastructure better.

Q: What is the future of local Indian publishing? Would you agree that in spite of the difficulties of the business, more and more players continue to enter the industry? Why?

AG: It is a positive sign that people are interested in publishing and more and more new players are entering into the industry. These new entrants should prepare themselves for the challenges and opportunities too.

The future of publishing is certainly promising. I am optimistic about the future of the industry, and look forward to people and the sector as a whole to do better. If you are into it, shape up your mind to do better, make more money, create more employment, produce worthy books, build a huge audience, maximize your sales and secure positive results.

Let's join hands to impart quality education to our children!

ASOKE GHOSH is Chairman and Managing Director of PHI Learning. He has been associated with the International Publishers Association (IPA) since 1974 and is currently a member of IPA's Executive Committee. He is also a founder-member and twice President of the Federation of Indian Publishers (FIP). He is currently a member of FIP's Executive Committee and Chairman of its International Relations Committee.

2

INDIAN PUBLISHING: TODAY AND TOMORROW

"The future of publishing lies in going up the value chain of learning"

Vikas Gupta

Q: What is the future of publishing in India in the context of the key challenges being faced by the publishing industry and publishers today?

Vikas: The most widespread challenge is online piracy or photocopy, both from the government or legal as well as the academic or student point of view. They feel that using a downloadable book is not a crime. Even the government and judiciary feel that university-level publishers' books are very expensive and so photocopying is fine. This scenario is making it increasingly difficult both for publishers as well as authors to make money. It is the aspiration of an author to be paid so that he feels motivated to write more. On the other hand, you have publishers who also need to run their business.

India has the unique challenge of piracy in print publishing. While, on the digital side, the challenge is even more daunting; people do not want to pay. Thus, publishing is struggling for its very survival; it is not around the future of technology or learning but the future of the entire ecosystem. Piracy and the use of copyright remain the main challenges.

Q: How is technology changing the publishing landscape?

Vikas: Why do you need books? Well, a book or content satisfies unmet needs. But, the book alone does not satisfy the needs of a student. Learning happens when a combination of multiple needs of a student is met with. If, as a publisher I only satisfy one of the ten needs, my business model will not work. The world of today is changing with technology, which provides stimulated learning, micro learning, video-based learning—all integrated with class learning. The business model of the book is not around the price of a book, but around a solution that we are providing with the book.

So the future of publishing lies is going up the value chain of learning. Publishers need to start offering multiple-level publishing solutions.

Publishers have the content and they need to leverage it. Soon, it would be a Google-like model, where the content is free but you charge for peripheral services. For example, there are test preps, which can be charged. That's where publishing is headed. The old book will remain but the solution will take importance.

Q: How will this work in fiction and what can be done to stop piracy in fiction?

Vikas: Digital piracy is killing fiction too. But, there's a solution. Can you create a digital book, which is a combination of different scenarios—for example, after a chapter, ask a question, giving options? Each option has a different story; you have many stories within a story. If you can create that platform—that's the future of fiction. So in a single novel, you can keep on writing new chapters, adding new scenarios—keeping the readers engaged and engrossed. We all need to embrace technology and stop the problem of piracy and distribution. We have to find models where we can make money.

In case of reading for pleasure or reference, innumerable new and exciting models are available with technology, such as: personalized and infinite endings; immersive experiences such as communicating with lead characters; multiple plots and perspectives, non-linear storylines as per reader preferences; crowdsourced books; fact checking features and alternative references; and social reading and shared libraries.

Q: What is the future of higher education (HE) publishing in the next decade, with a special focus on the next three to five years?

Vikas: I see print books are disappearing in higher education and will continue to disappear. Piracy will not allow the higher education business to flourish. But, school books will continue to grow as new schools are opening every so often. Since the availability of internet is not so strong in India, schools will rely mostly on print books. In future, I see the higher education publishing companies and edutech companies joining hands to create and offer a solution. Publishing companies have content, while technology companies have technology....They need to marry each other to offer a complete solution.

Q: Are today's challenges different from those in the past, with a decline in the reading habit in 'book format' and competition for attention from increased 'screen' time by millennials?

Vikas: According to *Edelman Digital's 2017 Trends Report*, weekly share of time spent watching TV and video on mobile devices has grown by 85 per cent from 2010 to 2016; while on fixed screens, consumption has decreased 14 per cent over the same period. It would not be out of place here to point out the fact that almost all businesses and companies today are in the business of content—be it software or technology or educational companies. Hence the competition is brutal and the path to reaching the end user is complex.

There has been a major change in how people read. Even in a newspaper, most people generally read the headline and the bullet points under it. They like to quickly scan content. Their attention span is small and they want to learn more in less time.

Thus, publishing needs to be more visual and to the point. Same applies to academics also. Publishing is shifting to be more visual; it is actually a hybrid of print and digital.

Q: There has been proliferation of free access (versus priced access) to all kinds of content and formats. How will this affect the economics of publishing in a price-sensitive market like India?

Vikas: A lot of content is available free on the net. So, people will pay only for something they need, which is not available with Google and has value. If you can teach something in a better way, then the book is a hit and will be bought. If your story is different, again, people will buy your book.

A publisher can give flat content free and charge for the unique content. I can also create a model where the author says he wants to give his content free in an open access model. In such a case, a publisher can offer services. So, we need to have a mix of both paid as well as free content.

If we dig deep into the core model of traditional publishing, publishers demand premium for the various services they offer to their authors and readers—that of curating, packaging, marketing and distribution of content. These are still relevant today and are more complex problems to solve. Digitization has not only disrupted the methods to curate, package, market or distribute, but has also opened up new models to monetize the services—such as: Subscription models where one can get a select set of loyal customers buying constantly; Freemium model where one can let customers get a taste of the core offering and then charge for various relevant services to improve her outcome; and Value-added curator/reseller model where one can take available good content and build services around it.

This, no doubt requires new capabilities, but so does any business with changing times.

Q: Where is technology taking publishing in the near future; and what are the strategies being employed by publishers to cope with it? From your experiences in the Association of Publishers in India (API) and Federation of Indian Publishers (FIP), is there a difference between 'India' and the MNCs in this context?

Vikas: There is no denying the fact that book and print consumption is on the decline. On the other hand, newer trends in the content market indicate that consumers are hungry for live, real-time and interactive reading and learning experiences and content remains a key consumable commodity.

I would say that Indian publishers' route to technology in the first phase was more cosmetic. But, now things are changing. They are realizing that it is not just enough to have an online website; there's more. They now understand that there are a few things where technology plays a good role. Besides, publishers are using disruption in the technology of the distribution network as in India distribution is very fragmented.

It would be unfair to call digital disruption just a technology play. This is to do with complete transformations in business models and how we engage—in essence, the problem of getting noticed and getting paid. The same applies to various verticals of publishing.

Let us take the case of the education market. The expectation of a learner today is to learn anytime, anywhere, personalized to his or her learning style. So a one-size-fits-all education content model does not work anymore. Multiple innovative options are available to learners and teachers to choose from, based on their learning preferences and background—such as learning by doing, collaborative or social learning, anytime anywhere learning, learning through gamification and virtual reality, adaptive learning, mentored learning—the list is endless.

In this context, technology can become an influencer and enabler to reach end users in the format they are looking for, and make learning a personalized experience. However, technology alone cannot be the solution. Think of pure online learning such as massive open online courses (MOOCs)—a trainer teaches and thousands of students just hear. Majority of learners are unable to learn as it may not suit their individual learning style. It is again, in a way, a one-size-fits-all format.

This is why pure online learning is not always successful, especially in cases of test prep and certifications where the barrier to passing is high. While technology helps in making quality content available without any restrictions on time or geographical locations, the value of a learning (publishing) solution will always depend on: how learning is curated and authenticated for individual learners; how it is imparted and what the ultimate outcome is; what the learner experiences is what we are developing; how empowered a student is after the learning.

The value of publishers and educators in earlier days remained in making available knowledge into sizable formats and with associated aids such as visuals, exercises and other elements which made the outcome of learning relevant. Technology has given various new, even more flexible and interconnected formats now to further improve this learning outcome, and made it possible to learn anytime, anyway, anywhere, and as a personal experience.

I feel new technologies are increasingly taking market share, I am not sure what will happen in the next 3 to 5 years but in the next 10 years, absolutely digital will replace print.

Q: How is Wiley specifically future proofing its business in India?

Vikas: As a company, we are getting into solutions strongly. Importantly, we are also a publisher. So, we exist in all formats where content is consumed—print, digital, online.... We want to serve the need of each customer at the end of the spectrum. We don't know what the future will be; so it is best to be a player in all the three and shift from one to another whenever the time comes.

In this crowded knowledge and content economy, publishing could still remain relevant if our focus moves from creating great content in silos to ensuring that publishing creates and curates quality content which meets the user's outcomes by leveraging technology; is credible and authentic; is able to create a personalized, adaptive and user-centric experience; and leverages user, product and functional networks and connections.

Wiley is focused on leveraging its core strengths such as credibility and trust that its customers have; its rich author networks and long-established distribution channels to innovate on newer models and improve its customers' outcomes with effective and unique services. It is also trying to globalize as well as localize its offerings, backed with technology, so that users have a more personalized experience across geographies.

Q: How do you think India fits in the global publishing scene in the next few years given our demographic, etc.?

Vikas: India will play a very big role in science, technology, academic and medical publishing. This is because for areas like the Middle East, Africa, and South Asia, print content would be required and India will play a leading role. India will also play a major role in providing technological solutions to these countries. In the digital world, we will be as good as the US, at one-tenth the price. We may also become pioneers in our ability to serve customers around the globe.

However, we need to identify a game plan for where each of us want to play and what unique and specialized services we can offer to enhance customer outcomes that can be valued as premium.

VIKAS GUPTA is Managing Director of Wiley India and Immediate Past President of the Association of Publishers in India (API). He has led innovative product and business models for technology-driven learning solutions, research and faculty development, professional certifications and skills development. He has co-founded and led ventures in IT, medical electronics and publishing. Vikas is an ardent promoter of entrepreneurship and runs his own blog and video series to share his perspective on future business models and emerging issues in the technology, education and learning industries.

3

E-COMMERCE AND ONLINE SELLING

"Develop a book culture first and then the retail culture"

Thomas Abraham

Q: Share your views on the evolution of the book industry with particular reference to pre and post e-commerce and online selling.

Thomas: First, all my views will be confined to trade publishing only. It is interesting to see that for about 100 years, we have had a publisher to distributor to retailer model that broadly functioned in a linear unchanging way. The last decade and a half, however, have seen seismic changes that weren't there in the century before. Yes, the change began in the early 2000s from two disruptive waves that India got quite late when compared to the west. First it was the chains (though Landmark began in 1987 as India's first modern large format bookstore, the chains came into their own only about 12 years later) that were deep discounting, and at that time it was the Indies that were protesting. Post 2009, the disruption was from online sellers, and this time it was the chain that was hard hit. It's reached a point where more stores have shut in the past five years than in the previous 50 years. We tracked this and we've found that in the last five years or so, over 176 bookstores have shut down, resulting in a loss of over 800,000 sq. ft store space. Distribution too has been brutally hit with just two main trade players left standing—both of whom are also doubling as online marketplace vendors.

Both disruptions had one thing in common—they ended up pushing the base discount up considerably. So today a predominant, and rather unfortunate, market characteristic is that it's less about the book than about discounts and returns allowances. Whether publisher or bookseller, the focus is not how we should build and grow the market but how each link in the chain can insulate itself against risk.

Q: Is leisure reading moving online? Has India always been a non-fiction market or is this a recent development with the onset of ease of online access?

Thomas: Though it might not seem so, non-fiction has ruled the roost from the beginning if you're talking of India-originated books, though fiction may have got the limelight. If you add in imports, then yes fiction was top of mind until the early to mid-1980s. From the 1990s there has been a decline that I personally correlate with the dying out of the neighbourhood lending library which was the go-to leisure choice in most towns. Non-fiction has always been and will always be a priority given our read-to-get-ahead mindset. Yes, online access has made a difference in the reference segment, particularly the dictionaries, encyclopaedias and travel guides segments, but core narrative non-fiction has remained unchanged. With the advent of cable TV and the internet explosion today with Netflix sort of options, leisure-time priorities are moving away from books. I hope this is a short-term phenomenon and once the newness wears off, reading habits will return.

Q: Talking about disruption waves, do you see a change in reading tastes (commercial fiction) or what's being called the digital revolution in terms of reading—on devices, etc.? What do you see as its implications for the future?

Thomas: Yes, and these are not new. Every decade sees its disruptions but it will equally take a decade to decide whether it has any impact. So I don't yet see these as disruptions and (digital or self-publishing variants) affecting industry or other companies. The disruptions and/or inflection points I would list in a potted history of English trade publishing in terms of being transformational are: Tagore's Nobel; R.K. Narayan being published to acclaim in the west and launching Indian writing in English; the first distribution houses of India Book House (IBH); Rupa, etc.; Penguin India starting local publishing; Shobhaa De's *Starry Nights* and Vikram Seth's *A Suitable Boy* as commercial and literary bestsellers coming into their own, *The God of Small Things* winning the Booker; the death of the lending library; Chetan Bhagat; Harry Potter, the low-priced campus romance genre; the coming of Flipkart and later Amazon; Amish Tripathi's Shiva series; to the collapse of the chains.

Coming to digital, I've always been sceptical about that but was hoping to be proved wrong. There are two–three publishers essaying this route and let's wait and see. In India e-books never really took off, though at Hachette we've beaten the average trend. But that I will admit is because of the sheer depth and range of our catalogue, and not from any market we were able to tap differently. So worldwide, where base readerships were high, the numbers skyrocketed over about five years (e-book contributions had reached as high as 32 per cent) and then declined and now have settled at 15–17 per cent levels. In India the average never went above 5 per cent, with just a couple of exceptions like PRH (Penguin Random House) and us, where we hit 10–12 per cent but have settled down to 7–9 per cent levels.

What remains to be seen is whether Amazon, with its heavy advertising for Kindle as e-reader, will be able to bring about a shift in default reading habits here which still prefer paper (the way soft-drink companies did, transforming India from a lemon-drinking country to a cola-drinking one) or whether Kindle will just end up competing as another tablet device.

Q: How have e-commerce and online selling changed the landscape of operations? Is the burgeoning of online retail stores such as Amazon and Flipkart good or bad news for publishers? Do you see physical bookstores reviving at some point in the future?

Thomas: Both good and bad. Their scorched-earth policy is bad news because they end up shutting down brick-and-mortar bookstores without offering the curated replacement that is needed; and the really bad news is the fact that they have become safe havens for pirates. There are over a hundred pirate sellers on online marketplaces today doing serious damage. The good news is that there is availability of any book and hopefully they will extend their outreach to serve non city-markets which don't have bookshops. So we should see some market expansion beyond the cannibalization that is inevitably the first wave.

Yes, online can, up to a point, enhance bestseller sales and provide some cross-recommendations, but they can't provide that browsing experience; so in the future I hope there will be space once again for the indie who manages costs well and curates books well; and is therefore not affected by any medium-term deep discounting wars. It's the chain stores with the high rentals that need to rethink their strategy and reinvent themselves much like Waterstones has done in the west. You need to develop a book culture first and retail culture second if you want to succeed and create that differentiator.

Q: Do you feel a backlash in the conventional channels of the book trade? Should the government be intervening?

Thomas: This is not new and has been building up for some time. A decade ago, it was the independent publishing houses versus chains. Today, with the advent of the online market, it's brick-and-mortar against online because things have begun to hurt much more than before. In a country like India, which disrespects intellectual property rights completely, I am sceptical that the government will do anything. Unless the government legislates otherwise and brings about a level playing field like France has done, nothing can really happen legally. Earlier this year, France passed a new law popularly dubbed as 'The Anti-Amazon Law', to protect its iconic bookshop culture from American e-commerce giants. This law has banned rebates on book sales and free shipping by online portals. France has around 3,500 bookshops, one-third of which are independent stores, struggling to compete in an increasingly monopolized market. This law follows 1981's fixed book price law, 'The Lang Law', which allows for a maximum of 5 per cent discount to ensure a 'level playing field'. The government's view is bound to be that whether or not the industry is crashing, the consumer is getting books cheaper, so it can't intervene. I doubt if it will see bookstores as cultural institutions that need to be preserved.

So online came in and created a huge wave with some stunning growth. Today they are estimated to be between 45 and 55 per cent of any publisher's business depending on the sort of books that are your oeuvre.

Q: What about the role and involvement of the author in today's new market. Do you notice a change?

Thomas: Yes, there is a big change as authors get savvier about leveraging an online presence and social media. It is interesting that in the last decade or so many authors have created bestsellers through their own efforts online. Many of them began online as self-publishing discoveries (from E.L. James in the US to Amish here) and all of those have amplified their sales by then being formally published. But I do believe that no amount of marketing can create a lasting bestseller out of a dud. In trade publishing it is finally about word-of-mouth. And everything you do as a publisher or author can only help build that tailwind. Today authors take a lot of care to build social media and online presence and why not. Finally, it is the most direct and interactive connect to their readers.

THOMAS ABRAHAM is Managing Director, Hachette India. He was CEO and President of Penguin India during 2003-07, before he started at Hachette. He joined the publishing industry in 1994 as an editor with Oxford University Press India. He thereafter moved to marketing and left OUP to join Dorling Kindersley as Marketing Director in 2000. He joined Penguin Books in the same position following the buyout of DK by Penguin.

4

PUBLISHING SERVICES IN INDIA

"Preparing for the perfect storm?"

*Anil Chandy**

Outsourcing of publishing services to India began in the mid-1990s, when international publishers began to replicate what other domains (such as financial services, medical transcription, IT services and customer care centres for global businesses) had identified as a strategy that bought great operational value. India seemed to have the perfect combination of business enablers—advantageous demographic trends (a young English-educated population), a never-ending supply of IT professionals at different skill levels, and importantly the ability to provide cost leadership.

In India, the information technology-business process management outsourcing (IT-BPMO)/ KPO (knowledge process outsourcing) services sector purportedly creates 4 million jobs directly and generates another 12 million in allied or indirect jobs. I focus here on a subset of the large and varied KPO industry—publishing services in the scholarly and science, technology and medical (STM) publishing domain, possibly accounting for less than 10 per cent of this IT-BPMO/ KPO market and revenue share.

The Growth Story

The Indian publishing services industry's growth story involved the world's leading English language publishers organizing their content creation and page production processes in India. Publishing services in India continued on the crest of a wave when the digital publishing moment arrived in the mid-2000s. The deep domain expertise the

**All views expressed in this article are the author's own and do not reflect those of* Springer Nature *or its subsidiaries.*

industry had developed by then allowed it to make a seamless transition from simply providing typesetting services to recreating electronic products for its customers. It implemented publishing workflows supporting generic content creation that was both human and machine-readable (for example xml-first workflows) and leveraging document management best practices. The speed at which adaptation, cost leadership and scale were created in a short period led to the industry gaining a competitive edge over publishing services businesses in Europe and North America.

The segment has seen nearly uninterrupted growth since its inception, but post 2008 has had its forecasts curtailed. Here, I briefly touch upon the drivers of success and indicate what challenges the industry (and the academic publishing domain) is facing today to suggest some ways to outlive the trend of anti-globalization, disruption and market shrinkage.

Publishing services organizations in India arguably were original disruptors taking advantage of the opportunities in globalization. They picked up exactly at the point where European and American publishers found using similar services in their own regions expensive and restrictive in sustaining publishing volumes and growth. Outsourcing therefore became a critical component of the growth plan of most businesses to leverage efficiencies and move volume-driven and consistent tasks downstream and offshore.

The Indian publishing services industry positioned itself well, attuning to the pulse of this business imperative, and justifiably deserves praise on a number of counts:

- Actively utilizing available skilled human capital.
- Contributing to the IT-BPMO/ KPO India success story and bringing in foreign direct investment (without any focused government support).
- Leveraging technologies to build key business processes in dedicated offshore delivery centres.
- Designing workflows, increasing automation and performing complex tasks.

Pause for Thought

However, more recently a tone of negativity has crept into conversations and reporting on the Indian publishing services industry's future. While not dramatic, companies in India during the growth phase had also gone through their own share of consolidation. Firms that had successfully partnered with global publishers or other service providers continued to grow, even acquiring smaller companies. The problem with market size as always is that when slowdown hits, the larger you are, the more it impacts you.

Nonetheless the slowdown has not been as drastic as some other domains. Unlike other KPO sectors, publishing (and especially academic publishing) by nature is a conservative business where growth rates hover consistently around the low single digits. But it is also characterized by comparative stability. Its primary customers are academic libraries, whose operational environment is a lot more stable. So while scholarly and STM publishing still has large global players, which also have corporate elements in the way they conduct their business, it is not truly a corporatized industry when defined as a business exclusively driven by profit. The industry collaborates closely with academia and so is bound by the latter's normative and social traditions around creation, communication, dissemination and scholarly rigour.

Challenges Facing Global Academic Publishing

The STM publishing industry globally has also had to adapt—whether it is to increasing regulatory pressures (especially in Europe), the shift to Open Access globally, the rise of the internet search giants and ubiquitous nature of content, changes in business models, and more recently, organized piracy. The industry is possibly unique in that it's a space where there is a fair amount of self-reflection, critical analysis and adjustments to meet the needs of readers/ end-users and customers. While criticism continually decries that academic publishing is thriving on a historical model, the many initiatives that publishers launch each year should call out that is far from the case (for example, specific programmes aimed at developing markets, and more recently committed content-sharing initiatives, discovery support, and other services aimed at authors). As in all incipient approaches, there are examples which can undoubtedly be improved but taken together STM publishing continually demonstrates an ability to adapt and work with its key stakeholders. Since 80 per cent of the global STM publishing services market that supports this business may be in India, any tectonic shifts can directly impact industry players.

The potential impact of declining revenues from core publishing services should make industry leaders aware and adapt to the changes in the evolving STM market. By way of personnel, the industry in India has some impressive leaders who are as knowledgeable and aligned with global STM market developments as those operating upstream in the formal industry. For these leaders and their organizations, collaborating and expanding capabilities to solve critical challenges facing the STM industry will strengthen their competitive edge and ability to address a shrinking market and outsail the perfect storm.

Providing Maximum Value

It is important to re-identify requirements of the STM domain and position the services sector as a valued partner and stakeholder. The analytical and problem-solving skills of the publishing services sector are universally recognized and esteemed—capitalize on it. Further, address some of the dominant narratives and negativity surrounding outsourcing. To take three examples:

Quality. The continuing story among many editorial and publishing personnel worldwide is that quality has suffered as a result of outsourcing. There is (and frustratingly so) some truth in this more so, if you define quality rather narrowly as the ability to fine-tune scientific communications (for example, in terms of language and grammar). Many service providers have tried to fix this issue by hiring experienced science editors worldwide (in a sort of reverse offshoring). However, what is neither easily measurable nor readily apparent is the quantifiable engagement of such editorial professionals. In short, publishing services companies seldom highlight what they do to address such perceptions. This perception gap points directly at an important element in such cooperation—managing the expectations of clients as well as transparency in process and work.

Attrition Rates. The other issue that plagues the industry is the high attrition rate. Companies that move to manage attrition effectively will strengthen the industry's authenticity creating an environment that is advantageous.

In addressing this challenge, publishing services by way of developing talent should continually skill and train their personnel as also give them, for lack of a better word—'faces'. All publishing is relationship-driven and it is always of intrinsic value to the client to know that the contact at the other end is a partner capable of supporting and solving issues. Speaking from personal experience, I have seen many cases where influential international academicians expressed their appreciation not just for us, their publishers but also for the services team for the value they had undeniably contributed.

New Competition. When an offshore industry scales, some of the problems of the established markets, which first drove offshoring, get reflected back. As drivers of offshoring gradually become diluted—most importantly cost—coupled with the general economic situation of the region that the service is located in, new challenges emerge. Globally there is consolidation happening in publishing services and especially taken with the growth of capable rivals in other emerging markets (such as in Southeast Asia, East Europe, Latin America and even North America), the Indian industry will not only have to demonstrate that it can exercise continued cost leadership but also maintain the edge in technology and skilled resourcing.

Grand Challenges to Solve

Such grand challenges are no different from similar questions confronting other domains. The solution points at strategies aimed at developing overall competitiveness as well as opting for some tactics that help sustain the lead. Here are some suggestions:

Continue the evolution in technology, providing streamlined solutions and service depth. This is an imperative if competitive edge has to be maintained. Sure enough, as in all technology-driven environments, the initial investment may be high, but insightful operational scaling can pave the way for growth ahead. Much of this needs to address the challenges the STM industry as a whole faces. As a respected partner, the publishing services industry can come up or support many solutions.

Invest in high-level talent, and especially specialized talent. India possesses, whether in terms of editorial expertise, IT skills, or knowledge experts, a number of choices. Sometimes this leads STM publishers to simply offshore their own personnel or grow in-house programmes leveraging location, cost and skill which then drive their larger programmes and product development. Two examples I can claim familiarity with related to the scaling of my own programme as well as to other extended editorial management operations.

Leverage domain expertise to continually support high-value tasks. Beginning from simple page making, service capabilities have expanded to putting in place complex workflows, systems, processes, content development support, market intelligence research, data support, legal and contracting support, extended project management and full-life-cycle ownership of the publishing process. As requirements of global scholarly publishing change in an era of digital discovery, many services companies are also playing a significant role in ontology development, support in developing better content and metadata for the semantic web to technology and platform development.

Systematically manage knowledge (important in a high-attrition industry) and drive best practices: identification and adoption. Not simply to pay lip-service or to satisfy a management fad but to distil real world domain knowledge which then can be the foundation for the next set of strategic tasks. This was done once before and needs to be done continuously. Developing deep knowledge, leveraging statistical and data research depth, and throwing out the 'way around' mentality means to be taken seriously. If despite growing to several billions of dollars worth and supporting a global industry, negative perceptions at the start still persist, then they need addressing.

Demonstrate agility. For clients a key issue is requesting course corrections in linear workflows for product improvements. Customers are as concerned as service providers that if you miss-step then chances of a cost-neutral change are low. Processes have to be manifestly adaptable, compartmentalized, and also modifiable if the need occurs (again possibly investment-driven), but it will keep the industry in tune and focused on the developments in media and content that are now arriving, whether they be dynamic publishing and or real-time updating while maintaining high quality.

Invest in the right skilling programmes that one can harvest. There is business to be had from multi-language publishing and translations, even non-European. The lack of good language learning programmes in India has always meant that even skilled graduates have been behind this curve. Can it be addressed or improved?

There are several other areas to potentially focus on, while keeping core strengths functional through continuous improvement and streamlining. In sum, build capabilities to produce and deliver content across media and markets. Build relationships exclusively through trust and transparency, which is the key to sustaining fruitful global partnerships.

To end, I ask a question: could the industry get disrupted?

If developments globally are any indication, the answer is most likely that it could. But it need not be, or one could leverage the disruptive moment to build something unique.

ANIL CHANDY is Vice President, Major Reference Works at Springer Nature, where he leads Springer Nature's global reference publishing programme including the well-known scholarly reference brands Springer Reference and Palgrave Macmillan Reference. He is based in Singapore.

5

BOOK DISTRIBUTION IN INDIA

"The book trade is a fulfilling business"

Ramesh Chandra Jain

Q: How and when did your journey in the book world start?

RCJ: My eldest brother Satyaprakash was a Gandhian; he built up a very good library on Gandhiana and other things like nature cure. After a while, he ran out of money and space both, so he started selling the books. Because he had collected more than one copy of many books, he decided to dispose of the spare stock by setting up a shop at home. He started getting good response. The year was 1962, and customers would come by appointment. Soon a loyal clientele grew. And then one day we decided, why not start a book-selling outlet? That was in the mid-1960s; I graduated in 1964 and joined him. When it first opened in 1967, the shop was known as Prabhu Book Service. It was the second branch of its namesake; the original Prabhu is in Gurgaon, known for rare old books. A printing press came up nearby and, in 1967, we opened a shop on Ansari Road. A year later the family business was divided up and, as part of the settlement, I got the Ansari Road establishment. So I renamed it after my father, Manohar Lal Jain.

Q: What are the changes you have experienced over the years in book-distribution patterns and how is the journey so far?

RCJ: It has been a wonderful journey. When I started, most of the PhDs were in history. Everybody was studying political or administrative history, but now it's multi-disciplinary, we have people studying social history, history of wine or education. Earlier authors and scholars were focusing on personalities. Famous Indian historian Sarvepalli Gopal also continued as a student at Balliol, earning his DPhil on the vice-royalty of Lord Ripon in 1951. Now people are writing on sati, intoxicants, military history and other new topics.

When I was growing up in the book trade, there were a few distribution houses, which were distributing imported titles. India Book House was one big name, which was primarily importing academic books from the UK and America. And then there were other distribution houses that were distributing paperback fiction, popular literature—all imported. Indian publishing was nowhere; it was very small, and most of the books were imported. Since we were coming out from colonial domination, we still had titles, which were written long back.

In the 1960s, there was one publishing house—Asia Publishing House—which was Bombay based. And others were Calcutta based. But gradually all of them disappeared and later new publishing houses like Vikas, etc. were established. In late 1960s and 1970s, Indian publishing expanded exponentially. So it was the time we needed distributors to sell these books. A Kanpur-based company, UBS, opened its office for academic and textbooks distribution; they did really well for nearly 20 years. And we had two others publishers—Munshiram Manoharlal Publishers Pvt. Ltd and Motilal Banarsidass, who were publishing a lot of stuff to be distributed. So it was obvious that dedicated distribution houses were needed.

Q: What are the challenges experienced in the past and how does the situation look now?

RCJ: The initial years as an independent bookseller were tough. Help came from the US, where about 18 universities set up academic centres of Indian studies around that period. Scholars who joined these centres needed specialized books on India. I would send catalogues to the American universities. Word-of-mouth publicity helped.

Challenges are always there; 10 years back everyone said printed books would disappear and e-books would replace paper books; thankfully that phase also got over. I feel logically it's not possible to have e-books every time. They are good for reference. And most of our readers are also comfortable with printed books; they are not happy with the idea of reading 600 or 800 pages on any screen. And now online selling is causing substantial damage to the book trade. Most of the business has been taken over by online booksellers; their competition is unhealthy. It's all about discount and not about quality.

Q: What is the current situation of distribution houses in India?
RCJ: Coming to distribution, I feel we still lack good distribution houses for Indian books. Now what is happening is that every publishing house is looking for distribution houses, which are not catering to a large number of publishers. For Indian titles, it is difficult to find good distribution house; every publishing house is looking for individual distribution channels, like Penguin goes to Prakash Book House and OUP doesn't distribute through anyone. But if we have one good consolidated distribution house, where we can find around 40-50 publishers under one roof, it will be a good option for buyers. If one wants to acquire books for a library, one needs to visit 10 different places or sources to procure them, which is very tiresome. After UBS, no one attempted to have big distribution house, DK Company Distributors, have tried, but now they have nearly folded up.

Q: How has the emergence of technology impacted distribution?
RCJ: Working model has changed substantially; previously it was all offline. Now online operations are more prevalent, but distribution channel is still very important for academic titles. Out of so many changes, there are several improvements as well, like logistics was never simpler. We can maintain the whole data and see the number of titles sold in any particular territory. So I feel the distribution channel is much more efficient and easy now.

Q: Book distributor or publisher, which one will you choose?
RCJ: Distribution and publishing are two different ballgames. You need a good manuscript to have a good book, which also needs lots of professionals like editors, designers, marketing team to bring it out. Whereas distribution is simple: all you need is a good number of titles.

Finding a good book or manuscript to publish is very difficult and different, but getting one is easy. I enjoyed both.

Q: You have spent 50 years in the book trade, how do you feel?
RCJ: I feel publishing is a noble profession; I thoroughly enjoyed my entire journey. Only anyone who is serious can stay for long. I feel a lot of work still needs to be done. We are bringing to light good work done by scholars; they need to be published. I enjoyed my publishing career so much that I still want to be surrounded by books even after 50 years. It's a very fruitful and fulfilling experience. God gives us one life, so we have to give back to society. I have published more than 1,500 titles; it's so fulfilling.

RAMESH CHANDRA JAIN is the founder of Manohar Publishers & Distributors. Initially selling only rare and out-of-print publications, Manohar soon branched out into local sales and export of new books published in India, and thereafter into publishing scholarly works under its own imprint.

6

DISTRIBUTION AND SUPPLY CHAIN MANAGEMENT

"E-commerce has impacted traditional supply channels"

Ramesh K. Mittal and Pranav Gupta

Q: How has the book distribution network evolved?

RKM: Traditionally, the publisher used to sell books to certain recognized wholesalers, and these wholesalers would sell them further to bookstores or suppliers for onward sale to the end customer. Over a period of time, with the advent of internet and other market facilities, the role of book wholesalers continued to diminish, and the publishers themselves began selling directly to bookstores and even to the end customers.

Q: Why does it remain so Delhi-centric even now? What happens for regional markets?

RKM: Up to around the country's independence, Kolkata used to be the hub of publishing, which shifted to Mumbai, and continued there until the 1970s. Ever since the 1980s, Delhi happens to be the main centre of publishing. Perhaps, because the weather conditions for printing as well as preservation of books are favourable; and second, because it is the capital city. Regional markets are also thriving because majority of regional publishing happens in the language of that region, besides English.

Q: Has the same changed over time?

RKM: Yes, it has changed over a period of time, as indicated above. There are high-end bookstores in some of the regions, and those publishers, especially from the textbook industry, having good market share in any particular region, come up with branch offices in those areas.

Q: What are the current challenges and the road ahead?
RKM: Like each industry, the book industry is also facing challenges. School textbook publishers are coming across with the government's policy to introduce more books published by the National Council of Educational Research and Training (NCERT).

Piracy has also impacted a great deal, since a lot of books (especially school and college textbooks), are either pirated or photocopied to fulfil the needs of the students.

Copy-paste publishing is another challenge for well-researched publications. The book industry has, and will continue to, improve content besides keeping textbook prices moderate. Publishers who have a good standing give due significance to well-researched content, good editing and good production.

Q: What are the challenges of collections, if any? Getting money from the book trade has always been tough: why is this the case and can it be addressed?
PG: Getting money from the book trade has always been a problem for publishers, and more so in recent years. The reason behind this is that there is no proper registration required to start or close a book business. There should be some sort of registration (regulation) for publishers and booksellers, where certain mandatory compliances are regularized. The laws to protect the beneficiary from bounced cheques have to be stringent. The book industry should also come together to ensure that nobody ditches any of its stakeholders as far as payments are concerned.

Q: How has e-commerce impacted traditional supply channels? Is it complementary, supplementary or replacing?
RKM: The advent of e-commerce has definitely impacted the traditional supply channels. E-commerce is indeed complementary and helps in making any book available to even the remotest corner of the country/world, including those places where there are no bookshops. Moreover, one can find a greater number of books in an e-store than in a physical bookstore. As such, the end customer has more choice when

it comes to buying. E-commerce is, however, replacing bookshops. As a result of which, a number of bookshops have closed down or are diversifying their interests to other areas of business.

Q: Has the supply chain improved over time?
PG: The supply chain has certainly improved with the use of electronic orders, queries, invoices, fast couriers and excellent transport services.

Q: What have been the major changes in printing technology?
PG: There has been a lot of improvement in printing technology over the past couple of decades. Automation and precision in the industry have changed/improved the quality of books a great deal. With the possibility of keying in and pre-setting the entire book using state-of-the-art software, it hardly takes a couple of hours for a book to be ready for printing. Also, printing itself does not take as much time as compared to the past.

Q: What is more—print-on-demand, offset or digital? What are the opportunities you see in the same?
RKM: Print-on-demand is generally used for books where smaller quantities are required by the market. It could even be as little as one copy. Whereas, the majority of printing takes place through offset process. E-books are altogether an independent product meant for a certain section of customers who prefer digital over printed material.
PM: While print-on-demand is growing, offset printed books will also continue to have a good market. Despite the fact that e-books have impacted the printing world, at least with respect to certain section of consumers, we believe that all three modes will continue to exist and survive.

Q: Do you think quality is a consideration in the books market? Quality versus Price—what would you say is more important?
RKM: Quality definitely is a big consideration in the market. But, at the same time, the consumer always looks at the prices. Though the cost

of content writing, editing and paper differs a lot in terms of quality. But in terms of printing, the difference is not expected to be much. So publishers should maintain a feasible price structure, while continuing to keep up the quality of their books.

Q: The number of books printed and publishers have increased in spite of the advent of e-books. What future do you see in the next five years?
RKM: Yes, the number of books printed and the number of publishers have been increasing continuously despite the advent of digital/e-books. The future of printed books still continues to hold well. In fact, statistics from developed countries show that sales of e-books have been declining slowly.

RAMESH K. MITTAL is Director of D.K. Agencies, an exporter of books and publications since 1968 and bibliographic services provider since 1973. He is also Director of LiFi Publications. He is Immediate Past President, CAPEXIL and ex-Chairman, Books, Publications and Printing Panel, CAPEXIL. He is Secretary-General of the Afro-Asian Book Council and the Indian Reprographic Rights Organization, and Advisor to Akhil Bharatiya Sanskrit Prakashak Sangh.

PRANAV GUPTA is Director of Prints Publications, an exporter of Indian publications since 1966. He is Member, Regional Committee, Northern Region for the Books, Publications and Printing Panel of CAPEXIL; and is also on the Executive Committee of the Federation of Indian Publishers. Pranav is Director of the Afro-Asian Book Council, and regularly participates in various social welfare programmes.

PART

2

Indian Publishing Looking at Itself

PART II • INDIAN PUBLISHING LOOKING AT ITSELF

AUTHORS AND THEIR PUBLISHERS

LITERARY AGENTS

LITERARY FESTIVALS AND BOOK FAIRS

TEACHING PUBLISHING

INDIA IN THE GLOBAL PUBLISHING COMMUNITY

INDIAN PUBLISHING LOOKING AT ITSELF

Arguably, relationships are the bedrock of publishing and this section looks at the evolution of the most sacred of all publishing relationships. The author-publisher relationship, based as it is on mutual respect and trust has endured and sometimes has a life beyond the book. The role of the editor has of course changed in line with current dynamics of publishing but remains vital. The first three pieces are eloquent odes to the joys of this relationship in publishing.

Yet, as authors have become more aware and savvy, they have expectations that can be filled effectively by literary agents and this profession is therefore gaining credibility, according to the next two contributors.

After publishing, comes outreaching to readers and a wider audience and that's where book fairs and festivals play a key role. The next four interactions with the founders of three major festivals and the iconic National Book Trust (NBT), tell their significant place in connecting readers to books and their authors.

How are publishing professionals created? Can you teach skills relevant to publishing or can they only be learnt on-the-job? We talk to both, one of the oldest, most enduring teaching programmes and another one, that is amongst the newest.

How does the global publishing community view the Indian market? Key members of the German Book Office (GBO) and the Publishers Association (PA) tell us how they immerse in and interact with our market.

7

THE AUTHOR–EDITOR RELATIONSHIP

"Involved yet detached!"

*Karthika V.K.**

After twenty-one years in this industry, I can say with certainty that the best thing about a career in publishing is the people you get to work with. Colleagues, writers, reviewers, academicians, booksellers, literary agents, and of course the readers you get to meet or talk with—there are so many who are as invested as you are, in the fate of the written word.

At the centre of this web is the author-editor relationship that has been the mainstay of acquisition and publication of trade books anywhere in the world. Or so I had always thought and said to younger colleagues and aspiring editors. Until a new factor emerged in the equation: the primacy of marketing in the publishing process. Earlier, writers were keen to negotiate advance and royalties; the new focus is on marketing budgets and a publicity plan that could become the deciding factor for choosing one publisher over another.

Does that mean editors have become redundant in a time of self-publishing and aggressive marketing? I had always imagined that the passionate commitment of an editor to a work and its creator was fundamental to the success of a book, but is that even true any more?

I decided for the purpose of this piece to ask a few writers what they thought of their relationship with, and expectations from, their editors. Here are some examples of what came back to me.

'My editor', said one writer, a novelist and poet, 'needs to be a sounding board who can evaluate my book idea for its potential and

**With grateful acknowledgement to Anita Nair, Aparna Jain, Manu Pillai, Kishwar Desai and Ruchir Joshi.*

possibilities even if it's just a mere thought; a fellow traveller who can help me get back onto the path when I veer too far away from it or get hopelessly lost in the journey with a book; a friend who has faith in my writing and in my ability to tackle a subject even through the darkest days and especially when I find myself asking—why bother?'

Another writer of non-fiction summarized it thus: 'My editor is the one person I trust implicitly while writing. This, however, is a relationship built over time.'

'I am sure to get a considered response, sometimes as excited as I may be or sometimes different to my line of thought. Since we both are invested in the right outcome, it's easy to take suggestions on board. In many ways, for me, my editor is like an artist. It's not about the commas and periods. Their assured yet deft touches and insights can make a manuscript sing.'

That's quite a tall order for anyone, I was thinking, when this popped up in my inbox from a young historian and author:

'The ideal editor is that increasingly rare creature—one who "gets" your work but also knows just what will transform it from good to great. For writers, substance is often the primary motivation, but the editor helps give that substance its shape and final texture. Writing, after all, is a marriage between craft and art, your conscience and your creative energies, and an editor is your bridge, your first reader, your critic, and your friend who holds your hand where needed, guides you, and when it is necessary, shakes you up in the right way.'

But what if the relationship doesn't go the way it's intended to? Here is another author who emphasizes the connection between a writer and an editor but has also felt the lack of a connection:

'I think it starts like a blind date in which you either get along or you don't. If you are smart, you will spot the differences in the first meeting, but usually it takes a few chapter edits to figure it out and then it may be too late. It is not only about a copy edit, but also about understanding the "soul" of the book. The author has very high expectations, which are often at quite another level from that of the editor or "book doctor". And if the "book doctor" is constantly giving out the wrong remedy, it may become a relationship that gets increasingly difficult—and yet it may be tough to break off because the author and editor are tied together by the book and a publishing deadline. I have had a couple of editors whom I simply had no rapport with. I found they did not understand the book I had written and so I could not really respect their suggestions. Nor could I accept many of their suggested changes. But when the author respects the editor, and the editor immediately gets what the author means (even if he or she disagrees with them), then it's a good relationship. Also, I do think that this understanding grows over the years.'

A fifth writer expanded on these ideas of shared commitment and responsibility when he wrote that the relationship between a writer and their editor is 'akin to that of a sportswoman/sportsman with their coach. Not exactly, but in that zone, so to speak. So, for instance, if I'm writing a novel, it's a bit like running a marathon or cycling on the Tour de France, say (with no other competition, only my own previous times to beat) and the publisher, ideally, appears at the pit stops, bearing reviving juices, organizes the massages and the repair-work on the body, gives advice on how to proceed on the stretches that await. The trainer/coach cannot run or cycle the marathon for you, but they can keep you feeling that you are not alone in this crazy endeavour.'

'When the piece of writing is "done", as in maybe first full draft, or nearing completion, then the editor-publisher is more like a dramaturge, this position that Germans specially have in their theatres. The dramaturge is not the producer, director or actor, s/he doesn't "tell" the director and cast how to play a scene or perform a play. They explicate or remind the theatre crew of the context, of what has gone before, of where they are placed in the creative world, they help cut out the self-indulgences, the potential bad mistakes, if necessary they help re-jig the whole production, but always keeping at the forefront what the director/cast (read writer) were attempting to pull off. In other words, the editor-publisher doesn't write the novel for you, they try and help you to arrive at the best shape for the novel that you are trying to write.'

'Once the text is ready to be put between covers and sent out into the world, then the role of the editor-publisher shifts, weight is transferred from the editor part of the role to the publisher side. Some writers are confident, bullish about what they have produced, others are less so, or the complete opposite. In any case, self-praise and crude self-promotion sit badly on a writer's shoulders, no matter the current fashion of many writers talking like tennis stars ('I was great, my serve worked really well, my backhand was amazing,' etc.). Hopefully, the publisher and their team would do the trumpeting, the flag-waving, the imaginative and energetic promotion of the book or piece of writing.'

Writer after writer seemed to articulate their idea of a working relationship as an intensely personal, all-encompassing friendship that extended beyond the page and the written word. Male or female, fiction or non-fiction writer, one-book down or fifteen-books-and-counting, they all looked to the editor to be critic as well as champion, and expected them to stay in their lives well after the editorial process was finished on the current book. They also signalled a desire for their editor to be more than a wordsmith in helping to shape their text, they wanted them to save some energy for the cheerleading that was required afterwards, when marketing plans were being written up and implemented.

The word, or at least the sense of it, that kept coming up over and over again in conversations with writers, was integrity. A deep unshakeable integrity that demands complete honesty at every stage. There is nothing to be gained from too much tact or forestalling of conflict, and everything to be lost. A writer I work with, walked out after a slug-fest of a meeting where we had struggled to find common ground between her aesthetic expectations and my financial compulsions and said, 'Well, that was a muscular conversation as usual!' We laughed and made up because both she and I knew we wanted exactly the same thing at the end of the day: a brilliant, beautiful book, which we could both be proud of.

Integrity, honesty, commitment, responsibility, confidentiality, as well as the original given, of skill and professionalism—if these are the expectations and the standards by which writers assess their editors, there is no doubt that every editor expects the same of their writers. And therein lies the beauty of this world we inhabit, where we demand and give unstintingly of the best we have within us. There is not one editor I know who does not feel hurt when an ungenerous review appears in the media or when a writer is disappointed by less than satisfactory sales. There are many writers I know who would put everything aside to provide a shoulder when their editor needs one. And each time I hear of, or see, or experience an instance of this sincere affection that lies at the heart of the publishing enterprise, I am reminded of why I am simultaneously challenged and at peace in this constantly changing world of publishing in India.

KARTHIKA V.K. is Publisher, Westland Publications. She started her career as an editor at Penguin Books India, and thereafter moved to HarperCollins India where she was Publisher for ten years. She joined Westland Publications, an Amazon company, in January 2017 to build a list that prioritizes literary fiction and narrative non-fiction. Over the course of her twenty-year career, Karthika has edited and published books in different genres including fiction, non-fiction, poetry and comics, and has worked with a number of award-winning authors.

8

THE AUTHOR–PUBLISHER RELATIONSHIP

"Strong relationships of mutual trust with authors"

Ravi Singh

Q: Share your experience of moving from a publishing giant to a new venture.

Ravi: If the move had been from one large multinational publishing company to another, or from one boutique subsidiary of a large company to another, the experience would have been less satisfying. There would have been the same pressures to play it safe, to crowd the list with commercial and literary stars, which means turning away from new voices—unless they, too, mimic the stars in style, content, sensibility. There's also a tendency in the larger houses to glamourize books and authors—even the business of publishing. There's some merit in all that, but overall it discourages risk-taking, finding and nurturing new talent, and staying with veterans who aren't the flavour of the season.

In a smaller, independent company there's greater room for diversity, and room for some mavericks, too. That's the kind of publishing my colleagues and I enjoy. Of course, we need to be profitable, that's crucial, but if we can learn to live with reasonable profits and not be chasing huge margins all the time, it's liberating. All of us at Speaking Tiger earn less than what we used to, but there's greater satisfaction.

Q: Share the opportunity and challenges you faced.

Ravi: The opportunity is in being a little freer of market trends and pressures. We can—in fact, we have to—think up interesting books, find fresh voices. And we're able to build a balanced list.

The greatest challenge is money—we lose some good books, especially those represented by foreign agents, because we can't win any auction. The corporate-backed companies will always outbid us. So we almost never consider books offered by foreign agents.

Another challenge, also to do with resources, is that we are a small team, and that is not likely to change, so we're always working overtime.

There's also the question of brand—there are authors who'd want the Penguin logo on their books, for instance, because of the global history of the brand. But we've been lucky in that we've acquired a distinct profile and some fantastic authors prefer to be on our list than any other.

Q: Tell us something about author relationships in this context.
Ravi: As I've said, there are authors who prefer to work with us—their support is crucial. We wouldn't survive without strong relationships of mutual trust with our authors. Which is why it's extremely important to try to give every book equal attention.

Q: How have you managed a good relationship with your authors, right from your time at Penguin to Aleph and now Speaking Tiger? How do you ensure they keep coming back to you for their next release?
Ravi: I haven't thought much about that. I suppose the thing to do is to respect your authors, work closely with them and not lie to them—about the quality of their work or your own limitations and constraints. Get to know them well, and the best way to do that is to read them with commitment and interest. But it's also important to remember that only a few authors will be friends, from whom you can expect genuine regard and loyalty. Never, ever let them down. The others come and go.

Q: Share your branding strategy and the establishment of this new imprint.
Ravi: It's easier building an identity if you're focused on a specific area or genre of publishing—writing by and about women, for instance, or art books. But we wanted an eclectic list. So we knew it was a certain sensibility that would define us—a clear commitment to diversity and quality, and being equally clear about the kind of books we would *not*

publish. Taking chances that the others may not—because the subject is tricky or a little radical or the theme or the author isn't marketable—that's important to us. Publishing translations of non-fiction—like Daya Pawar's memoir, *Baluta*—when most others privilege fiction; publishing Wendy Doniger, the brilliant scholar and writer whose books two publishers had chosen to withdraw rather than defend; publishing short-story collections and poetry, which are traditionally considered hard to sell; bringing great new fiction to Indian readers from Africa, South East Asia and Eastern Europe—these are some of the initiatives that have helped us build a distinct image.

Q: How do you handle demands for censorship and banning of books? Speaking Tiger has just published Wendy Doniger's new book: how was it dealing with or responding to withdrawals of her earlier book by Oxford University Press and then Penguin?
Ravi: We've had no problems. *The Hindus* is widely available. Our view at Speaking Tiger is simple—once we've taken a considered decision to publish a book, we'll defend it. If we must fight the battle in court, we will. If the higher courts rule that we cannot continue to publish a book, we'll have no choice, but we won't withdraw books under pressure or do secret deals with people seeking bans. If there's threat of violence, we'll take precautions—we certainly don't want to put our colleagues and associates at risk; but it's the police we'll turn to first, it should be their responsibility to ensure our safety.

Q: In a highly competitive as well as fickle environment with readership declining, how did you manage?
Ravi: Well, every day is a bit of a battle, but every day we also grow a little more confident. What's working for us is that for the most part we strike a balance between new voices and established names. And while we'll always take risks, we'll also always look for books that have the potential to be bestsellers but aren't the usual, lazy mass-market stuff.

We've found that it's also important to give every book equal attention—focusing on a few big books and star authors and neglecting the rest, which will always be the larger proportion on any list, is bad strategy.

As for readership declining, I'm not convinced about that. There are readers out there, but we won't find them if we think of them as a homogenous mass and if we all publish the same kind of books. It makes good business sense to publish across a range of genres and styles, identify different segments and cater to them.

Q: What are the trends you foresee, going forward?
Ravi: More non-fiction—especially the kind that doesn't sacrifice readability for scholarship and vice versa. And genre fiction will continue to grow.

Q: What will be the trends in Indian writing in English?
Ravi: I think Indian writing in English will remain diverse, but the middlebrow will grow, and good middlebrow is something to be valued, so this should be welcome. There'll be more solid yet accessible non-fiction, as I've said. Though there isn't likely to be much genuine variety in fiction. Indian fiction in English will be almost entirely urban and middle-class. But that's been the case for many years now.

Q: How has online selling impacted sales?
Ravi: Overall, I'd say positively. Things may change later, if discounts go too high. While online selling does tend to work best for the bestsellers—it's a bit like making the rich richer—the range of books that is available is huge, which is a great thing. And the bigger online sellers pay publishers on time, so we value them greatly!

RAVI SINGH is Publisher at Speaking Tiger, a Delhi-based independent publishing company he co-founded with Manas Saikia. In the past, Ravi has been Editor-in-Chief and Publisher at Penguin India, and Co-Publisher at Aleph Book Company. Over 23 years he has worked with most of South Asia's finest writers.

9

THE EDITOR: THEN AND NOW

"It was initially the editors who were in control"

Adil Tyabji

For an idea of what it meant to be an editor in the days when I was aspiring to be one in distant 1968 and how that role has changed since, one needs to examine how publishing has fundamentally changed. Publishing then was perceived to be a profession clearly differentiated from a business: a gentleperson's genteel engagement with earning a living, but just about achieving the latter. Very few people knew what a publishing career meant so it had a certain cachet, particularly when you threw in mysteriously that it had to do with books, an even more mysterious commodity, provided you did not need to reveal what you actually earned; fortunately, not many stooped to ask you that, at least on casual contact.

Publishing then was a low-key, low-paid profession shorn of the razzamatazz that surrounds it today, but those within it believed they were performing a service of great value and thoroughly enjoyed engaging with it. Notwithstanding the low salaries there was very little staff turnover. I occasionally mourned that if no one left, there would be no room at the top to which to aspire!

Having broadly set the scene we come to what the editor actually did. As in all professions, where you work and with whom makes an enormous difference to your functioning and responsibilities. I personally worked for only two publishers: first with Orient Longman(s) (OL), as the Orient BlackSwan of today was then known (three years), and Oxford University Press India (OUP) (20).

Fortunately, and in a sense surprisingly, both in the main functioned more or less identically. Both had a head office in Delhi and branch offices in Bombay, Madras, and Calcutta, and each had an academic/general list which attempted to earn its keep and more but there was no acute scrutiny of that because it was the flagship or loss-leader. The real earnings came from, (1) the educational list (school and college textbooks), annotated college anthologies prescribed by various state educational boards (if there was a somewhat seamier side, this was it!), and supplementary reading material; and (2) reprints of reference material (dictionaries in the main), at various levels, largely generated by the respective UK parent companies (although OUP stoutly maintained that it was not a company but a department of the University of Oxford, and we wore that as a badge of honour! and attempted to live up to it).

In OL then there was no strict bifurcation between the academic/general and educational departments so an editor could be simultaneously working on academic/general and educational books, although usually a broad bifurcation came about depending upon skills and preference; in OUP specific editors were assigned to each department but come the last minute rush preceding the academic year and most editors pitched in with the educational list, the academic/general editors usually working on supplementary reading material. There was no specialization within these broad categories either until later years when it crept in to a degree.

As a largely academic/general editor, in OUP I was either assigned a manuscript by the then chief editor/general manager (Ravi Dayal when GM, for many very fruitful years, combined these roles) or generated it myself on the basis of an idea or proposal, with of course the concurrence of the former, and where necessary a specialist report. There were visits to the university for inspiration and bookshops for feedback.

Manuscript in hand you were on your own without any external interference, no time pressure except from within and occasionally from the author. Ivor Lewis for instance, a charming sprightly individual of 80+ years from the Isle of Wight, who became a great friend and spoke eloquently about the charms of the nuns at the convent where he stayed when in India, was forever threatening to die and once, just as we were approaching the end (not of him but the book!), in a state of depression, wrote lightheartedly that he would sue me. Then it was an intense 6-to-8-month engagement (although Irfan Habib's *An Atlas of the Mughal Empire* took three gruelling years and Ivor Lewis's *Sahibs, Nabobs and Boxwallahs*, two!) with the MS to be edited, detailed queries and suggestions exchanged with the author, the focus on expression and presentation but also on structure, discrepancies, repetition.

Then the proofs arrived and moved between editor and author accompanied by carefully crafted letters, drafted and typed, with more queries, pleasantries, and humour, providing the author, frequently anxious and impatient, continuing reassurance and support. The relationship at this point was frequently very intense, albeit transitory.

In addition to the interaction with the author there was close coordination with the production department. I was extremely fortunate for most of my time at OUP to have the able and sage guidance of Dipen Mitra, a soulmate, as production manager.

They did the costings, chose the typeface, designed the text, and selected the most suitable press. When considered necessary, the press was jointly visited where I was privileged to watch the magical sight of molten metal pouring down to form letters and pass through successive generations of evolving technology: hand setting, monotype, linotype and admire the exceptional skills of the people who operated them and occasionally rescued us from the brink of disaster. Sadly, a sterling and dying breed of professionals defeated only by technology. Publishing and printing presses were then inextricably intertwined.

Those are glimpses of the past, what of the present? I have observed that in publishing it was initially the editors who were in control, and that was the period with which I naturally empathize, then the baton passed to the accountants, and eventually to the sales and marketing people who have since maintained a stranglehold. Although from a purely economic point of view the present arrangement makes eminent sense, should publishing be subject to purely financial criteria? Does publishing in its present form adequately play its essential role of having the author at the centre and providing the mutually enriching services necessary to enable the organization to get the best out of him/her and publish the best possible books in the most attractive form possible?

What brought about this dramatic change in the structure of publishing and even infected the renowned university presses whose fundamental role it is to *nurture* authors and scholarship. Some time in the 1980s I think, publishers overseas, followed astonishingly even by the renowned university presses, decided that having copyeditors on their payroll was a waste of money. They occupied too much expensive space, spent far too much time worrying about commas and split infinitives, so why not hire them in their own space at rates they (the publishers) thought they were worth. They succeeded in some measure because in consequence there were hundreds of experienced copyeditors on the limb with few other alternatives. Also, given the scale of many of their operations they were able to have an entire department monitoring the performance of their external copyeditors. OUP UK, for instance, which in the first flush of enthusiasm fired a substantial clutch of brilliant editors, has I believe an elaborate and very well-organized one.

A decade later, when the Indian general managers, by now rechristened managing directors! with a background in sales and marketing, with no interest in or inclination to fight for the traditional independence of the Indian branch operations, this organizational blueprint was transported to India.

To my mind this was an entirely misplaced move; the situation in India was very different. There were relatively few experienced editors and with the model being adopted by a large number of publishers, the catchment too narrow. In OUP we could by no stretch of the imagination claim to have had the best editors but what was important was that they were on the payroll and responsible to the management and the authors for the books they produced and how they produced them. A reasonably competent in-house editor, responsible to the organization for results, I think, produces better outcomes than someone out of the blue, generally underpaid, underqualified, and no sanction beyond not getting a second assignment from a particular publisher. I would imagine, and given my experience as a freelance editor of a couple of decades, the commissioning editors of today frequently do not have the time or the ability to evaluate the quality of the work offered.

I had naturally seen these winds of change and decided that my interest in working on manuscripts far exceeded that of merely planning and soliciting them. Perhaps the nature of the change can best be illustrated by a brief exchange I had with a charming lady from OUP's International Division at a party to welcome her to India. Touching on the future, she informed me with the utmost gravity: 'You will not be an editor you will be a product packaging manager.' Needless to say, much as I admire individuals who tirelessly and splendidly package our goods, I did not envisage that as my future. My new avatar overnight as a freelance copy-editor was somewhat daunting with only a meagre provident fund and gratuity in the bank, and those took a month or more to arrive. I was rescued by my editorial colleagues in OUP, first Rukun Advani, the then editorial director, academic and general, and when he himself resigned, Nitasha Devasar, who kept me almost continually in work, albeit at the near starvation wages that were then available, for over a decade.

A freelance editor does not have to prepare him/herself to rush to office in the morning, has the luxury of working uninterrupted in the comfort of home, can concentrate single-mindedly. On the other hand, there is an obligation to adhere to prescribed schedules, there is no guarantee that the morrow will see a manuscript on the desk, and if, as I do, s/he works on a single manuscript at a time, promising offers have to be declined, and it is more than likely that in consequence follow-up ones will not be forthcoming. The other disadvantage is that unless you are working directly for an author there is no contact with her/him whatsoever. The commissioning editor emails a manuscript, you edit and return it with broad comments and suggestions, text-related queries highlighted within the text, email it back, and wait for a cheque to arrive a month or so later! You, more often than not, do not know what the book looks like, when it is published, how it was received/reviewed. When a trifle diffidently (time had passed, memories were hazy) I agreed to write this piece, the first few lines were tapped out on my mobile phone on a Saturday afternoon at the bar of the India International Centre. A little Dutch courage is always useful in igniting resolve! This is only relevant here because it vividly illustrates how technology has dramatically changed the palate in terms of the editorial function, communication, and author–editor interpersonal relations, largely for the better, certainly for convenience and efficiency, and in some respects perhaps for the worse. Throughout my years with OUP there were no computers whatsoever, except during the last few years when a large, handsome standalone Mackintosh was acquired for design purposes which I admired from a safe distance! Then everything was done by hand. Manuscripts (ironically, the very word means book written by hand) were edited with fountain pen or ballpen, depending upon preference, proofs were corrected in the same way, letters were carefully crafted by hand unless you had a forte for dictation, and then typed and retyped.

For years after computers became omnipresent and ubiquitous, I obstinately maintained that editing by hand produced superior results because the slow pace of the operation permitted greater time for thought and consideration. It was only quite late into my editorial freelancing days that I bought a laptop on a whim and was persuaded by its convenience, and that conversion itself was gradual, for some years both methods going hand-in-hand, depending upon clients' preferences. Today I would regard hard copy as an enormous imposition but still miss the convenience of flipping the pages backwards and forwards. How times change!

Another significant change that technology brings is the instant availability of information. While in the past the editor scoured her/his reference shelf, and those of others, for references/words/meanings or queried the author, today the click of a button and there on your mobile phone is your dictionary, thesaurus, Wikipedia, Google, the last giving birth to that frightful term 'googled'.

Again another major change wrought by technology is in author–editor interpersonal relations. Because in the past correspondence, both in the writing and its conveyance (with the humble postman a star actor), was so much more time-consuming and infrequent, if utilized effectively it could create a great bond between author and editor. It is difficult to replicate the same personalized effect with today's instant electronic communication, which has taken a toll too on the art of correspondence and the pleasure of receiving a letter. Alas, no longer can 'Lost in the mail' be proffered as a convenient excuse. On the positive side, everyone is constantly in touch with everyone else which, if it lacks magic it is convenient and efficient but with that comes the price of an enormous overload of information which is often difficult to digest and maximally utilize.

In conclusion, a couple of thoughts and questions run through my mind. Where will future generations of copyeditors come from and with what background? Will future generations of commissioning editors be in a position to evaluate the quality of copyedited MSS they receive? What effect will the new arrangement have on the traditional, mutually enriching relationship that existed between the author, the editor and the publisher, now that the functions of the traditional editor have been cleft in half?

ADIL TYABJI joined Orient Longman as an editor in 1968 before moving to Oxford University Press India in 1972, where his roles included Assistant Manager of the Bombay branch and thereafter Senior Editor till 1992. He has since been working as a freelance publishing editor for a wide range of publishers, organizations and individual authors.

10

EMERGENCE OF LITERARY AGENTS IN INDIA

"Some local agents have started making giant strides"

Kanishka Gupta

In January 2016, Jaipur Bookmark, a publishing event held in conjunction with the famed Jaipur Literature Festival, organized a panel on agenting titled *Of Gatekeepers and Enablers*. The participants included, among others, two Indian agents and two agents from the West, one of whom represents the Booker Prize-winning Ben Okri. The panellists discussed the scope, peculiarities and challenges of the job, but without presupposing a complete ignorance on the part of the audience, something one definitely wouldn't have noticed around seven to eight years ago. There were two other interesting takeaways from the session that lasted nearly 45 minutes. First, there are certain commonalities in this highly specialized profession that cut across markets, territories, and, at times, even language. Second, the Indian agent has come so far as to share a platform with his far more experienced international counterparts.

Not too long ago, the Delhi edition of the Times Literary Festival included a session on agenting in India moderated by the bestselling writer Ashwin Sanghi. At the Delhi-government sponsored Delhi Literature Festival, held a few weeks before the Jaipur Bookmark session, a panel on publishing for aspiring writers included an agent as well. The Indian agent seems to have become an important part of the local publishing ecosystem.

While the first agency in India started in 1997, it was only in 2007, with the setting up of the Neville Tuli-backed Osian's Literary Agency, that the profession assumed some sort of formal shape in the country.

Although the agency soon folded up because of financial difficulties, it managed to discover some acclaimed and bestselling writers like Omair Ahmad, Saeed Mirza, Madhulika Liddle, Karan Bajaj, and others. This was followed by the Jaipur-based Siyahi, Writer's Side, Lotus Lane, Purple Folio and Book Bakers. In 2011, much to everyone's surprise, the UK-based Aitken Alexander Associates set up an India office. This last line would have surprised many industry watchers a decade ago, but not now when, due to a multiplicity of factors such as increasing reader base, setting up of local divisions of big multinational publishers, and the advent of the mass-market bestseller, sales and, subsequently, advances, have increased manifold. A debut fiction writer with no credentials can easily get a Rs 1,00,000 advance. This figure could go higher for a debut non-fiction writer. Fiction and non-fiction by established, award-winning, and celebrity writers can get Rs 10,00,000–15,00,000 as advance against royalties. Bestselling writers can get upwards of Rs 50 lakhs and, sometimes, even a crore. In 2013, the Khan market-based Red Ink Literary Agency, in operation since 2006, made it to the front page of all the top newspapers by securing a million-dollar advance for publishing phenomenon Amish Tripathi. It remains the highest payout to an author, Indian or otherwise, by a domestic publishing house.

Although it is true that in India, agents aren't valued that highly because of the widespread culture of direct commissioning, several published authors, established journalists, and even celebrities, who seemingly don't need agents, nonetheless sign with them for various reasons.

According to senior journalist and columnist Aditya Sinha, 'Going through an agent saved me the embarrassment of haggling with people I know and leaving this necessary activity to a third party. Plus, the agent knows all the publishers, and where my novel might make a proper fit. Also, I don't have to worry about follow ups and can just focus on my writing.' Amrita Tripathi signed her first book *Broken News* directly with a publisher and yet chose to go through an agent for her second book. 'Having Shruti Debi, then with Aitken Alexander, as my agent not only offered me some validation, but also (and perhaps more importantly) raised the bar for me. She helped me enormously as an editor during the writing of *The Sibius Knot*.... I suppose I also thought an agent was a prerequisite to be taken seriously, and to even think about breaking onto the international scene.'

A vastly underrated role of an agent is that of a sounding board and someone who actively develops book ideas with prospective authors. Both senior journalists Chitra Naryanan and Pranjal Sharma developed book ideas with their agent and didn't use him just to get a deal. For Aditya Mani Jha, a seasoned literary critic with a major newspaper, and thus in direct touch with most top publishers, an agent is a lot more than someone who just connects an author to a publisher. 'I look at the job of a literary agent as a combination of talent manager (in the Western, Colonel Tom Parker sense of the phrase), literary sounding board (on some days, everything you write will be horse manure), chartered accountant (although I've always loved math, not all authors do) and soothsayer (never underestimate the value of those). It is a confluence of skills and as a debutante [*sic*] author, I did not feel like I could do all these jobs (to say nothing of my actual day job) and still give the book the attention that it deserves. So I thought, why not let the specialist take over?'

Many authors go to publishers directly not because they are averse to working with agents but because of complete lack of awareness of their existence. One such author, the bestselling film writer Yasser Usman, was always under the impression that the usual way to reach out to a publisher was to get his/her contact details or email id from a published friend or colleague. Luckily for him, one such connection led to a contract for his first book on Rajesh Khanna. Ironically, he now completely understands the role and importance of an agent, but feels that introducing him/her at this point in his writing career may cause confusion and embarrassment for his publisher, with whom he gets along very well.

Manu Pillai is another well-known author who went directly to a publisher with his first book but is not closed to the idea of working with an agent. 'Not having worked with an agent, I can't comment on Indian agents in general. But I have been advised more than once about the advantages of working with someone who knows the publishing industry well, and can negotiate better prospects (and stouter financial terms!) for my work. I didn't necessarily feel the lack of an agent while working with HarperCollins on my first book, but for my next, whenever the time comes, I will think more seriously about working together with somebody who can, frankly, take care at least of those conversations that authors are not always well-equipped to handle themselves. The author's relationship is with the editor; for much of the other business that the process of publishing involves, an agent would be a welcome ally.'

In fact, even authors represented by foreign agencies, such as the pioneering investigative journalist Josy Joseph, see some positives to Indian agenting. 'Indian agents are visibly more aggressive in the market, and make an extra effort to find new writing talent. They are playing a crucial role in the booming publishing world because of their willingness to go hunting for new talent, and operate at all levels of the food chain,' says Joseph. Some award-winning authors, like Hansda Sowvendra Shekhar, have reposed faith in Indian agents to handle even the nearly unachievable foreign rights for their books. 'I just received a message from Jayapriya (of Jacaranda Literary Agency) telling me that she had read both my books, *The Mysterious Ailment of Rupi Baskey* and *The Adivasi Will Not Dance*, and she had faith in my books, and would like to represent them in territories excluding the Indian subcontinent. So, it was Jayapriya's faith in my books and my faith in Jayapriya that made me sign up with her.'

One problem Indian agents face is that of retaining authors they discover since editors may have developed a good rapport with the writer, who might consequently fail to see any value addition by the agent in future deals. According to prolific translator and novelist Bhaskar Chattopadhyay, 'Redundancy is an agent's biggest enemy. As long as the agent is doing his job and bringing in results, I don't mind paying him. The day I realize that he is not getting me the best deal that I could have possibly got, including the one I could have clinched on my own, his role becomes redundant. And why just an agent, that's true about anyone making a living. The only way an agent can survive is by ensuring that he always, always acts in the best interest of the writer, gets him or her the best possible deals.'

'With my agent I can express myself more freely and he can negotiate on my behalf. Also it makes my job easier about following up with the publishers regarding publishing dates, media coverage and money. It's not just about the initial contract but several other jobs that an agent helps you out with. That's why I continue to work with an agent,' says Pakistani anthropologist Haroon Khalid.

Although it will take another five years for agenting to become fully mainstream in India, some local agents have already started making giant strides, their turnovers surpassing those of highly reputed, medium-sized publishing houses. According to HarperCollins India CEO Ananth Padmanabhan, 'I think agenting in India came at the right moment when both publishing and the quality and diversity of content from authors began to grow both in depth and breadth. Ten years ago there was no commercial fiction, for example.' Although he feels there is room for better quality he adds, 'Submissions have changed as agents better understand publishers and the kind of books they seek.'

KANISHKA GUPTA, a writer and publishing commentator, is Founder of the literary agency Writer's Side. His second book is forthcoming from Speaking Tiger in 2018.

11

THE ROLE OF LITERARY AGENTS

"Literary agents are here to stay!"

Anuj Bahri

Q: How did your journey as a bookseller and then publisher lead you into Literary Agency?

Anuj: I have been a bookseller as per family tradition and it was a natural progression for me to add a publishing division to our core competence business…hence the publishing. Though we still consider ourselves a small publisher of few titles, quality is of importance for the kind of books we work on.

Negotiating rights is something I had been doing since the year 2002, but officially became a literary agent in 2009 and involved myself fully into negotiating rights, placements, and advances on behalf of authors within India and the world market.

Q: Is there a gap in the author–publisher linking that you feel a literary agent fills?

Anuj: It is only the literary agent that can fill this void in the relationship between author and publisher. We work as the bridge between the two. Authors are meant to write well and publishers must only get the best from every table. Here, we act as the bridge that connects the two thoughts and also work as the first line of editorial between good writing and the not-so-good.

Q: Many general books publishers do not entertain proposals sent by individual authors but only work through agents. Do you think this trend will grow further?

Anuj: The need and its processing are different in different markets.

Internationally, if a publisher advertises that they do not entertain any unsolicited works, then they mean what they say and do not entertain any proposal sent directly to them. However, in the Indian market I have seen a lot of publishers 'advertise' the same, but in practice they all sift through the 'slush pile' and certainly entertain the reasonably acceptable writing that can come to them directly as freebies.

Many Indian publishers also try to dissuade the author from engaging an agent for their writing, if they want to entertain the author directly. I have no idea if this will grow further, but the authors have certainly become more aware now.

Q: Does this extend to academic publishing as well? And if so, what does this mean for authors and for agents?

Anuj: Some academic publishers have started looking at rights through agents, that is, they have no problems in accepting works from agencies, but as the offers are still not big enough, they shy away from making an offer or a bid on the work.

Q: Why do you think it is important that a publisher should go with a literary agent? What according to you are the genres of books which require a literary agent?

Anuj: Good writing will always remain good—through the agency or directly to the publisher…and it will always be found one way or another, no matter where it is sourced from. Most publishers have no time to look at the large quantity of submissions that come to their doorstep every day. Hence a lot of them rely on agencies that they work with for the best to be shown to them, leaving out the not-so-good at this first level itself. There is no specific genre for good writing and all good writing deserves to be represented, otherwise the world will not know what it has missed!!

Q: Why do you think it is important for an author to take assistance from a literary agent? Could you give us some examples and experiences?

Anuj: The author's job is to write and not worry about offers, contracts and paperwork. Also, the literary agent is an expert on all these issues and can make an author's life much more comfortable and a great experience as a writer.

Most authors let their agents work freely after the rules of the relationship have been agreed upon, making the experience smooth and enjoyable—however, there will always be writers that keep interfering in the affairs of the agency and like to run their own ship. Relationships with such patterns sometimes work really well but often do not last too long.

A classic example are the agents of Harper Lee and Dan Brown who have stayed with the author since their first writings; however some other authors who like to take charge, change agents frequently.

Q: There are some foreign agencies that have set up shops in India as well. How do you view this development?

Anuj: Foreign agencies being here is a good sign because they have finally realized that the real flavour of the Indian writing is in its local market only. Home agencies will always work because they are clued into the local flavour. The foreign agencies only need the big names and that is all they look for because their interest in local writing is limited, but the fun is in making the local small author's name BIG!!

Q: We notice you are into selling Indian-language rights for foreign bestsellers. How did that happen? What is the success with it?

Anuj: There is more money in languages than anything else—the market is far far bigger in the languages than English. It's an amazing ride, so let's enjoy.

Q: What are your views on self-publishing and the road ahead for the literary agent in the next five years?

Anuj: Self-publishing is both good and bad; it all depends on how successful the book becomes. Indian publishers do not regard it well, but the international publishers have no issues with it. In fact, it is the agents that finally find the gem from among self-published works and make the works great. Agents often have to polish the original work, but can only do that if the book has substance to make it sparkle. Agents are here to stay!

ANUJ BAHRI heads the BAHRI Group. A third-generation bookseller and literary agent, he worked at the New Delhi's Bahrisons bookstore for more than 20 years under the tutorship of Balraj Bahri. Thereafter, he looked at other avenues in the book trade and added a small publishing division called Tara-India Research Press, and a literary agency called Red Ink, to the BAHRI business.

12

NATIONAL BOOK TRUST

"Promoting reading and a culture of books"

Baldeo Bhai Sharma

Q: What is the role NBT India plays in popularizing books and reading habit across India?

BBS: The responsibilities of the NBT include book-promotional activities, promoting reading habits and promoting a book culture. We are constantly working towards these responsibilities. We do not just publish quality books at affordable rates but also publish in more than 30 different languages.

For book-promotion activities, we organize not just the New Delhi World Book Fair but also several smaller book fairs in different cities across the country. This way books can be promoted in far-off areas as well. We even try to reach out to tribal areas where it is not possible for publishers to reach on their own.

For promoting a book culture, we use buses—Books on Wheels—to reach places where it is impossible for books to reach. This programme covers areas on district level across different states. This way we reach villages where there are no bookstores. There is huge enthusiasm amongst villagers when our buses reach there, which is very heartwarming. This shows that the reading habit has not declined; people are interested in reading but it is required to bring the books to them and they should be affordable. Villagers cannot come to cities to buy books, so we have to take books to them. We have 10 buses which are always on the run. We have one bus each in the East Regional Office, South Regional Office, and West Regional Office, plying across their zone.

In our Grant-in-Aid programme, we work with NGOs, where we give them funds to promote the reading habit. They go and organize district-level book fairs to promote a book culture. They also organize seminars and meet-the-author events where authors can meet children or young population.

Another important activity is our translations programme, where good literature from one language is translated to another language, so that more people can read it and know about their culture more. For example, we have translated *Thiruvalluvar*, Gita of Tamil, into Hindi so that the Hindi-speaking community can read and learn about this epic. It is getting very popular. All these activities are for promoting reading habits.

Q: How much focus needs to be on regional languages for the above to be fruitful?

BBS: Not just reading, NBT India is also striving to encourage regional languages which have very few books. Recently, we organized a workshop for children's books in the Kokborok language in Tripura. In this workshop, both authors and illustrators worked together and some of these manuscripts will soon be published by us. As many as 21 books have been published in three languages in Bihar—Magahi, Maithili and Bhojpuri. When children see books in their languages, they are inclined to read them. It is very successful and many areas like Jharkhand have asked us to bring out books in their languages. We have started working in these languages as well.

Q: How much of what the NBT publishes is in English versus regional and does it bring out multilingual works?

BBS: In fact, NBT publishes more books in Indian languages than English. We do not do multilingual books.

Q: You have 80,000 book club members. How has this been achieved and, more importantly, how is it sustained?

BBS: We have a different wing called National Centre for Children's Literature (NCCL), which organizes book clubs so that book lovers from far-off areas can be joined together. This centre is working to establish readers' clubs for making reading and teaching more interesting in schools, non-formal education centres, libraries, and education centres run by NGOs. Readers' Club is an activity centre based on reading books. Children, teachers, book-loving people of the society and parents came forward to set up and run such centres. A simple form has to be filled for membership of the club. Books worth Rs 500 are gifted to each new Readers' Club so that, apart from textbooks, other books are available for reading. Besides, a monthly bulletin is sent free to them. So it is like an extended family of the NBT. We are always trying to increase it further. We also monitor it regularly.

Q: Tell us something about the New Delhi World Book Fair?
BBS: The New Delhi World Book Fair is a kumbh of books. It is the largest book fair in the Afro-Asia region. Book lovers from not just Delhi and NCR but all over the country wait for one year and come to this book extravaganza. Books that they cannot find anywhere else, can be found at the book fair. So it has a big role to play in the circulation of books amongst the masses. It also has a big role to play in the promotion of a book culture. It has now expanded a lot. Earlier, it was a biennial show but since 2012 it has been an annual show. Book lovers come to this fair in large numbers and there have been a lot of developments in terms of the services and facilities provided. In the last two years, the number of book lovers to this fair have been more than 12,00,000.

Q: Where do you see NBT India five years from now?
BBS: NBT has recently completed 60 years of its existence. For this, new programmes have been developed and these will be carried forward on a continuous basis.

We have taken a few new initiatives to promote a book culture in faraway places in the country under our 'Har haath ek kitaab' (one book for every hand) campaign. For this, NBT India has tied up with Snapdeal Sunshine, a corporate social responsibility (CSR) initiative run by Snapdeal. The campaign is a nationwide online books donation drive especially targeting underprivileged children, and aims at inculcating a reading habit among them. As part of the campaign, Snapdeal will encourage its customers to buy and donate books published by NBT

India. People can choose to donate anywhere between 10 and 2,000 books by simply visiting www.snapdeal.com/offers/har-haath-ek-kitaab and clicking on the donation plan they prefer. NBT will dispatch books to NGOs across India working towards educating India's underprivileged children including Teach for India, Goonj, Bhumi, Aarti, Idea, Impact, 17,000 ft, Books for All, Turnstone Global, Guzarish, Educate Girls, PYDS (Purkal Youth Development Society), Pratham, Vimukti Sanstha, Deepalaya, and the Indian Dreams Foundation. We have already dispatched books worth Rs 3 lakh under this campaign.

For the first time, NBT India published a book in Sanskrit. We also organized the NBT Rashtriya Sanskrit Pustak Mela in Varanasi, where publishers showcased books in Sanskrit as well as in other languages.

To bring more and more people of rural areas closer to books, NBT is also planning to organize National Panchayat Book Fairs by involving Panchayati Raj institutions—the first one will be held in Srinagar, Uttarakhand.

Another new initiative is Rashtriya Bal Pustak Mela in Pune, where there will be a two-day seminar on what kind of books should be developed for children to inculcate a reading habit among them.

In order to encourage young women writers below 40 years, NBT has launched the 'Mahila Lekhak Protsahan Yojana', under which we will publish original and unpublished works of young writers. Besides, NBT has added several new series to its publishing profile, including Women Pioneers series, Veergatha series and Navalekhanmala.

As another first, NBT has conducted book publishing courses for girl students under the government's skill development programme—the first one was held at Aditi College.

Senior media personality and thinker, BALDEO BHAI SHARMA is Chairman of National Book Trust. He has served as Editor of dailies such as *Dainik Swadesh, Dainik Bhaskar, Amar Ujala, Panchjanya* and *National Duniya.* He is known for his participation in socio-political discourse on various news channels and has long been associated with Akashvani through numerous programmes. He also works with various social institutions.

13

JAIPUR LIT FEST

"Literary fests make ideas accessible"

Namita Gokhale

Q: Trace the history of the Jaipur Literature Festival (JLF) since its inception.

Namita: Described as the 'greatest literary show on Earth' and the 'Kumbh of literature', the ZEE Jaipur Literature Festival is a feast for the mind. The past decade has seen it transform into a global literary phenomenon, having hosted nearly 2,000 speakers and welcoming over a million book lovers from across India and the globe. The Festival's core values remain unchanged: to serve as a democratic, equitable platform offering free and fair access. Every year, the Festival brings together a diverse mix of the world's greatest writers, thinkers, humanitarians, politicians, business leaders, sports people and entertainers on one stage to champion the freedom to express and engage in thoughtful debate and dialogue.

Looking back, I feel extremely satisfied and a bit surprised by the way events have turned out. I am very gratified with the outcome. JLF had begun as a very tentative initiative years ago. In 2002, I helped to set up the first international festival of Indian literature in Neemrana with the Indian Council for Cultural Relations (ICCR). It had a fantastic turnout, with writers of the stature of Amitav Ghosh, Vikram Seth and Gopalkrishna Gandhi. At that time, I had insisted that we also bring in all the famous Indian writers in the major Indian languages. So we had U.R. Ananthamurthy, Sunil Gangopadhyay and Ashok Mitra.

Until then, English writing was more popular than Indian-language writing and the Indian-language writers felt a bit hurt by the fact that they were not taken seriously in the national media or by the national publishers. There was a sort of a confused snobbery in the English writing scene. So, when I was asked by the Jaipur Virasat Foundation in 2006 to help them establish a festival, I made it clear that I would do it only if it was to have the festival centered on the Indian languages. They were very happy with that and that's how we started.

Then in 2008, when Sanjoy Roy and Teamworks took over the festival formally, I continued with the same approach. For me, the main purpose was to forefront Indian literature, as much as I could in the Indian languages.

Now when I look back, I feel that purpose, to a very large degree, has been established. There are so many wonderful publishers operating in India and when they think of Indian literature they no longer think about it in isolation in terms of the Indian English writer. Perumal Murugan is as much part of Indian literature as Mahasweta Devi. The business of translating into different languages and making literatures accessible to each other is a reality. So I no longer need to push the writers the way I used to. There are a lot many people doing this. Our purpose of showcasing Indian literature and belief that India had a great literary moment ahead, if the languages can be in conversation with each other, is happening.

So the aims of the festival have also slowly changed and evolved. For me, the purpose is now to make ideas accessible to a new generation and of course to the older generation. There are so many young people in our audiences now, who are so very intelligent, articulate and so very engaged. Like it or not, people are afraid to say what they think. I think the JLF is a place where India can hear what it thinks. We have public conversation around many subjects which are not binary, which are not right or wrong or confrontational, which are not left versus right, but which have a larger, more intuitive look because so much change is happening in our country and that change needs to be recognized and understood and channelized. And that's the job of books and ideas!

Q: According to you, what are the reasons that the JLF got so big?
Namita: I remember, in 2008, we had wonderful programmes but we hardly had any audiences. So the very next year, the team and I worked

very hard in outreach. I remember if we had a Bangla session we would reach out to leaders in the Bengali community in Kali Bari, asking them to have a representation. The year we had our first Sindhi session, which involved a lot of Sindhi writers from India and Pakistan, we made sure that the Sindhi community knew about it. In that sense, we made specialized outreach programmes wherever we could. Over the years, the word spread and there are people who are curious to see what the JLF is all about, and we also have our regulars...people with a sense of community and solidarity as book readers and book lovers. The JLF can be intimidating because of its humungous size, but there are people who have figured it out—how it works, they look at the programme and plan their day—so they are able to make the most of it.

I think, if a person is not familiar with the inner dynamics of the festival, if they are lucky, they will land a wonderful session of their choice. Some people do get disoriented and disgruntled because the whole world has suddenly decided to visit the one inch of space!! But every year we expand the space, we run it intelligently to make our crowd management efficient. We have been on the course for two years at the Harvard Business School and been taught there as an example of cultural entrepreneurship. But I also think someday just the crowd management in Jaipur will deserve a study. So when our former President Late Dr A.P.J. Abdul Kalam came in 2015, we were completely taken by surprise....There were so many schoolchildren and they clambered on to trees to have a look at their idol. That was a life-changing moment for us! Similar was the case when Oprah Winfrey came to the JLF in 2012....There were thousands of people outside waiting to get in and get a glimpse of her.

Q: How has the engagement with readers/visitors changed over time?
Namita: There was a divide....The English-speaking ones did not go to the regional languages so much. There were more barriers and compartments within the audience, which has changed. The audience is much more flexible and listening to one another. And I think this has happened because of the literary festivals and here is really a literary community that has emerged.

It feels wonderful to see so many young people at the JLF. Out of every hundred children, even if two or three minds are sparked, if they get that inspiration that will unlock their capabilities and capacity, then I think it's worth it and wonderful.

Q: How has the nature of authorship changed over the years?
Namita: We had the immensely popular writer Chetan Bhagat at the JLF in 2009 and 2010 which sparked animated discussions over whether or not he deserved to be at a literary festival.

Now we have Amish Tripathi and Ashwin Sanghi who are bestsellers in a different formula. In 2018, we had Rupi Kaur, who represents a different kind of authorship which extends its hold across social media and also languages. So there are different authors who reach out to aspirational readership, each of them has a different formula....The fact is there are new and varying formulas around.

I also see some very wonderful literary writers, such as Perumal Murugan, who were thrown into the Indian consciousness because of an unfortunate event and went on to make their mark because of the excellent quality of their writing and wonderful translations available. The crossover to another language really depends on the quality of the translation. A bad translation can kill a book.

Q: What is the role of publishers at such fests?
Namita: At such fests, the role of the publisher is to help make books accessible and to make the less-known writers visible to the festival directors. Though it is great to have the authors of the top ten books of the year, there are many writers who are wonderful too and have written thoughtful and unusual, off-the-beaten-path books. When the festivals are able to highlight these writers too, that is their best function, because these writers also get visibility, audiences and readership. Besides, the audiences and the festival itself have more diversity and range.
Q: Across the nation, we say people are reading less, but on the other hand, book fests are growing. What is your take on this?

Namita: I don't think people are reading less; the publishing industry has so many economic problems: GST (goods and services tax), distribution, industry status, etc. The industry struggles to make it viable every time and most publishers are there because they believe in publishing not only as a financial proposition but because they believe in it. Keeping these constraints in mind, I think people are reading and people are reacting. I think it is a reality around the world that people do want to hear their writers speak, and it is a part of their old tradition. Writers are public figures. There are writers who are performers and writers who are non-performers. But I think that when people go to a festival and hear an author, it helps them bridge that approach to a book/set of books. The bookstore at the JLF—Full Circle—does extremely well in terms of sales. The fact that most publishing centres on December or January releases is because the major festivals, including Jaipur, happen around the same time.

Q: There has been a boom in book fests across the nation? Do you think this trend will continue to grow? Why/Why not?

Namita: Our festival has sparked off so many other festivals as well and I think that it is wonderful, because every town and city now has two or three festivals. Most of them follow the Jaipur model—while they get international writers, they also celebrate their local languages writers, thus bridging the distance between our Indian languages and English. It is really unfortunate that in India, like the class divide, the caste divide, the regional divide, language divide also exists. People with access to English tend to have a privilege. The more the Indian languages are celebrated, the more these distances will be bridged. Therefore, one of the reasons for the Jaipur BookMark is to work towards translations and to meet the international publishing industry and have conversations around the subject.

Also writers from different parts of India and abroad, writing in different languages, spend time together in these festivals. The off-time opportunities at the JLF give them time to meet other writers and to interact with them. There is an intellectual exchange of ideas.

Q: What is your opinion on e-books?

Namita: I am a physical book person. There is no doubt that e-books have a wonderful space. But, 'I live in a book shelf.' The habit of reading in a digital mode is also very compulsive because it is easier to carry and you can have multiple books in one device, then there is backlighting. Also, there are enhanced books with so many extra components of audio and video. I have no doubt that it is a feasible and important format for the future. But I love my physical books.

Q: What future do you see for book fests?

Namita: There are two kinds of book festivals—ones which are run with selfless passion/love for books and others are motivated by egos and celebrity culture. Book festivals which run with great depth, empathy and feeling have a bright future indeed! Human interaction with writers, thinkers and creative persons is a great catalyst and stimulus to reading and original thinking.

NAMITA GOKHALE is Festival Director for the Jaipur Literature Festival (JLF), and is JLF's co-Founder-Director along with William Dalrymple. Her debut novel *Paro: Dreams of Passion* was published in 1984 and she has written 14 books of which eight are fiction. Namita published the Bollywood film magazine *Super* right after dropping out of college.

14

HINDU LIT FOR LIFE

"Book festivals are a great addition to the reading culture"

Rachna Singh Davidar

Q: Trace the history, purpose and benefits of the Hindu Lit For Life (LFL) since its inception.

Rachna: The Hindu Lit For Life held its first festival in 2010 to commemorate the 20th year of the *Literary Review.* A literature festival contributes to the cultural fabric of the city and the country it is part of. I'd like to think that the LFL, in the eight years that it's been around, has made its own contribution to Chennai and the Indian literary festival circuit. I believe our festival gives writers and readers a tremendous opportunity to interact with each other. As we pride ourselves on being a festival of ideas, we also try to create a space in which ideas can be generated and reflected upon. In the 21st century, the cacophony all of us generate is deafening. So what we are trying to do, among other things, is to create a forum where, in addition to high-quality debate and presentations, people with conflicting viewpoints can get together to discuss contentious issues and think deeply about what is being said. Be that as it may, at the heart of the festival is literature: we showcase the best literature in India and the rest of the world. Nothing is taboo, the only basic criterion or filter we use is that the ideas and literary creations that find a place in the LFL line-up are world class and thought-provoking.

Q: How has the nature of authorship changed over the years?

Rachna: Writing and writers in India continue to evolve (and I only speak for books published in English, since that is what I know about). We're a far from mature market, unlike the UK for example, so there is plenty of scope for experimentation and for our writers to get to grips with the unparalleled source material they have at their disposal in our country. Already, we have some of the most interesting books and writers to be found anywhere in the world, and I am confident that in times to come, there will be more and more outstanding books that will be written here. One noteworthy aspect of the book scene, in the past decade or so, is the explosion of commercial writers. Selling them in high numbers is not uncommon. Still not enough though, and other than the top ten commercial writers we still don't have large sales, which is a major disappointment.

Q: How has the engagement with readers/visitors changed over time?
Rachna: There are many more readers and writers at the festival. Both have become even more diverse and that has made the festival so much more vibrant. We have many more students and younger folk at the festival. And this year we started a kids' festival as part of the larger festival.

Our numbers are growing every year. About six years ago, we had less than a thousand visitors to the festival. In 2017 it was close to 30,000. Over three days, we had 120 speakers, 60 sessions that were packed to capacity, 10 workshops, and a kids' festival. The visitors to the LFL come from all over the country and in the last couple of years we have attracted the attention of festival goers from many parts of the world, so now we get folks from everywhere. As entry to the festival is free, anyone wishing to attend is welcome. A lot of the people who have visited have remarked on how much they have enjoyed listening to some of the finest minds of our time. I must single out Chennai audiences as being among the most engaged audiences I have ever seen. They are well read and informed and love to interact with visiting writers. And because we're still small enough, there is something that is very satisfying about the way in which members of the audience engage with writers.

Q: What makes the Hindu LFL different from others?
Rachna: I spend very little time comparing the LFL to other festivals. I like to focus absolutely on making our programming the best it can

possibly be. That is at the core of the LFL. For example, one of the things I don't focus too much on is restricting to themes, which seems to be the flavour of the month. What I would rather do is make every single session count, and have as wide and deep a mix of writers and subjects as possible so that there is a great deal of diversity and energy and range to what the festival is able to offer those who visit it. In addition to the English-language programming, we have incredibly strong regional programming, which comes in for high praise from Chennai audiences.

Q: What is the role of authors at the festival?
Rachna: Authors are the beating heart of the festival. Most of them are superb at communicating with their audience. We try to make sure they are comfortable and enjoy their sessions as also get to meet their readers, and fellow writers. I get a kick out of seeing them sitting in the audience to listen to other writers once their own sessions are done. So they don't simply come to the LFL for their own sessions. And the highest compliment we get is when many of them say they would like to return —there is nothing more rewarding than to get a note from a writer asking to return to the LFL.

Q: What is the role of publishers at the festival?
Rachna: I'd like them to introduce their new books to me, come up with new ideas for the festival. And they're doing that. Many of them will get in touch with me as early as March to meet and discuss how we might collaborate for the following year. More and more publishers are coming to the festival either as speakers or as readers. I love when they come to the festival just to listen to the sessions. I know that they can do so every single day, especially in a city like Delhi, so when they make a special trip to Chennai to listen, you know you're on the right track.

Q: Across the nation, we say people are reading less, but on the other hand, book fests are growing. What is your take on this?
Rachna: I don't quite agree with the notion that we are reading less. We are still reading. The readership is growing, even if it's from a tiny

base. We might be reading differently and in different formats, such as digital readers, but I'm fine with that. It is also a fact that the physical book thrives and sales of printed books still outnumber digital sales. Book festivals are a great addition to the reading culture, no matter their size. They are a treat for any reader and a fabulous new way of being introduced to new writers and writing, thoughts and ideas.

Q: There has been a boom in book fests across the nation. Do you think this trend will continue to grow? Why/Why not?

Rachna: The number of book fests has gone from zero to about 70 in a short space of time. I'm not sure if it will grow further, or if this is just a fleeting trend. Nevertheless, whichever way you look at it, we have a lot of festivals. Inevitably, the quality of the festivals isn't always up to scratch, but no matter; it's great we have so many of them around—they foster the culture of books and reading and that cannot but be a good thing. We might lose a few over the years, because of lack of sponsorship and the like, but that's okay; what we'll be left with are the better, more solid festivals. I'm delighted to see that literature festivals have come to be seen as cool places to be. There's so much competing for the attention of the urban consumer that it is good to see literature holding its own against other forms of entertainment and culture.

RACHNA SINGH DAVIDAR is a literary consultant based in New Delhi. She has worked with books and writers for 30 years in India, the UK and Canada. She started her career with The Bookshop in New Delhi, which her family owns. She is currently the Programme Director of Lit For Life, the literature festival of The Hindu.

15

BOOKAROO

"Creating a lifelong love for books"

Swati Roy

Q: Share the genesis and purpose of Bookaroo.

Swati: It was in 2003 that Venkatesh and I set up Eureka Bookstore, an independent children's bookstore in Delhi. At that time there were no indie bookshops such as ours. The idea was to create a space where children were free to choose what they wanted to read. We would only make the best of Indian and international books accessible. Over a period of time, we started holding meet-the-writer or illustrator sessions in the bookshop. This eventually expanded into other areas for lack of space within the shop. From local gardens to playschool halls to community centres, we would take our sessions to any place that was ready to host us. Looking at the hunger for more, we decided, in 2008, to create a bigger platform. Since then, the last weekend of every November, in Delhi, has become a calendar event for parents and children in the city.

Q: How has the journey been in the last 10 years and how has Bookaroo expanded to different cities?

Swati: Over the last nine years, we have consistently expanding the scope of the festival. The first foray outside Delhi was into Srinagar in 2011. Thanks to a steady partnership, we have been able to celebrate the joy of reading in Srinagar for four years now.

Bookaroo has so far travelled to nine cities and held 27 editions. Apart from Srinagar, the other cities are Pune, Goa, Kuching (Malaysia), Ahmedabad, Jaipur, Kolkata and Bengaluru. Bookaroo is the only children's literature festival in India to have travelled abroad.

Apart from the weekend festival, Bookaroo also has a very strong outreach arm. In every city that we visit, we take speakers to schools, care homes, hospitals and underserved institutions. This is an expansion within the city.

Q: Tell us about the award you won recently.
Swati: Bagging the International Excellence Award in Literary Festivals at the 2017 London Book Fair was a huge validation and affirmation of the work we do in bringing children and books together. The achievement was even more special as it was a children's literature festival that won the award in a general category.

Q: What, according to you, are the benefits of Bookaroo to children?
Swati: It has created a lifelong love for books in all children whose lives we may have touched. We have established that reading for pleasure has its own benefits and charm.

Q: With your insight and expertise, tell us how we can develop the joy of reading and ensure children read more than textbooks.
Swati: As mentioned earlier, Bookaroo aims to bring books alive in a fun and enjoyable way. We believe that there is a book for every child and Bookaroo serves as the medium to connect the two. When parents, teachers, and those who usually decide what children should read, see children blossom and feel happy in the festival listening to speakers, asking questions, drawing images, creating innovative extensions from books through craft, the idea of reading for pleasure stays in their minds.

Q: How has the engagement with readers/visitors changed over time?
Swati: Not much has changed in terms of engagement. Visitors are as keen as ever to participate in Bookaroo every year. Children who have outgrown the festival come back as volunteers to support us. New genres have been introduced in children's literature. These are well represented in Bookaroo. Several publishers plan book launches during Bookaroo.

Q: Across the nation, we say people are reading less, but on the other hand, book fests are growing. What is your take on this?
Swati: We cannot comment on adult reading. As far as children are concerned, the footfall has increased; there is greater curiosity and thirst from parents, children and schools alike. The festival bookstore's performance year-on-year reiterates the fact that children's books are growing in popularity.

Q: What is the role of authors at such fests?
Swati: Writers, illustrators, storytellers, poets are the soul of our festival. They bring to life characters, scenes and ideas that are written in their books. These speakers get instant feedback for past work and ideas for future work.

Q: What is the role of publishers at such fests?
Swati: Publishers are a huge support base for Bookaroo. Their support helps us curate and execute our mission.

Q: What is your take on e-books?
Swati: Books in all forms are welcome. Content is prime. The mode of delivery is incidental.

Q: Would you like to add anything else?
Swati: After ten years of struggling to get adequate funding, we think that the corporate world should sit up and take notice of this segment. The corporate world needs to take cognizance of this growing market and support it adequately for future generations. Without support, it is very difficult to create a good festival. We wish there was more representation of children's books and literature in media.

SWATI ROY is Founder and Festival Director, Bookaroo. She is passionate about children's books and, through Bookaroo, makes books come alive for children. After organizing 27 editions of Bookaroo and spending 15 years in the business, she thinks there is no place better than this. She started with Eureka, an independent bookshop exclusively for children, in 2003 with her partner M. Venkatesh.

16

TRAINING PUBLISHING PROFESSIONALS

"Editing is a must for every publisher and required in publishing forever"

S.K. Ghai

Q: How has Institute of Book Publishing (IBP) evolved and what is the student profile?

SKG: The Institute of Book Publishing, New Delhi, is the first of its kind in Asia. Responding to the growing needs for professionally trained and well-honed personnel to feed the expanding book industry in the country, the institute was founded by my late father, O.P. Ghai, the Founder Chairman of Sterling Publishers Pvt. Ltd., in 1986. At that time, he started a post-graduate diploma in book publishing in the first year. Abul Hassan was the Director then. In the first year, we had five students—one was a chartered accountant, another a doctor and three were from the publishing industry.

Later, IBP developed a condensed course for publishing professionals, and the first course was conducted in 1988. It attracted 22 participants, out of which 8 were from outside India. We continued this annual condensed course for 26 years. In 2007, we started an intensive course for editors in book publishing as we felt that people were less interested in a condensed course.

At that time, people thought that printed books will finish and e-books will take over. So, to educate the people, we held a seminar on e-publishing for three days. We told them that editing was a must; you cannot produce a book without an editor, whichever platform it may be. So we concentrated on the Intensive Course for Editors in Book Publishing and the 10th course will be held in May 2018.

Q: What are the skills in publishing that can be taught, and which are the ones that must be built through experience and learnt on-the-job?
SKG: Editors have a lot of knowledge and the editing process has certain procedures. Interaction with the industry is essential for any course. All the skills in publishing learned in the classroom have to be refined while working. Unless they are put into practice, all teaching goes waste. In the post graduate diploma in book publishing at IGNOU, we made practical training compulsory before giving the diploma.

Q: What is the uniqueness of IBP? How does it compare with other publishing programmes?
SKG: The course comprises lectures, group discussions, workshops and hands-on exercises designed to give the trainees a well-rounded exposure to all aspects of editing. A part of the session is utilized for practical training, exercises and field visits to a printing and publishing house. The course faculty is drawn from a panel of highly qualified and professionally experienced editors from the Indian publishing industry. After attending lectures on editing skills and strategies, the participants work individually and in groups to apply what they have learnt.

The course in DU fizzled out because there was no connection with the existing publishing industry. It was only theoretical. No practical knowledge was given. But at IBP, we focus on practical knowledge.

Q: What contribution has IBP made to the publishing community?
SKG: From time to time, we hold seminars on various subjects, the first one being on promotion and marketing of books in India and abroad, followed by another on sale of translation and other subsidiary rights. Besides, we also conduct short-term courses for various national and international publishing bodies, including those in South East Asia, South Asia, Africa, Europe and also recently in Italy.

We conducted a workshop on book publishing in association with Sri Lanka Book Publishers' Association, Colombo, organized a special course for officers of Educational Publication Department, Sri Lanka and a book and sales marketing workshop for the World Health Organization at Kasauli. We also organized short courses on e-publishing, book publishing, book editing and designing, and an elementary course in electronic publishing. So we are contributing to the industry in our own way.

Q: What about the faculty?
SKG: The faculty at IBP is very cooperative. They are people from the industry and they don't come here for payment; what we give them is an honorarium. It is very creditable of them and I thank our professionals for helping us run this course efficiently.

Q: What are the challenges of running such a programme?
SKG: The students have decreased over time and so we are not able to take the institute to the heights it should reach. We do not get any subsidy from any source, so cannot promote and advertise the course in the media. We have to keep the course fee in line with the industry practices. We have been taking the help of publishing associations for promotion of the course. Sometimes, we get good participation from organizations like the Publications Division, National Book Trust (NBT), MBD, and so on. It definitely gives us a boost.

Q: How are yours different from, say the courses at NBT or Jadavpur, which have endured over time?
SKG: Ours is a focused course. The faculty is sometimes similar to the ones at the NBT or Jadavpur, but there is a lot of difference in the total environment of the course. There is no director of the course at NBT. But here we have a director for the course, who is present at all times to support the faculty members. In his or her absence, I make it a point to be there. We also encourage students to ask questions so that they understand the discussions fully and get the maximum from the course faculty.

Q: How are you teaching technology in publishing?
SKG: We are planning a course on e-publishing but we need to decide up to what level we should go in technology as it is a very vast field.

This is a current trend and there will be a lot of scope in this. But we also believe that books will always be there, though the delivery platform might be different. So editing will always be required.

Q: How do you see the future?

SKG: The publishing industry will decide the future. If the industry grows, we will grow. It all depends on the industry. I enjoy what I am doing and will continue to do so.

S.K. GHAI is Chairman of Sterling Publishers and other group companies, as well as Chairman of the Institute of Book Publishing. He has been associated with the institute since its inception in 1985. He was Chairman, Books, Publications and Printing Panel, CAPEXIL during 2008-11. He is also Executive Committee Member of The Federation of Publishers' and Booksellers' Associations in India. Mr Ghai has authored many books on the publishing industry, and is Editor of the e-journal *Publishing Today*. He is on the course faculty of National Book Trust and a member of the Expert Committee (Publishing) at IGNOU.

17

NEW WAYS OF TEACHING PUBLISHING

"Aim to create publishers, not just editors and designers"

Bishan Samaddar

Q: What are the skills in publishing that can be taught and which are the ones that must be lived and learnt on-the-job?

Bishan: We believe that mostly technical things can be learnt at the Seagull School. We teach our Editing students the details of grammar, language, house-style practices, reference systems, indexing, and so on. Design students learn the use of design and photo-editing software such as QuarkXPress, InDesign and Adobe Photoshop. An overall view of the different aspects of the publishing industry is also provided to students through extensive classes as well as master classes by visiting faculty that comprises national and international publishing professionals. However, once graduates begin working in publishing houses, they have to learn on their own, and through guidance from seniors, such practices as dealing with authors, meeting deadlines, and, eventually, looking for authors to publish and building a viable list for the publishing house. Freelance designers also learn on their own how to procure clients, how to negotiate fees, how to deliver projects on time, how to set up one's own venture. Of course, at the school, we do share our experience on all these matters. Yet, a lot has to be learnt on-the-job.

Q: What do you think makes the Seagull School of Publishing unique?

Bishan: The Seagull School aims to create publishers, not just editors and designers. Every editor or designer trained at the school has holistic knowledge of all aspects of publishing—from manuscript preparation to rights management, print and production, and sales and marketing. It is essential for those working in the publishing industry to have this breadth of knowledge, so that the decisions that they make as editors or designers or publishing entrepreneurs are always informed decisions. We believe that the Seagull School is unique in providing this kind of rounded, comprehensive knowledge to its students. Furthermore, our focus is on hands-on practical exercises, rather than lectures. This prepares the students for the everyday life of an editor or designer. This is yet another unique aspect of the school. The school derives a lot of its human resources from Seagull Books and the latter's relationships with the international publishing world. This leads to publishers, editors, authors, translators from around the world (especially the US, UK, Germany, France, Norway) visiting the school and teaching master classes, facilitating workshops, and interacting at length with the students. As a result, those trained at the Seagull School emerge as potential global publishers—their knowledge of the industry is not limited to the Indian context.

Q: Your experience in running the programme: how has it evolved—what is the student profile, how many fresh and how many already working in the industry?

Bishan: Over the past five years, we have seen that the majority of students who enrol are fresh graduates from college or university. Some have worked in diverse fields (from law to journalism to corporate management) but seek a complete change in direction in their careers. A small minority happens to be already working in the publishing industry. The courses we teach at the school have evolved subtly through our interactions with the students—by understanding their needs, we have framed many of our lessons and exercises. However, the focus remains on what we believe is the ethos in the school—which is to provide an all-round knowledge of the publishing industry.

Q: In terms of outcomes: how many have joined larger publishing houses, how many have joined the smaller independent publishers, and how many have set up on their own?

Bishan: More that 80 per cent of Editing students who graduate from the Seagull School have joined different publishing houses as editors. It is difficult to ascertain exactly how many have joined mainstream houses and how many have joined independents. We believe there would be a 50–50 division, but we are unable to give you exact numbers. One of the entrepreneurs who emerged from one of our early courses and has successfully set up her own publishing venture is Ruby Hembrom, the founder of Adivaani (www.adivaani.org). Several designers have their own small ventures, too, through which they freelance for some of the best-regarded publishing houses in the country.

Q: What kind of ventures are your ex-students working in?
Bishan: Graduates from the Editing courses at the Seagull School have been working in various publishing houses such as Oxford University Press, Sage Publications, Zubaan Books, Niyogi Books, Bee Books and Ratna Sagar. Design graduates have been working (as freelancers) for houses such as Routledge and Orient BlackSwan.

Q: How are you teaching/learning technology in publishing?
Bishan: We teach Design students details of QuarkXPress, InDesign, Adobe Photoshop and related software. This gives them a thorough knowledge of contemporary design software necessary for designing book covers and inside layouts as well as typesetting. We also have a special module dedicated to digital publishing and our Design students graduate with comprehensive knowledge of how to create e-books as well. Even our Editing students learn the basic functions of QuarkXPress, so that they have a more wide-ranging idea of the role of design in book publishing.

We teach our Design students to create e-books in Mobi and iBook formats. These e-books can be read on devices such as Kindle, iPad, iPhone as well as within the Kindle app on any device, including Android smartphones, laptops and desktop computers.

Q: What is the role of design in book publishing?
Bishan: Among things we teach our students is that book design is a functional art—design in books must not only attract the reader to

the book but also make his reading of or engagement with the book a pleasurable experience. It is important to maintain that balance.

Q: What are the challenges you face and what would your progress be in the next five years?

Bishan: We believe that the Seagull School has already made a mark in producing thoroughly trained publishing professionals who have entered the industry and are being cherished by the publishing houses they are working for. We are getting more and more applications from across the country and abroad for each of our courses, which means that more and more young people are looking at publishing as a career and they recognize that the Seagull School courses will give them an advantage when they enter the industry. We expect this trend to continue over the years. Our challenge is funding. We have, for the past five years, been generously supported by a grant from the Royal Norwegian Embassy, New Delhi. However, that funding has come to an end. We spend a lot on our courses—on creating an inspiring environment for the students, on bringing in international publishing experts—and yet we do not want the course to be too expensive for the students. In order to maintain the quality of our courses as well as to keep them affordable, our challenge now is to look for alternative sources of funding. But we are confident that if the world understands and appreciates the need for an institution, it finds ways of supporting and nurturing it somehow. So we are full of hope.

BISHAN SAMADDAR is Editor and Book Designer at Seagull Books, and Instructor in Editing at the Seagull School of Publishing. He has worked at Seagull Books for more than seven years, and has edited books by numerous authors including Gayatri Chakravorty Spivak. He is a keen traveller and a phone photographer.

18

INDIAN PUBLISHING FROM THE GLOBAL PERSPECTIVE

"India has the greatest potential for a thriving 'reading' nation"

Emma House

Q: How does Publishers Association (PA) view the Indian market/ publishing industry in the context of the global publishing industry?

Emma: Nielsen estimates the Indian book sector to now be worth US$6.76 billion and to have over 9,000 publishers, and it's no surprise that we'd say that India has to have the most exciting publishing industry in the world. With the myriad voices and languages, genres, styles and formats, it's one of the most important countries for publishing.

With over a billion people and an emerging middle class, as a market, India has to have one of the greatest potentials for a thriving and growing reading nation. The book fairs and festivals are fantastic evidence of the appetite for literature that Indians share and anyone who works in publishing around the world must visit the Jaipur Literature Festival. With e-commerce now becoming widespread and literacy improving, books can now be put into the hands of many more readers and we also have the potential to hear from even more colourful and important voices.

Q: How do the PA's activities in India compare to those in other emerging markets like China and Africa?

Emma: The PA has some activities in India, mainly around supporting our fellow publishing and publishing association colleagues with their activities, but also supporting our UK publishers who want to do business in India. We provide useful market information to UK publishers to help them navigate the market. We also support our Indian colleagues with information to help support their own lobbying activities, be it around copyright, piracy, or generally promoting the value of publishing. We work very closely with the UK Embassy and British Council in India, especially the IP (intellectual property) attaché, creative industries and literature teams. Being the UK–India Year of Culture, 2017 was an exciting year and we welcomed an India Spotlight to the London Book Fair. As the market becomes more mature, our role is ever changing. More UK publishers are setting up offices or distribution partners. We have a good partnership with the Federation of Indian Publishers (FIP) and Association of Publishers in India (API) which evolves over time as well.

We work very similarly in China, with fellow publishers and also with UK publishers who operate in China. These are our two biggest markets for international activities outside of Europe.

Q: You work closely with the API in India whose members have their head offices as members of the PA. How does this dual relationship pan out?

Emma: We work closely with the API and their membership is shared with the PA membership, the multinational companies who have offices in both countries. They don't have any full time staff as we do in the UK and therefore we aim to help and support as much as we can in providing information and insight. Equally, they provide enormous support to us by giving us valuable information on the market that we can communicate to our members. The relationship gives the API good access to the UK Embassy in India which can assist with lobbying activity.

Q: You also work closely with the FIP in India. What has been your experience in dealing with key publishing concerns in this context?

Emma: The FIP is the Indian member of the International Publishers Association (IPA) and the PA is the UK member of the IPA and so we work closely in the international community. This is very much on top-level industry matters such as copyright and freedom to publish, which are really important to both our countries. Both associations have been in existence for a long time and are keen to ensure publishing is a buoyant and thriving industry. We work hard to overcome obstacles and challenges that would threaten the industry and also support our members to help them do what they do best.

Q: For several years you have been working closely with the API and FIP on piracy- and copyright-related issues. What has been your experience? And what do you see as the future course, especially after the verdict in the Delhi University (DU) case [1]?
Emma: Copyright is the bedrock of the publishing industry, and is also so much more. Copyright fuels publishing, which in turn helps with literacy, education, social mobility and well-being. The PA, API, FIP, and publisher associations around the world are often finding themselves needing to explain copyright, to defend it and to challenge those who threaten to destroy it. The three associations work closely together in this area to explain to the multiple stakeholders what copyright actually is, why it matters, and what publishers contribute to the world and to society, thanks to copyright.

There is a huge amount of work to do in India post the DU case on promoting the value of copyright and why it's important. There is also work to be done to explain why creators and publishers should be rewarded for their work and that publishing is an industry that employs thousands of people and contributes to a multitude of other industries. Most important is the need to explain why a good copyright regime means a good education system, and that educators play a role in championing published resources. There is a broad expectation that books should be free and we need to change this perception.

Q: Your role has always been to work closely with publishers. How has this relationship evolved over time and have the issues and discussions changed over time?
Emma: I joined the PA in the year 2009, so have been working with

it for nine years. I previously worked for the London Book Fair for six years so have now 15 years' experience in global publishing which doesn't feel that long when we are surrounded by publishing gurus who have been in the industry for decades. I started off looking after international affairs and moved to cover other areas such as educational publishing and open access in journal publishing, and I am now Deputy CEO.

Our members are at the heart of everything we do and we work hard to ensure we provide them with insight, influence and services. A big part of my role is to understand the needs of publishers and how we can provide them with information or services to help their business, be it seminars, workshops and trainings through a new legal service we are launching to help prepare for a new data protection law coming into force.

It's equally important we understand what is happening on the policy and legislation landscape so we are able to influence this in favour of publishers and the wider publishing industry. This hasn't really changed over the years as at the end of the day we rely on member subscriptions and we must provide value for money. The issues we deal with have also stayed relatively similar, revolving around copyright, the supply chain, demonstrating the value of publishers and publishing.

Q: What are your impressions of the landscape of Indian publishing and publishers now and in the future? How do you see it in comparison to other markets like China and Africa?

Emma: Indian publishing has a long history and I see it having a very long future, especially internationally. The internet has made the world a much smaller place and people are much more curious about other cultures. The Indian diaspora around the world is now able to enjoy reading Indian authors much more than ever before and so the potential for export of Indian published works is enormous. Digital publishing and e-commerce have also meant that books are very accessible and can be enjoyed all over the country and at a range of different prices.

Indian publishers are talented, passionate, determined, dedicated, and it comes from the heart. I certainly think there are more family-run publishers in India than anywhere else in the world. Freedom of expression and freedom to publish are very important to the future success of Indian publishing and the industry must work together to defend the principle. When you think of India, you think of stories and storytelling that has evolved over thousands of years, you think of the politicians, the Bollywood actors, the cricket players who have stories to tell, you think different languages and different religions.

Q: From an international context, looking at Indian publishing within the frame of the global publishing industry, where do you see the pitfall and opportunities over the next few years?
Emma: India's standing in the global ranking of publishing nations can only improve as publishers become more sophisticated, more reliable statistics become available, and the distribution network continues to improve.

The only obstacles I see to India's progress are a weakening rather than strengthening of copyright and its enforcement and a tightening up of freedom to publish regulation. The Indian government's strong emphasis on education and its importance needs to extend to a strong emphasis on copyright. Publishing is often stifled in other markets through tight government control, censorship, or when the government decides to assume the role of the publisher, especially for education.

We should also talk about the role of technology in publishing and how this will impact the future of publishing. The fact is, we have seen technological developments all over the world, and whilst this has changed the way content is delivered and consumed, either through e-commerce or the devices for enjoying reading, it fundamentally has not changed the role of the publisher.

Innovation in publishing means different business models, different modes of reaching the reader, and greater access for those with visual impairments or those who simply don't have regular access to books. As such, Indian publishers can only benefit from embracing the opportunities that technology brings, comfortable in the knowledge that the fundamental publishing skills that have been honed over generations will still be essential for the future success of the industry.

[1] DU case: Three foreign publishers filed a case against a Delhi University photocopying shop for large scale photocopying of their content. They lost both the case and the appeal in 2017 after which they are working to improve copyright awareness rather than pursue the legal path.

EMMA HOUSE is Deputy CEO of the Publishers Association, the trade body in the UK for books and journal publishers. Emma has worked at the PA for 9 years, having previously spent 6 years in international roles at the London Book Fair and 6 years in international magazine publishing.

19

INDIAN PUBLISHING IN GLOBAL BOOK FAIRS

"A huge equity in diversity!"

Prashasti Rastogi

Q: How does the German Book Office (GBO) view the Indian market/ publishing industry in the context of the global publishing industry?

Prashasti: The book is dead; long live the book! In 2012 e-books were the rising stars of the book world and a shockwave ran through the industry projecting that digital will take over 80 per cent of the sales volumes. In 2017, print is living and publishers have evolved relatively stable business models. On the other hand, online retailers are making it possible to increase the reach by overcoming traditional distribution challenges. In this renaissance of print, Indian literature, especially Indian writing in English is getting the international publishers very enthusiastic. The Indian book market is the sixth largest in the world and the second largest for English-language books. The western economies are recording stagnating sales. India presents itself as a high-potential market with rising literacy. In terms of potential customers, the Indian market is twice the size of the UK's and hence it becomes imperative for international publishers to consider the Indian market in their global strategy. It's also visible in the trajectory that Penguin Random House, HarperCollins, Springer, and other global publishing houses are following in India with a huge concentration on promoting Indian fiction. Hybrid publishing houses like Juggernaut are leveraging the fact that India ranks topmost in terms of mobile data usage.

This is a unique example of how Indian publishing is agile, tech-savvy, disruptive, and yet traditional and culturally rich. India is a market that the West can't ignore, not only in terms of content, but also in innovation in the publishing services industry. The growth of service providers for digitization and print is making the world consider destination India. On the literary exchange front, publishers in the West want to be more international, and the Western markets seem ready for foreign books that are not by the usual suspects. Diversity is the buzz word of the season and India has a huge equity in the sphere that can be leveraged.

Q: Do tell us something about the GBO's activities in other emerging markets like China and Africa.

Prashasti: China is an aggressive market for rights buying and book printing. Printing with integrated port to door services at competitive prices makes it enjoy the largest share of the book printing pie. In China, our colleagues support the outreach and internationalization activities of Chinese publishers and allied professionals. The Frankfurt Book Fair has also found long-term partners in China with China South Publishing & Media Group (CNS) coming on board as investor in IPR License. Another cooperation running with China is at the new ARTS+ forum of the Frankfurt Book Fair. ARTS+ is the platform that brings together representatives of the culture and creative industries and innovative players from the technology sector.

Frankfurt is increasing its engagement in the African markets as those markets have started to respond to international stimulus only recently. A new entry at the 2017 FBF were the collective stand Publishers from Africa and Haiti. Also new in 2017 were debut appearances at Frankfurt of Niger, Madagascar and Gabon.

Q: Please share the specific experiences that the GBO has had with respect to its various initiatives.

Prashasti: I still remember the reactions of publishers at the rights and licensing workshop that we organized at GLOBALOCAL 2013. A number of publishers had questions that were very basic such as which rights to specify or what are subsidiary rights actually. Almost all publishers realized that their contracts were not enabling the potential that the rights market presents or were silent on most aspects regarding trading copyrights. Also notable was the fact that publishers hadn't thought about milking the domestic potential by selling translation rights into other Indian languages. We continued conducting the rights workshop at GLOBALOCAL year after year and also included it in our Young Publishers Training Programme every year. The scenario has changed very effectively over these years and many book fairs and literature festivals are trying to set up rights meetings to facilitate this exchange. Also the fluidity of literature from one to the other with Seagull's Bengali list or Harper Perennial has made English a good outreach point. The power of 1:22, with 22 officially recognized languages, needs to be more aggressively harnessed. I feel that the literature festivals are a great platform to showcase writing in languages other than English and would act as a catalyst in promoting stronger exchange if more and more Indian language authors are integrated in the programme of the major festivals.

Q: Why is the Frankfurt Book Fair relevant to Indian publishers even now? What do you consider as its USP for Indian publishers?
Prashasti: With the growth of multi-platform content, short-form consumption, the licensing business is becoming even more aggressive. The Frankfurt Book Fair provides that ecosystem and hence is important for Indian publishers to reach out to markets in Latin America, South East Asia, the UK, Australia, the Middle East all under one roof. We don't see ourselves as an exhibition but as a service provider to the publishing value chain that can help people and businesses grow and be future-ready. Keeping informed on the market, competitors, consumption geographies and making connections different from your address book is where the long-term game is.

We're also witnessing an interesting trend that's a contra wave to the global politics of nationalism—thirst for diversity. Foreigners are likely to accept an Indian book, as diversity writing is the flavour of the season. Especially the English-language markets are very curious about literature from India which presents enormous opportunity for small and mid-sized publishers from India, because they can really take their lists global. International publishers with offices in India already have mechanisms in place to ensure that the books travel in geographies they operate in, but the shift in interest towards diversity has opened doors for other players too.

Q: With the emergence of the London Book Fair as a credible alternative, why do you think Indian publishers will still go to Frankfurt?
Prashasti: In an industry that is so dynamic, comparisons of one fair with another lead to shrinking the share of the pie that you'd want Indian publishers to have. The Frankfurt Book Fair is like a hypermarket, a one-stop shop for global products, global relationships and the engine is the licensing business at a scale which no other fair has been able to replicate. With over 700 agents and 7,300 publishing companies from 102 countries coming together in Frankfurt for 5 days to talk business, it'll take a highly disruptive business strategy to give it a miss.

Q: What is the key role of the GBO in India? Has this evolved/ changed in recent times? Do share with us your personal journey with the GBO for last four to five years. How has the same evolved and where does your role fit into the Indian publishing context?
Prashasti: I joined at a time when the industry worldwide was going through a slow phase and there was a huge discussion around the singular digital future. In the education sector, the business models had graduated to looking at tech solutions as aided-learning programmes and not as core products. Over the years, print has proved to have the proverbial nine lives, with double-digit growth registered in most developing economies. There are more publishing houses in India now than there was five years ago. The market is crowded, with conglomerates and independents, giants and start-ups, reading forums and publish online platforms. The questions have changed over the years—from a query on e-book production to multi-format content, from social media branding to digital outreach strategy, from retail to e-commerce, from book launches to reader engagement and discoverability!

Looking at these developments, at the GBO we've always pitched in with insights, training and forums to build networks to address the pain as well as growth points of the industry. The publishing programme at IIM Ahmedabad was a significant contribution towards the professionalization of the sector. To fill the skill gap in publishing, we initiated the Young Publishing Professionals Programme in 2014, addressing topics ranging from digital rights trading, book to film licensing, new product development, and commercialization of IP. Through GLOBALOCAL, we bring together Indian and international publishers in roundtables and business matchmakings to trade products and ideas. JUMPSTART, the GBO's annual event on children's content, which has completed eight editions, has been a first-of-its-kind cross-industry forum for children's content which provides inspiration as well as facilitates skill development through master classes. We extended JUMPSTART with three satellite editions in Bangalore on demand from many loyal authors and creative professionals. Our role though is not limited to this we're also the node of the Frankfurt Book Fair in the region and connect the subcontinent to the German and international publishing industry. Translation promotion has always been top priority for us and we regularly invest in capacity development of translators and facilitate translation from German to Indian languages and vice versa. To summarize, the GBO is a service model for the entire publishing value chain, wherein we engage in capacity development of authors and translators and business development of publishers.

Q: How do you see Indian publishing and publishers? How is it in comparison to other markets that the GBO is in?

Prashasti: The Indian publishing industry is very vast, diverse and fragmented. With its constituents so different from one another, it's difficult to find one voice to represent it on the global stage. This could be addressed by crafting a joint global strategy and breaking it down to specific needs in working groups of different factions who promote their individual interests as well as aid in augmenting the outreach for other groups. An excellent example of this was the Malayalam Pavilion steered by Dr Jayakumar at the Frankfurt Book Fair 2016. The pavilion promoted literature, technology and printing services along with establishing Kerala as a cultural destination with support from the Kerala tourism department. They were also very welcoming by providing meeting space to publishers from India who were not participating with their own stands. They also organized press tours and a book launch to ensure visibility for their activities. It's a great example of how one can synergize and maximize outcomes in competitive environments like the Frankfurt Book Fair. I feel that the Korean or the Chinese model will also be relevant to India with collective yet independent representations by the digital service providers, printers, publishers and distributors. They run individual programmes and meetings and yet stand collectively to appear as a service destination of capacity and calibre. Internationally, there are many such examples from Bangladesh, Canada, Mexico, Brazil, France, Turkey, and hopefully there will be examples to quote from India too by the time this collection goes into its second edition. I'd really look forward to the Brand India being presented and spoken about on international publishing forums more often.

PRASHASTI RASTOGI is Director, German Book Office of the Frankfurt Book Fair in New Delhi. She works at the cross-section of publishing, technology and entertainment to create networks that will build the future of content. Her recent initiatives include the Young Publishing Professionals Programme and a translation portal to provide community orientation to German-language translators. She has previously served as Head of Communication and IT at the German Academic Exchange Service South Asia office.

PART

3

Policy Landscape

PART III • POLICY LANDSCAPE

INDUSTRY ASSOCIATIONS AND THEIR ROLE

POLICY LANDSCAPE

The publishing industry is faced with many challenges in our market and needs to garner support from government agencies and policies to deal with them. Industry associations have a vital role in this context. The current and past executive members of the Federation of Indian Publishers (FIP), the older professional body, the Association of Publishers in India (API), which represents multinational publishers, as well as the more recent FICCI Publishing Committee, tell us about their priorities and how they support their members.

Beyond this, the wider importance of publishing to society and its contribution to building ideas, educational and research repositories and growing the nation, are part of their advocacy. A key issue in this context is that of copyright protection which is, erroneously, now seen globally as an inhibitor of creativity rather than an enabler, with hostile judiciary decisions towards content creators. Our next two contributors both experts in the field, highlight the key points in this fraught issue from a global and local context. Our next piece covers a related and equally important requirement, for authors and writers to be aware of publishing ethics, including the checks and balances, required while writing, either for academic purposes or for pleasure. Another issue with similar societal impact is that of censorship and freedom to publish. It is addressed here by the leaders of the movement at the International Publishers Association (IPA).

In this tough environment, our final conversation—on the range and breadth of reading movements sprouting around the country—uplifts and brings much needed optimism to the publishing-writing-reading ecosystem.

20

FEDERATION OF INDIAN PUBLISHERS

"FIP looks after the interests of its members"

N.K. Mehra

Q: What have been the key focus, achievements and challenges for the FIP in the last few years?

NKM: The focus area of the FIP is primarily looking after the interests of its members. One major focus today is to tackle the GST (goods and services tax) problem, which though not applicable to books, is applicable on journals to the tune of 18 per cent. As it is, libraries are short on funds and an additional 18 per cent burden is too much for them. Besides, publishers face a reverse charge of 12 per cent on royalties paid to authors. According to the government, the education system is supposed to be kept as inexpensive as possible, but with the additional reverse charge on royalties, publishers will have to increase prices.

Moreover, the recent judicial pronouncement that for educational purposes one can make a photocopy, has further added to our woes.

Another problem which the FIP is tackling is that though the Central Board of Secondary Education (CBSE) did not have the mandate to publish books, it was doing so. National Council of Educational Research and Training (NCERT) books, which were not available in sufficient quantities, are now available in ever larger numbers. Though it is not compulsory for schools to use NCERT books for Classes 1-8, many schools, which depend on government funds, have started opting for them, thus making it difficult for private publishers to survive in the K-12 segment.

Besides, the Federation also provides facilities for publishers to interact with foreign publishers. For this, we organize meetings, book fairs and trade fairs. Earlier, we used to get help from the government to sponsor these activities, but even this has been cut off now. With this funding, we used to offer 50 per cent of stall charges to regional-language publishers at our flagship exhibition, the Delhi Book Fair. We also facilitate publishers' associations' meetings during the Delhi Book Fair and also offer Awards for Excellence.

Q: What is the relationship of the FIP with other industry bodies? Are there any points of convergence?

NKM: We have good terms with all major associations like the Association of Publishers in India (API) and the Federation of Publishers' and Booksellers' Associations in India (FPBAI). We work closely with each other to address our issues with the government. We meet the same people, talking the same language. We do have our differences, but that does not matter. Together, we have asked the government to set up a publishers council, but it is yet to be announced.

Getting an ISBN was a problem at one time, but it has been sorted now. All the associations worked together to make the process of getting online ISBNs easy.

The FIP organized the 32nd International Publishers Congress in New Delhi in February 2018, at Taj Palace Hotel. The FIP is a member of the International Publishers Association (IPA), which is the world's largest federation of national, regional and specialist publishers' associations. Its membership comprises 70 organizations from 60 countries in Africa, Asia, Australasia, Europe and the Americas. We are getting good support from all the associations in India.

Q: What about copyright protection? It is a fraught issue: how is the FIP approaching this challenge for the publishing sector?

NKM: Copyright protection is a big problem. The copyright law exists and the Indian Reprographic Rights Organisation (IRRO) has been authorized by the Government of India to issue licences. So, for a small fee, the IRRO gave licences to Delhi University and institutional libraries, so that money collected on copyright can be divided between the publisher and the author. But the problem is that the IRRO has not been able to distribute money as people have not made any claims.

N.K. MEHRA is Managing Director, Narosa Publishing House and President, Federation of Indian Publishers (FIP). He started his publishing career in 1959 and set up two companies, Narosa Book Distributors and Narosa Publishing House. Nandi, as he is popularly known, has been on FIP's Executive Committee for over ten years, and has also served on the Executive Committee of the Federation of Publishers' and Booksellers' Association in India where he was President for two terms.

21

ASSOCIATION OF PUBLISHERS IN INDIA: THE EARLY YEARS

"The formation, objectives and journey of API"

Sesh Seshadri

Q: Share the formation, objective and journey of the Association of Publishers in India (API).

Sesh: When this association was being formed on 9 July 2001, there were three other national associations for the publishing/book selling industry—the Federation of Indian Publishers (FIP), the Federation of Publishers' and Booksellers' Associations in India (FPBAI), and Federation of Educational Publishers in India.

Nevertheless 14 people got together and put on record 26 aims and objectives and formed the association under the Societies Registration Act 1860. Some of its important aims were:

- Promotion and advancement of global publishers in SAARC (South Asian Association for Regional Cooperation) countries.
- To consider, promote or oppose legislative and other measures affecting global publishers.

Having said that, the primary reason cited was the attack on export processing zones (EPZs)[1,2] printing. That led to supposedly kindred publishers (read MNCs) grouping together to form an association. Some of the interesting records in their Memorandum of Association are:

- No addition or amendment shall be made to this Memorandum of Association.
- Membership shall be available only to global publishers having business establishments in India.
- The membership is by invitation only.

Q: What were the challenges faced, given that the FIP already existed? How has the relationship with FIP and other industry bodies been in the early years?

Sesh: It will not be fair to use the term antagonistic. However, other industry bodies perceived it that way. Some of the API members at that point of time, or even to this date, are members of other associations.

Q: What were the key issues covered in the early years and why?

Sesh: The one issue that was (maybe) overplayed for many years was piracy. Others include EPZ printing and other educational issues. The API was and remains a largely education-facing body with very little nuanced understanding of trade. The classic example was office-bearers not even registering the impact of parallel imports, and they would have let the controversial 2m Amendment[3] go through. 'We just missed it' was one office-bearer's view.

Q: How has the API evolved over time?

Sesh: With the main problem (EPZ printing) resolved, the API has ticked over tackling the main issues confronting educational publishing with an occasional look-in at trade publishing. Less than a decade ago, a trade sub-committee was formed, and the decision was taken to have one or two office-bearers from trade. However, the office-bearers appointed have not called for even a single trade meeting.

Q: What is the key role played by the API for the publishing sector since it was set up?

Sesh: MNCs/International publishers are large by turnover, and hence the association gets some play from a reflection of the companies within it. But the truth remains that the association itself (outside EPZ and the 2m battle where we had non-API members at the finish tipping the balance) can hardly point to any major change effected or policy drafted and say we did that. The publishing associations (all of them, not just API) are largely bureaucratic organizations concerned with events and seminars rather than real change...and hence what can be achieved by writing letters is done (for example GST [goods and services tax] representation for children's books where everybody wrote in), but where change means real lobbying and sustained push (GST on royalties, anti-piracy government involvement, copyright protection, legal metrology, freedom of speech, decriminalization), the associations can effect no real change and the API mirrors this.

And let me forestall the inevitable—those who complain should become office-bearers and walk the talk—argument. That is a complete cop out. The fundamental principle of efficiency would be to appoint a CEO or president who does this full-time. This was mooted some time ago, but was dropped.

Q: Have the issues and challenges changed or do they remain similar today? Why?

Sesh: The issues of the 1990s remain even today with new twists added from the onset of digital and the increased misuse of laws embodying freedom of speech. It is telling that the API has not chosen to engage in even one freedom of speech issue or ask for change in laws.

Q: One of the key demands for publishing has been to get industry status. Why do you think this has not happened?

Sesh: This is because of a lack of will within the industry. The government will take you seriously if it registers the contribution you make—by revenues, by socio-cultural impact. The industry has effectively conveyed neither. At every stage, the mindset is of the small trader preferring cash trade and keeping business secret. So we have no concrete data; we have less than 50 per cent of the retail book trade willing to be mapped by Nielsen. We have an industry almost unanimously wanting the freebie of 'tax-free' status when that status is legitimately merited only by textbooks publishers.

Q: What are the prospects in this regard?

Sesh: I see none…because publishing prefers staying a fragmented cottage industry. The day the associations merge with full-time office-bearers will be the day publishing will have taken a step forward. Until then the API remains a body that will have some activities ticking over to no real purpose or targeted conclusion. But something that is needed there…just in case we are threatened again as MNCs.

[1] EPZs are spatially delimited areas in which manufacturers produce goods that are largely aimed for export markets. EPZs generally offer export-oriented investors a host of advantages in relation to the domestic investment environment. These units operating under certain specific schemes such as EPZs/ special economic zone (SEZs)/ export oriented units (EOUs) are expected to carry out their activities within a customs-bonded area. Any area which is not under the jurisdiction of a customs-bonded area is called a domestic tariff area.

[2] The Government of India provided an opportunity via EPZ to encourage printers to get more overseas business and publishers in India to reduce the end customer price.

[3] The major opposition to EPZ was from most Indian publishing and bookselling associations claiming that there was no level playing field. They wrote to the Ministry of Human Resource Development/Commerce Ministry formally opposing EPZ.

SESH SESHADRI is Director of Lonely Planet India. He played a key role in Lonely Planet's entry into the Indian market in 2012. In addition to over four decades of publishing experience, Sesh is an entrepreneur and consultant. He established the publishing consulting company O.V.E.R.L.E.A.F. in 1997, and is a trustee of the Neelbagh Group of Schools. He was also Founder-Director at Textech that specializes in providing content solutions to publishers.

22

ASSOCIATION OF PUBLISHERS IN INDIA: BUILDING PARTNERSHIPS

"All industry associations help to connect with the government"

Rohit Kumar

Q: How has Association of Publishers in India (API) evolved over time?

Rohit: The API, over the last several years, has evolved in many ways to play a role that helps the government to take the publishing industry seriously. Over the last several years, we have worked together with other industry bodies to make sure that the industry works together to counter situations like GST (goods and services tax), piracy and photocopying. But when you have to work towards the improvement of the sector, these things take time. As the publishing industry continues to grow, we will see more improvement in the industry.

As the President of the API for two years (2013–15) and Secretary before that, I can very well say that API members successfully collaborated in getting the Nielsen report published about the size of the publishing market in India. That also makes it easier in government discussions or any discussion of any stakeholder, whether in India or abroad.

Q: One of the key demands for publishing has been to get industry status. Why do you think this has not happened?

Rohit: Publishing industry is recognized as a small-and medium-size industry—this categorization was done several years ago. The Federation of Indian Publishers (FIP) obtained this status 10 to15 years ago. The reason for asking for industry status is to get better financing. But there are other issues which need to be addressed, like GST, taxation and reverse charges. If you do an Industry poll, industry status will come at number 3 or 4.

Q: What has been the Federation of Indian Chambers of Commerce and Industry's (FICCI) role in improving government and industry connect?

Rohit: FICCI plays a very key role as the government listens to FICCI. Being part of both FICCI and API, has helped the industry as it gave us a way to reach the government through multiple channels. Whether it's the FIP, FICCI, or API—all these industry associations help us to create awareness with the government.

ROHIT KUMAR is Managing Partner of Guiding Star Digital Publishers LLP and its subsidiary Chapter Apps Inc, where he is building and leveraging mobile technology platforms to improve productivity for professionals and students. Prior to starting his entrepreneurial ventures, Rohit was Managing Director, South Asia, Health Science Division, Reed Elsevier India. He was President of the Association of Publishers in India during 2013-15, and Co-Chair of the FICCI Publishing Committee during 2013-16.

23

ASSOCIATION OF PUBLISHERS IN INDIA: LOOKING TO THE FUTURE

"We work towards making India a knowledge economy"

Ratnesh Jha

Q: What have been the key focus and challenges for API in the last few years?

Ratnesh: In recent times we have been embracing changes that have had a fundamental impact on how the publishing industry operates, be it incorporating the GST or advocating the cause of copyright and quality learning to take India to excel as a knowledge economy.

API has matured as the voice of the industry and is playing a crucial role to articulate the views and concerns of the publishing industry in India. With the ongoing engagement between key stakeholders, policymakers and other industry bodies, API is now being actively called upon for their opinion and participation in taking forward the charter of developing India as a nation par excellence. Today API works along with FICCI, DIPP (Department of Industry Policy and Promotion) and collaborates to put together a point of view on Intellectual Property that is represented at WIPO (World Intellectual Property Organization).

I am proud to see API working in tandem with the Federation of Indian Publishers (FIP) and building a coherence of thought and approach. As a key player of the knowledge industry, we are striking a fine balance to ensure we contribute to build India's success story by enabling our generations with the right knowledge and skill.

Having said that, I believe that there needs to be the right balance which not just caters to market and its requirements but also takes care of the publisher. We are a global organization that knows what the local demands are and present to our audience what they need in just the way they want it. With immeasurable local investments, we can humbly say that we contribute to job creation in the nation. Hence, API lends itself to working on developing a strategy which not only benefits the association, but also the learners, the researchers and the educators, which in turn acts to the advantage of India as a knowledge economy.

Q: What, if any, are the key issues that foreign publishers face today and have to collectively tackle?
Ratnesh: As value creators in India, we are instrumental in enhancing Indian research and making it available to the rest of the world. With policymakers partnering in our endeavours, we wish to be acknowledged as local players and present ourselves as agents of growth and contributors to the nation. We will carry on collaborating with the policymakers and make a mark for India on the global map.

Q: What is the relationship of API with other industry bodies? Are there any points of convergence?
Ratnesh: We work together with other industry bodies to solve myriad challenges as we share common values and work on common themes. The copyright theme can be highlighted as a case in point, we worked in close association with FIP, FICCI, DIPP and other agencies collectively. With concerted efforts and synergies, the collaboration worked to the advantage of all the stakeholders.

Q: As API President and FICCI Co-Chair of Publishing, how do you see this dual role working to the advantage of the industry?
Ratnesh: Common challenges like copyright, piracy, and many more can be catered to if we work together. API is an important stakeholder at PubliCon (FICCI flagship programme); this collaboration not only takes care of the industry but also representatives from across the globe. With efforts steered in the same direction, FICCI and API are together working towards carving a niche for the nation. As one of the leaders of FICCI and API, I attempt to help the industry in a joint set of

imperatives and objectives and ensure that issues are addressed collectively in a logical manner.

Q: Publishing does not have industry status; is this on the agenda of API, FICCI, FIP, etc.? How important is this in the long-term growth and survival of the industry?

Ratnesh: Mostly seen as a fragmented industry, we do have a classification as an industry but we are working towards being recognized as an organized industry. We need to work in diverse areas like taxation, consolidation, copyright, and individual as well as collective initiatives as an industry. As we work to be known as a superior knowledge economy, we are all set to move to the next level. We need to respond to policy measures in a positive manner and grow together.

Q: What has been FICCI's role in influencing the government-industry connect?

Ratnesh: FICCI as an industry body represents the industry to the policymakers. Understanding what we stand for and fully comprehending our requirements, it has always aided us to grow and fare well as an industry. Working in association with the government and policymakers, FICCI gives us a reach and ensures that we are recognized as an industry body. It helps us to positively contribute as a growing knowledge industry.

RATNESH JHA is Managing Director, South Asia, Cambridge University Press, and President of the Association of Publishers in India (API). His management career spans over two decades and he is passionate about the education ecosystem. He is Co-Chair of the FICCI Publishing Committee and a member of the Higher Education Committee. He also advises start-ups and works as a fundraiser and volunteer for NGOs.

24

FICCI PUBLISHING COMMITTEE

"Connecting the publishing industry to the government"

Sumeet Gupta

Q: How and why was the Federation of Indian Chambers of Commerce and Industry (FICCI) Publishing Committee set up? What are its objectives and how are these implemented?

Sumeet: Books have always been regarded as an important medium for the development and promotion of human values. They record new ideas, preserve and communicate knowledge, impart education and values, and aid the overall development of an individual. Books serve as the backbone for creation of knowledge economy. The book publishing sector in India is the second largest in the world in English-language publishing. Current statistics reveals that the sector is truly a colossus—a giant in slumber, which needs to be awakened and given its due status and identity.

Releasing the promise and potential that this sector offers, FICCI instituted the Publishing Committee in 2011. FICCI's publishing desk has the following objectives:

- Address key issues confronting the publishing sector, both in terms of policy and trade.
- Provide thought leadership in the area of publishing.
- Represent the Indian publishing community in various international forums and look for opportunities for Indian publishers abroad.
- Identify gaps and create opportunities for capacity building.
- Conceptualize and develop programmes for the support and benefit of the publishing sector.

Q: How are the members chosen and how has this evolved over time?

Sumeet: The members of the FICCI Publishing Committee represent all genres of the publishing ecosystem, K-12 publishing, higher education publishing, trade publishing, distributors and printers. We also have players who are from the digital space. They all are FICCI members. Besides leading publishing houses, we work closely with various sectoral associations. In fact, the Association of Publishers in India (API) is member of FICCI. The committee has evolved over the last few years. Due to the kind of work that we have done and the value organizations perceive in getting associated with us, we are getting quality membership.

Q: How does this committee fit with the other committees that FICCI has and is there any convergence or connect?

Sumeet: The Publishing Committee has some connect with the Education Committee, both school as well as higher education. Publishers are essential stakeholders in the education ecosystem, be it curriculum design or delivery mechanism. I see a large connect there. With the increase in digital content both in production and the way content is consumed, there is a trend towards convergence. Consumers would like to have the availability of content anywhere, on any device, and at any time. There is a connect with the entertainment segment as well. There are tremendous opportunities for content to be monetized across various platforms and in various forms. Books to screen is probably the most obvious model; however there are opportunities in new media as well like animation, gaming and licensing & merchandising (L&M). The mobile is emerging as one of the promising platforms to ensure reach and delivery.

Q: What is the relationship with other industry bodies? Are there any points of convergence?

Sumeet: As mentioned earlier, we work closely with other sectoral associations. The API is a FICCI member and we work with the leadership of API in driving industry agenda.

Q: What has been FICCI's role in influencing the government–industry connect? What are the key issues before publishers today and can FICCI help in resolving them?

Sumeet: FICCI has been playing a key role in policy advocacy with the government. We take up issues that are confronting the industry and try to get favourable decisions. There are various policy issues that we have taken up on behalf of the publishing sector—copyright is one such issue, another being ISBN. We have been involved with Ministry of Human Resource Development (MHRD) earlier and now with the Department of Industrial Policy and Promotion (DIPP) in areas related to intellectual property like anti-piracy and copyright. We have also been actively working with US Patent and Trademark Office (USPTO) in India as far as protection of copyright in the context of publishers is concerned. Our involvement is also with National Book Trust (NBT), India, as far as the creation of a book reading culture is concerned. We partner with NBT to provide overall fillip to the publishing ecosystem. In the past, we have advocated for industry status for the publishing sector. We have got engaged with the MHRD and other stakeholders on the issue of content liberalization on behalf of K-12 publishers. We have also done some advocacy around the proposed National Book Promotion Policy, which is still at the draft stage. We essentially provide connect to industry with government to articulate demands and expectations.

Q: What is the specific role in copyright advocacy?

Sumeet: Copyright is one of the most important areas of concern for any kind of creative industry; publishing of course is one. We have continuous engagement with the government on this front. We have organized various programmes on sensitization and awareness on protection of intellectual property (IP) specifically from the publishing perspective. We have come out with various policy documents, white papers and reports for advocacy. Besides the Government of India, we have also taken initiatives with the World Intellectual Property Organization (WIPO). We are currently working closely with the DIPP and have regular engagement on various aspects of IP concerning the publishing community.

Q: What have been the key focus areas for FICCI in the last few years which aid/provide support to the publishing community?

Sumeet: Besides policy advocacy, we have also been focusing on providing trade opportunities for publishing houses. We have tied up with the London Book Fair (LBF) where we organize India-centric sessions to explore joint opportunities with global counterparts. We also come out with FICCI rights catalogue, which is done in partnership with the LBF. This rights catalogue is distributed to all the rights managers present at the festival. The objective is to explore opportunities of rights trading, co-publishing, distribution, etc. This initiative has been well received. We have also done some activities at the Frankfurt Book Fair in the past. In the recent past, we have also engaged with the Kochi Lit Fest (KLF). In continuation of our endeavours to address the issues of copyright and piracy in South Asia, we have organized programmes in this region.

We have our annual programme by the name PubliCon, which has become the flagship event in the publishing sector. The programme witnesses a congregation of various stakeholders from private enterprises as well as from government, to ideate and debate on the key issues of the sector. We have also instituted a programme exclusively for K-12 publishing by the name of Scrapbook, which caters to issues pertaining to school publishing, involving various actors like schools, education boards, the National Council for Educational Research and Training (NCERT), MHRD, and of course publishing houses. In partnership with the NBT and MHRD, we organize a business breakfast for CEOs of publishing houses, CEOSpeak over Chairman's Breakfast, during the New Delhi World Book Fair. It is an exclusive and elite programme of the World Book Fair. The forum has emerged as a major platform for decision-makers of the publishing sector to share and exchange ideas. In addition to this, we keep on organizing various programmes related to issues of copyright, sharing of best practices, and capturing emerging trends. We have also started focusing on other important players in the publishing domain like editors and authors.

Q: PubliCon has been organized for a number of years. What has been achieved via this forum? What are the gaps and the way forward?

Sumeet: PubliCon has become a flagship industry programme in publishing. We have tried to address different aspects of publishing during various editions of the programme. Topics ranging from digital publishing to IP protection including digital rights management (DRM), content monetization, export markets, school publishing, publishing services and book marketing have been covered in our previous programmes. Over the years, PubliCon has become an ideal platform to advocate policy issues, share best practices, explore business opportunities, networking and marketing. From the last edition, we have tried to bring a fresh outlook in the programming of the event. We have also brought authors to not only participate but articulate their perspectives. We have increased our focus on capacity building as well. Now we are reaching and catering to the wider audience. We have also instituted FICCI PubliCon Awards, for which we have received encouraging response from the industry. The shortlisting and screening process is under way.

Going forward, we intend to address more areas like printing, libraries, publishing services and capacity building. There is tremendous scope in Indian-language publishing and the promising area of translation. The idea is to address various genres and serve them appropriately.

SUMEET GUPTA is Senior Director, FICCI where he heads Publishing, Homeland Security, Private Security, and Geospatial Technologies. He has over 19 years of experience in domains including science and technology, security, media and publishing. He was instrumental in creating the first international animation awards in India, and worked a report that formed the backbone of the second phase of FM radio privatization in India.

25

TAX AND COMPLIANCE ENVIRONMENT

"Keeping books affordable for all – difficult with GST!"

Sanjiv Gupta

Books are considered to be our main source of knowledge. India, as a developing country has always aimed to develop skillsets to spread knowledge and readership across the country (at accessible costs?) in order to reach more people. To enable us to keep books at more accessible price points, books have always been kept out of the tax arena. Books have traditionally been exempt from sales tax or service tax, and the same was expected under the new Goods and Services Tax (GST) act.

How is the price of a book determined?

To provide some context: prices of books are determined by several factors including sales volumes, printing and design costs, design royalties, and inventory obsolescence. After implementation of GST, costs are going to increase since GST will be levied on royalties and printing costs at an abnormally high rate of 12 per cent. As GST is not charged on sale of books, publishers cannot claim input tax credit (ITC). This increase in cost will likely lead to publishers increasing prices of books.

The GST's objective was to keep cost neutral. The costs of books will rise under the new scenario.

To increase readership and share knowledge, we need to keep the prices of books affordable. The government can play a pivotal role by not taxing royalties and printing services. It would result in keeping the prices of books in an affordable price range.

Credit period: Another challenge

Book publishers have to provide long credit period to their distributors/

customers, hold large inventory for a long period, and struggle to keep prices of books low to ensure affordability. As our credit period is the longest compared to any other industry, the entire value chain works on publishers funding, until the time the reader buys the book.

For most businesses, the credit period is usually thirty days and sometimes payments are received in advance before supplies are made. Not so in publishing: we have the highest credit period anyone can imagine. Such a long credit period was set historically many years ago when there was not significant local publishing. Books were shipped into India by sea, and the time taken to bring them to India was more than ninety days and hence credit period was what it was.

Other overheads...

Now, with digitization and upgradation of technology combined with simplification of import regulations, books by international authors are released at the same time as they are being released internationally. Book publishers can also print international titles locally under the export-processing zone. The publishers are burdened with high cash servicing cost since payments to printers are made prior to collection of payment from distributors.

How Penguin Random House tackles this

The physical inventory warehouse for Penguin Random House India is based in Dasna, Uttar Pradesh. It is a 140,000 sq. ft facility with state-of-the-art infrastructure and processes. This facility is the best warehouse in the country: zero dust and with efficient delivery mechanism—order to shipment in 24–48 hours. We carry approximately 3 million units at any given point to service our distributors. The inventory turnover is approximately three times.

We at Penguin Random House India are devising new ways of managing inventories. We have implemented the 'One Book Model' for a significant number of titles from our local list. Hence no book goes out of print—we can print one copy of a book in 48 hours and deliver it to the reader in paperback. This is undertaken at Repro Knowledge

Cast Limited in Mumbai at its state-of-the-art facility. We have a similar arrangement with Ingram for international customers—a book can now be ordered, printed and delivered internationally in a short time.

But we are facing challenges under the GST, for us to send free copies of our books for review to authors, media, etc. Every copy of a book shipped, whether free or otherwise, needs to have an invoice. This is adding to the paperwork and becomes inefficient for the industry.

Piracy: another menace

The challenges of piracy are widespread—pirated books are available at every traffic light, key markets in all the metros and multiple other places. A publisher launches a hardback title and a paperback on cheap paper is available on the roadside. The publisher loses out on sale/margin, authors on royalty and the 'piracy vendor' laughs all the way to the bank.

However, at the end of the day, all the challenges we face fade away when we get appreciation for our books from readers. And that is what keeps us going.

SANJIV GUPTA is Chief Operating Officer, Penguin Random House India. He manages finance and operations for the company and has over 25 years of experience across a spectrum of industries. Before joining Penguin in 2011 as Finance Director, Sanjiv was Director at Masonite Doors and was leading operations in India. He has previously worked with Hines India Real Estate, Bharti Group, Honeywell International, Honda Cars and DCM in various roles.

26

KEY FACETS OF COPYRIGHT TODAY

"Changes, conflicts and challenges"

Michael Healy

When did copyright become such a hot topic? For most of my career in publishing, it was talked about rarely. When it was discussed, it seemed to be the preoccupation of lawyers and academics. Everyone was aware of infringement and vigilant to the most egregious expressions of it, but for the most part senior leaders in publishing didn't have to think about it much, if at all. Copyright was one of those essential and immovable foundation stones on which the industry stood: safe, secure, dependable. Those comfortable days are far behind us and are not returning. The foundation has been shaking for several years and continues to do so. Everyone knows why. A global, ubiquitous content network, accessible every moment, has facilitated sharing to a degree unimaginable previously. Co-workers, students and teachers, friends and families now share content with ease and with little regard to the legality of the simple practices that technology has enabled. With technological transformation has come cultural change. The 'content demands to be free' mantra is a popular one among consumers, and it has powerful supporters in big tech companies and some governments. In quite a short time, copyright has come to be seen by many outside the publishing industry as an inhibitor to creativity and innovation instead of the enabler and protector it once was. Even many of those supportive of copyright, those who think that it's an important tool for encouraging writers to write and publishers to publish, say that it requires reform to keep pace with changing technology and social expectations and that existing licensing mechanisms are cumbersome and inefficient.

Although these are global phenomena, it's true to say that the consequent disruption to the publishing industry has been felt more intensely and for a longer period of time in some countries than others. Canada stands out in this regard. The late actor and comedian Robin Williams famously (and rudely) likened Canada to 'a loft apartment over a really great party'. The implication was obvious. All the action was in the US, while Canada was a place where very little happened. In the world of copyright, nothing could be further from the truth. For the past several years, Canada has been the front line in the world's 'copyright wars', a place of seemingly endless and very public confrontation. It's important to understand how this happened because it holds lessons for every country, including India.

Canada became the first major copyright battleground in recent years, the front line where rights-holders and educators fought so bitterly, and the focus for so many other countries considering the future of copyright. It started for most people with the Copyright Modernization Act, a piece of legislation introduced by the Canadian government in 2012 and widely interpreted by educators as allowing them to use copyrighted content without seeking permission from, or paying, the rights holders. Publishers and authors cried foul immediately. The legislation, and a series of subsequent judgements from the Supreme Court of Canada, were seen as devastating to their business interests and very damaging to Canada's wider cultural industries. Some publishing companies closed down entirely. Others reduced their output or diverted resources away from educational titles. Some US publishers pulled back, shuttering their Canadian operations. They, along with many commentators, complained that the pendulum had swung too far, that the essential and delicate balance between incentivizing and rewarding rights holders on the one hand, and making content accessible and affordable for Canada's teachers and students on the other, had been broken. Estimates of the loss to rights holders were put as high as $50 million per year.

Five years later and the battles are still raging on many fronts. In 2017, the Reproduction Rights Organization in French-speaking Canada,

Copibec, publicized its class action lawsuit against Université Laval, alleging that the university '*infringed the patrimonial and moral rights recognized under the Copyright Act*'. The class action, authorized by The Québec Court of Appeal in February, was filed on behalf of 'all authors and publishers from Québec, the rest of Canada, and other countries'. Copibec's equivalent in Anglophone Canada, Access Copyright, has had its own litigation battles going back several years, most notably with York University.

But the significance of what happens in Canada extends far beyond its borders and the noisy debate reverberates around the world. That's why a worldwide audience is watching what happens next. The 2012 legislation has to some extent been the basis of proposals for new copyright laws in other countries, notably South Africa and Australia, provoking fears among many rights holders that anti-copyright sentiments—what they call 'the Canadian flu'—might be infecting other jurisdictions. In Australia, rights holders and their representatives have been fighting proposals by the country's Productivity Commission to introduce a US-style fair use exception into its copyright law. Publishers, authors and other creators were relieved by the news late in 2017 that the Australian government had merely taken note of the recommendation and would begin a new round of public consultation on copyright exceptions in 2018. The very high-profile campaign mounted in Australia by its creative industries may have helped publishers and authors 'dodge the bullet' on this occasion, but no one there is complacent about the final outcome.

India itself is no stranger to the 'copyright wars' being waged between content owners and educational institutions. In March 2017, three international publishers, Oxford University Press, Cambridge University Press and Taylor & Francis withdrew from a long-standing and highly contentious litigation with Delhi University that centred on copying copyrighted content for course packs. The highly publicized dispute saw reprised in India many of the confrontations and distortions familiar from other battles in other jurisdictions; authors and publishers on one side, teachers and university administrators on the other.

It's difficult for authors and publishers surveying the copyright world today to find much solace. Wherever you look—whether it's in India, Germany, Belgium or Brazil—you can find evidence of judicial decisions profoundly hostile to the interests of content creators. Decisions, for example, that offer no protection against systematic and unremunerated copying of educational and scholarly content; decisions that refuse to recognize publishers as legitimate rights holders for the purposes of receiving monies from copying levies; new laws and regulations that have the effect of widening the exceptions to and limitations on copyright. The news is by no means all bad for the publishing industry, but there are more than enough discouraging signs for publishers and authors. The good news is that the industry is more alert to the problems than ever before. Awareness has increased and with it the realization that copyright is critically important, not just for the health and prosperity of publishing companies but for the wider creative industries on which so many economies depend more and more for jobs and exports. With awareness has come effective action. Individual companies and trade associations have stood up, shown real leadership, and fought for their own and the wider industry's interests, committing significant time and money in the process. That leadership and commitment deserves to be acknowledged and applauded, but there's much more that needs to be done.

The industry needs to come together to invest as a matter of urgency in a sustained, international programme of copyright education to inform and educate users about the value of copyright and about their rights and responsibilities in regard to the content they consume. Copyright infringement is not a victimless crime and users, made aware, can be brought to an understanding that high-quality content, whether it's for education, research, professional advancement or entertainment, requires substantial long-term investment. But we need to do more than inform and educate. We have to learn from other sectors, such as music and video, and make it easier for everyone to buy and license the content they want. We need to put in place easy-to-find, simple-to-use tools that deliver content in the workplace, in the classroom, in the library, and in the home in exactly the forms that consumers demand. The challenge facing publishers and authors is to make it as easy to buy and license as it is to infringe. Informed and aware consumers, global content networks, and ubiquitous licensing services: that's the future towards which the publishing industry should be working.

MICHAEL HEALY is Executive Director (International Relations) at the Copyright Clearance Centre (CCC). Prior to joining CCC, he was Executive Director of the Book Rights Registry. He has also worked for more than 20 years in UK's publishing industry. Michael has been closely involved in developing standards for the international book trade and has been Chairman of the International ISBN Agency. He currently chairs the International Standard Name Identifier (ISNI) Agency and is a director of the UK Copyright Hub.

27

LEGAL ASPECTS OF COPYRIGHT

"There is lack of awareness of the importance of copyright"

Saikrishna Rajagopal

Q: What is the role of copyright for the publishing industry in India?

Saikrishna: Copyright is, of course, critically important to the publishing industry since its business models are based on being able to protect the content it publishes from being copied and used without permission by those who do not invest in creating it. Publishers act as de facto promulgators of both culture and education in many ways through their publications, and they are able to effectively fulfil this function only when they are supported by a robust legal framework which, in theory, acknowledges their exclusive rights in the content they publish, and by enforcement mechanisms through which their rights are protected in practice on the ground.

Without both such substantive and positive protection, which copyright provides, it would be challenging for publishers even to contemplate being able to protect their content. Without copyright protection, their content could become freely available for anyone to use and exploit. While there are sections of society which may cheer such a development, especially if free use were by the readers of books, the fact of the matter is that, without effective copyright protection in place, untrammelled and unregulated exploitation of content would not just be by the isolated reader seeking knowledge. It would also be by the unscrupulous middleman seeking to exploit the investment by another to make commercial gains for himself through the mass production and sale of content without reference to and, certainly, without the permission of the content creator.

Although the case of unjust commercial enrichment is a far greater concern than that of the lone individual who makes limited use of content without authorization, both cases chip away at a model where publishers use copyright, and the gains they make through copyright are invested in the creation of further content, which in turn contributes to the enhancement of both cultural and academic spheres of public life.

Q: How is the situation in India different from elsewhere?
Saikrishna: A lot of the content which is made available in the country is reprinted from publications abroad at special, lower prices for India. This is true not just of academic content for which special editions for the Indian subcontinent may be published through licensing arrangements but also of general fiction which is often available in India at prices which are much lower than those at which the same books are sold in the West. Thus, while the content available in India may not significantly differ from the content available elsewhere, publishers have ensured that prices often differ in order to make content accessible to people in India keeping in mind the purchasing power and per capita income of Indians.

Although doing so certainly makes good business sense, it also functions as a public service. In such a scenario, copyright becomes more important than ever since it is important that publishers are able to contain copies meant for sale in India, and ensure that they are not sold without authorization beyond the country's borders. If that were to happen, it would cause tremendous losses to publishers as the price points in the West are higher.

It is with reference to this territorial differentiation of rights that the Indian scenario significantly differs.

Q: Can you tell us about a few key judgements globally that have influenced the way copyright is viewed and used?
Saikrishna: Copyright as we know it is a few hundred years old. Although the copyright traditions of continental Europe are more author-centric than those of England and other common law jurisdictions, they are not incompatible with each other. Having been a British colony, we unsurprisingly follow the traditions of English law although, in recent years, we have significantly diverged from its specifics, particularly in our

attempts to restructure copyright law to create a more level playing field for all of those who participate in the film and music industry.

That said, the basics of copyright law have been thrashed out over centuries in jurisdictions as far apart as England and the United States. We have judgements which stipulate that copyright cannot be perpetual, that news or a fact alone cannot be copyrighted, that ideas by themselves merit no protection, that copyright can subsist in independently created similar works, that a copyright owner may lose the right to control the subsequent sales of a specific copy of a protected work after the first legal sale of that copy. All of these concepts, some of which have cohered into doctrines, are now fundamental to the practice of copyright law. They are not restricted to the legal inventions of a specific jurisdiction but have emerged in jurisdictions across the world, and are generally accepted across the globe. They now form what could be considered the backbone of the mechanisms of copyright protection, and indicate how both publishers and authors may use a prior work, where they require permission to use existing content, and where they may make use or refer to content without authorization.

Q: In the wake of the outcomes of the Delhi University (DU) case, what do you think is the way forward for various stakeholders here?

Saikrishna: There does exist a legal mechanism through the offices of the Indian Reprographic Rights Organisation (IRRO) which enables photocopies to be legally made. The DU case aside, photocopies of works are often made in India without the payment of any fees to the content creators. Ideally, functioning mechanisms need to be set up and used to ensure that fees are paid for photocopies for legitimate purposes such as education. This would not burden students too much; it would ensure that publishers are paid for the use of their work; and it would ultimately contribute to enabling publishers to ensure that academic content continues to be available in the Indian market. Such an outcome would be to the benefit of all the stakeholders including publishers, students and authors whose royalty payments are directly dependent on the income which their books generate.

Q: Given the proliferation of photocopying in our educational institutions, how do you think the existing law can be used to protect copyright holders' interests?
Saikrishna: As we've just discussed, the way forward likely involves not attempting to stop photocopying in toto but in attempting to ensure that photocopying is legal and with remuneration to publishers. Facilitating the distribution of paid-for authorized photocopies is a path that takes care of the interests of all the stakeholders simultaneously. I think it is a fallacy to frame the issue as one of academics or students against publishers. On the contrary, it is one of how academics, students and publishers can all work together and contribute to an ecosystem in which academic content is available and accessible in the market. That system, to my mind, involves facilitating the distribution of legal copies of works and, where required, legal photocopies of works.

Q: What about dealing with pirates? You have been supporting publishers with taking some action against book piracy. How has this panned out and what is the way forward?
Saikrishna: Our firm has been involved in a number of piracy actions which have helped stem the sales of pirated copies of books. As long as there exist pirated copies, it is worth considering continuing to engage in actions against piracy including actions in court. Copyright infringement is, of course, both a criminal offence and a civil wrong under Indian law. Where copyright is infringed on a commercial scale, it is worth advocating for the routine levy of punitive damages to the extent that it becomes unprofitable to engage in copyright piracy as a trade.

Q: What do you see as the main roadblocks or challenges?
Saikrishna: Following are the main challenges:
1. The ambiguities in the law or in the exceptions
Indian copyright law in terms of its statute, the 1957 Indian Copyright Act, is not particularly ambiguous, although there has been a trend in recent years to go beyond the letter of the statute, particularly with reference to acts which may be executed in relation to content without

the permission of the copyright holder. To my mind, this brings in a great deal of uncertainty to this realm of the law since it is very difficult to predict how a court would view an act of alleged infringement.

2. Lack of incentives to implement the law

There isn't so much a lack of incentives to implement the law as there is of resources. That said, there are relatively cost-effective steps which can be taken to facilitate the implementation of the law, such as the creation of comprehensible, functioning and accessible national databases to help track copyright infringement on a commercial scale when it takes place across state boundaries, which it often does.

3. Lack of awareness of the importance of copyright and of the law among key stakeholders

Awareness of copyright law and infringement is low, as is awareness of the detrimental effects of piracy on authors. This isn't a concern so much amongst publishers and authors as they deal with copyright routinely and understand its implications, but it is a concern when it comes to members of the general public who often do not understand how copyright works and who see the acquisition of copyrighted content primarily in terms of the money they part with for a specific copy, pirated or not. It is worth engaging in campaigns to increase awareness both in schools and in other public fora to explain the benefits of respecting copyright. One can only hope that with increased awareness, more members of the public would shy away from buying pirated copies which decrease authors' incomes and which inhibit academics and culture from flourishing by straining publisher revenues, and consequently publisher investment in the creation of new works.

Q: What, according to you, can be done to address these?

Saikrishna: Addressing the proliferation of copyright infringement has to involve a multifaceted programme. The motivations and understanding of the various persons who engage in copyright infringement differ. Commercial infringers, for example, are motivated by the desire for profits which they likely know are illegitimate. On the other hand, the individual consumer of a pirated work of fiction, for example, may simply be driven by the benign and even laudable aim of participating in the literary culture without necessarily understanding what the implications of consuming pirated works are.

Countering copyright infringement therefore cannot fairly treat all those involved in infringement on a par, and responses have to be tailored to their motivations. That is why a programme which seeks to counter infringement must encompass a range of actions right from the initiation of legal proceedings, where they are warranted, to increased interaction with the public to educate it about copyright law.

Q: As someone who has worked long and hard on this issue, with the publishing community and other industries as well, what would you say are the best practices that can be picked up and implemented?

Saikrishna: There are, broadly speaking, three arenas in which publishers and those in comparable positions in other copyright industries can take action. First, invoking copyright law, particularly in the case of commercial infringement. Second, raising awareness amongst the public. And, third, revisiting pricing models wherever necessary to ensure that they are tailored to the Indian market. These lines of action all have to be coordinated with each other, and it is worth having a point person to oversee the high-level response of a company to the occurrence of copyright infringement.

SAIKRISHNA RAJAGOPAL is Managing Partner of Saikrishna & Associates, a firm in the field of intellectual property. He has worked on a variety of intellectual property disputes in the past two decades and has appeared in many landmark cases. He has appeared before a Standing Committee of Parliament deposing with respect to the 2012 amendments to the Copyright Act, 1957.

28

PUBLISHING ETHICS

"Publishers are custodians of scholarly record"

Sushmita Das

Every year, Indian scholars contribute a sizeable amount of information to the already existing pool of knowledge in the form of books, magazines, academic journals and new articles. As per UNESCO's statistics, about 90,000 books were published in India in 2013. Another survey conducted jointly by Elsevier Publishing Group and the Government of India[1], showed that in 2013, India's scholarly output accounted for 4.4 per cent of global academic output, with a growth rate of 14 per cent, while the world average growth rate was 4 per cent. The study also reported remarkable impact of these contributions from India and the growth in impact showed an increase from 0.8 per cent to 1.2 per cent between 2009 and 2013. A few other reports, such as the Nature Index[2], also rate India among the contributors of high-quality scientific publications.

The high growth rate in scholarly contributions from India can be attributed to numerous factors such as increase in literacy rate, high competition in the job market, and amendments in governmental policies and guidelines for publication. In the current scenario, scholarly communities feel that there is an 'inbuilt pressure' to publish as appointments, promotions, and tenure are linked to publications. Early-career researchers are even more under pressure as many of the universities offering PhD programmes state that students must have one to three publications before they can defend their thesis.

With the pressure on scholarly communities to 'publish or perish', publishers are witnessing a surge in scholarly submissions. Publishing styles are changing dramatically with traditional publishing models being upgraded and new ones innovated to cater to the submissions. As 'gatekeepers' of this huge influx, it has become imperative for publishers to put in place robust publication processes and maintain ethical standards to thrive on the delivery of high-quality and trusted content.

Over the past few years, numerous incidents of scholarly misconduct by authors, sometimes high-profile scientists, have been reported in the Indian media. A study by Professor T.A. Abinandanan[3] reported that about 70 scholarly articles published from India have been retracted or withdrawn from peer-reviewed journals due to various types of publishing misconduct ranging from plagiarism to self-plagiarism and data fabrication. Numerous other reports show that the most common issues are authorship disputes, allegations of plagiarism and dual submission, allegations of data mishandling/fabrication, author/reviewer conflicts of interest, reviewer bias, or an editor adding content without the consent of the author. Manipulative and intentional behaviour could be one of the reasons for the rise in misconduct, but aspects such as the lack of awareness and training on publishing ethics, ignorance, and lack of affordable editorial services, statutory controls and clear government policies also contribute towards these practices.

Publishing ethics are guidelines that authors, editors, and reviewers should adhere to and comply with during a scholarly communication. It is a collective responsibility of all stakeholders that high standards of publication process are ensured and the integrity of the scholarly record is maintained.

Authors should ensure that they have substantially contributed to the conceptualization, design, data analysis, drafting or revising of the article, and its final approval for publication. Unethical practices of 'gift authorship' raise serious concerns when an inexperienced author believes that adding an academic heavyweight's name as co-author would help in getting the article reviewed more favourably. It is extremely important that all co-authors consent to the work presented for publication. Duplicate submission or publication of the same or identical work in one or more publication is considered unethical and is a serious violation of copyright law.

The role of reviewers in the publication process is very important as they are the experts in the field of the submitted work. Their appraisal of the work and feedback help in improving the quality of the work. The comments aid the editors to make an informed decision on the submitted work. Reviewer misconduct can range from minor issues, such as rude or unconstructive reviews to major issues, such as the appropriation of author's ideas or data. If the manuscript under review is that of a rival or a competitor, wrongful practice by the reviewer, such as submitting a biased review or inappropriate comments, could lead to delay in publication. It is very important that the reviewers disclose competing interests, such as working in the same area of research or belonging to a competing institution.

Editors play a vital role in safeguarding the integrity of the peer-review process and ensuring that all submitted manuscripts get the same treatment during review and publication. The editor must protect the confidentiality of all material submitted for publication and all communications with reviewers, unless otherwise agreed with the relevant authors and reviewers. It is ethically important for the editor that she must not be involved in decisions about papers which she has written herself or have been written by family members or colleagues or which relate to products or services in which the editor has an interest.

Editors should ensure that the policies, guidelines and instructions to the authors are clearly mentioned in their journals. They should keep themselves abreast of the possible misconducts and should know how to detect and deal with them. They should sign up with organizations such as the Committee on Publication Ethics (COPE) and International Committee of Medical Journal Editors (ICMJE), which provide advice on all aspects of publication ethics and on how to handle cases of research and publication misconduct through guidelines, case studies, flow charts and sample letters. They should collaborate with their publishers and publishers should provide editors with online peer-review systems like ScholarOne Manuscripts and Editorial Manager to allow authors, editors, peer reviewers and editorial offices to manage the submissions and peer review of manuscripts. Software such as Crossref Similarity Check, powered by iThenticate; and Turnitin could be used in preventing scholarly misconduct and, specifically, unattributed copying of previously published work.

Publishers are the custodians of scholarly record and any allegations of misconduct could diminish their reputation and trust among the scholarly community and society at large. Publishers are ensuring that publication processes are robust and the best practices are being followed by authors, reviewers and editors, so that the content produced by them matches global standards. To ensure publishing ethics, publishers conduct awareness and training programmes at regular intervals. They disseminate material on ethical publication through both print and online media. Authors are made aware of the procedure and practices that are required to be followed while submitting their work for publication. Editors are trained on how to handle potential instances of misconduct, how to notify authors about the risks and how to contribute in preparing the procedure and policies of the journal they are handling. The publishers often play an important role when ethical questions arise and are better equipped to provide legal review and counsel, if necessary.

Elizabeth Wager, ex Chairperson of COPE, noted that all players in scholarly communication have ethical responsibilities and complacency in compliance will not reap substantial benefits. Efforts are required from all stakeholders to fulfil the aim of providing quality content to the readers.

[1] International Comparative Performance of India's Research Base 2009–2013. Link: http://www.nstmis-dst.org/PDF/Elsevier.pdf

[2] Subhra Priyadarshini. 2016. Nature Index India analysis reports surge in publication. Link: http://blogs.nature.com/indigenus/2015/12/nature-index-india-analysis-reports-surge-in-publication.html

[3] T. A. Abinandanan. 2013. Scientific Misconduct in India: An Analysis of Retracted Papers in PubMed. Link: http://www.imsc.res.in/~ethicsmeet/abstracts/abinandanan.html accessed on 22nd Dec 2017

SUSHMITA DAS heads the Journals Peer Review team for Taylor and Francis India. Her team handles over a hundred journals and is responsible for authenticating articles, peer review and publication. She has trained journal editors and authors on peer review systems, and has led workshops on publishing ethics, plagiarism and copyright. She has 17 years of experience in knowledge management and publishing functions.

29

FREEDOM TO PUBLISH

"Publishers must have the will and the ability to challenge established thinking"

José Borghino and Kristenn Einarsson

The International Publishers Association (IPA) is committed to defending and promoting the freedom to publish, which is under worldwide siege today. Freedom to publish has been one of the IPA's two primary policy drivers since the creation of the organization in 1896—the other being the promotion of copyright. Our organization believes that the unique contribution of publishers to enabling freedom of expression, debate and dialogue by disseminating the works of others, deserves recognition and protection.

If we are to create and maintain free, healthy societies, then publishers must have the will and the ability to challenge established thinking, preserve the history of our cultures, and to make room for new knowledge, critical opposition and challenging artistic expression.

Publishing has always operated in a social and cultural environment that is constantly changing and where the publishers themselves—through their commissioning or selection of material and as a result of the works they decide to disseminate—influence both what is discussed in society and how those works are received. Freedom to publish means that publishers must be allowed to publish all that they deem worthy of publication, even and perhaps especially if those works challenge the boundaries established by the society they operate in. As the French Enlightenment philosopher and writer Voltaire is often credited with saying: 'I disapprove of what you say, but I will defend to the death your right to say it.'

The conditions governing and restricting freedom to publish vary around the world. In some places, it is governments and state regimes that prevent the publication of material or works deemed to be 'dangerous' or 'inappropriate'. In other cases, there are pressure groups (religious, social, commercial) trying to prevent publication of certain information. Increasingly, large technology companies are influencing, often secretly or behind our screens, what we as readers and consumers can and can't see. The significance of this sometimes overt and at other times insidious manipulation of what we are allowed to read is simple: laws that prevent freedom to publish must be constantly challenged—there are actually very few instances where public welfare is increased or maintained by the blocking, removal or censoring of information.

In the educational sector, a growing concern is the interference by government in the production of learning materials. The IPA's Educational Publishers Forum is monitoring the rising trend of educational authorities aiming to produce one authorized book per subject per student. This is not only an impediment to the freedom to publish of educational publishers who could produce a number of competing textbooks in any given subject area; it is also a grave threat to the free exchange of ideas. The best-performing education systems around the world, by and large, encourage educational publishers to compete in an open market, producing innovative solutions that meet local needs. This new trend of government interference, however, not only robs students and teachers of the opportunity of learning from the best-possible resources, it also creates a state monopoly in the production, dissemination and accreditation of certain ideas and interpretations of history. Such a situation is inherently dangerous, authoritarian and susceptible to corruption. The IPA's Freedom to Publish Committee is working with the Educational Publishers Forum to monitor and respond to this worrying trend.

Another common challenge to publishers in all countries is the question of self-censorship. Even in countries with few regulations on freedom to publish, publishers might have to consider the negative consequences of producing and distributing certain content. Prime examples of this are the draconian libel or criminal defamation laws in some countries which take no account of the public interest when a critical statement is made about people or even corporations, and instead place an extraordinary legal burden on authors or publishers. Similarly, a growing number of jurisdictions are punishing whistle-blowers and investigative journalists who expose malpractice, corruption or official incompetence, when the public interest is more clearly served by the protection of these writers and their publishers. In this way, the same fears that affect publishers and lead them to self-censor can also infect authors, booksellers and librarians. In the end, if these fears delay or stop the creation or publication of such reports and works, then it is we the readers who are deprived.

The IPA is currently working on a policy position that addresses such laws. It is important that the publishing community, all over the world, stands together and supports the necessity of challenging all laws and actions that prevent the publication of work or information for other than very strict reasons of public safety—and those reasons must be constantly questioned and scrutinized.

In the IPA, it is the task of the Freedom to Publish Committee to manage the association's work in this field by implementing programmes and activities in partnership with IPA members and other national and international organizations.

The IPA's Freedom to Publish Committee does this by:

First. Helping Our Members Fight for the Freedom to Publish

We support our members through legal advice and direct lobbying when laws that threaten freedom to publish are proposed by governments or other agents. We do this in concert with an extensive network of international non-governmental organizations (NGOs).

Second. Challenging Violations of Freedom to Publish

We raise the alarm when publishers and writers are in danger and we support them when they face wrongful prosecution. We liaise with global fora, such as relevant United Nations agencies, to ensure that the collective voice of publishers resonates in the free speech arena.

Third. Driving Dialogue on Freedom to Publish

We lead or support international engagements and conferences to raise the visibility of freedom to publish and foster a continuous international conversation about this underappreciated area of free-speech advocacy. We coordinate our lobbying efforts with an extensive network of NGOs and the media.

Fourth. Celebrating the Champions of Freedom to Publish

We award the annual IPA Prix Voltaire, which honours and celebrates the courage of publishers who defy their would-be silencers and enable writers to exercise their own freedom of expression—a freedom that is enshrined in the UN's Universal Declaration of Human Rights. For more than a decade, the IPA's Prix Voltaire and its predecessor, the 'Freedom to Publish Prize', have honoured brave individuals and publishing companies from all over the world: from Turkey, Vietnam, and Russia to Iran, South Africa, Belorussia, and Saudi Arabia. Unfortunately, and despite our best efforts, the nominations for the prize keep arriving every year—a testament to the dire situation that too many publishers find themselves in.

The championing of the freedom to publish is no easy assignment but there is no alternative—and to stop now would be a betrayal of this founding principle of the IPA. Ultimately, to succeed in consolidating freedom to publish around the globe we will need international cooperation as well as support from many individuals and organizations. The bravery of our colleagues, who regularly stand up against intimidation, legal threats and physical harassment, inspires the IPA to redouble its efforts every year.

JOSÉ BORGHINO is Secretary General of the International Publishers Association (IPA). He joined the IPA as Policy Director in 2013 and was appointed to his current role in 2015. He came to the IPA from the Australian Publishers Association where he served as Manager of Industry Representation. His previous professional roles include teaching journalism and creative industries at the University of Sydney, Executive Director of the Australian Society of Authors, and senior positions at the Literature Board of the Australia Council.

KRISTENN EINARSSON has been Chairman, IPA Freedom to Publish Committee, since 2016. His other roles include: CEO, Norwegian Publishers Association; President, Bjørnson Academy (The Norwegian Academy for Literature and Freedom to Speech); Board Member, Norwegian Literature Abroad; Chairman, RiksTV; and Chairman, Norges Televisjon. He was CEO of Norwegian Book Clubs from 1991 to 2010, Chairman of the Kunnskapsforlaget publishing house during 2000-08, and Managing Director of Kunnskapsforlaget during 2008-10.

30

PUBLIC LIBRARIES AND LIBRARY MOVEMENTS

"Delivering quality joyful reading material to all"

Himanshu Giri

Q: What has been the contribution of various public library systems, NGOs and private movements in creating reading space and opportunities? Do give examples.

Himanshu: StoryWeaver, Pratham Books's online digital repository of multilingual books for children, has enabled a number of organizations to create joyful reading material for children in tribal and minority languages, languages which are often overlooked by mainstream publishers. Suchana, an NGO working in Birbhum, West Bengal, has translated over 60 titles in the Kora and Santali tribal languages on this platform. Ten thousand copies of select books have been printed for distribution through mobile libraries.

In Goa, the Konkani Bhasha Mandal—a pioneering non-governmental institution striving for the cause of Konkani in the social, educational, literary and cultural spheres—has translated 102 stories in Konkani on StoryWeaver, keenly aware of the fact that children's literature is a means of ensuring the continued usage of the language. Plans are under way to print the books and distribute them widely across schools and libraries in the state.

In Mumbai, Vibha Kamat, along with two friends, started the MCubed public library. Most of the books are donations that have come by word-of-mouth, and the library has books in English, Hindi and Marathi. There are arts-based activities and engagements that are constantly taking place to attract newer readers.

Q: Do you think there is some revival in the public library system?

Himanshu: The Raja Rammohun Roy Library Foundation (RRRLF) was set up in 1972 by the Indian government to support public library services and systems. Currently, this foundation is supporting around 50 per cent of the 70,000 public libraries that exist; however, there is a huge pool waiting to be tapped. To revitalize this movement around public libraries, the Indian Public Library Movement (IPLM) has been created with the support of the Global Libraries initiative of Bill and Melinda Gates Foundation and hosted by the NASSCOM Foundation.

The idea is to make public libraries prime centres of information that cater to 21st-century needs of communities. The Delhi Public Library is an autonomous organization under the Ministry of Culture and was started as a UNESCO project in the year 1951 by the Government of India. The library has a network of zonal libraries, branches and sub-branches, R.C. (Resettlement Colony) Libraries, Community Libraries, Deposit Stations, Mobile Libraries, Braille Libraries, etc. spread all over Delhi. There are over 18 lakh books and it is believed to be the busiest library in South Asia. In order to bring more children into public libraries this year, a Summer Fest was also organized for children by the IPLM in partnership with the Delhi Public Library. Spread over a month, a host of activities were designed for children within the walls of the library.

The National Mission on Libraries was set up when the National Knowledge Commission recommended that libraries have to be developed keeping in mind the needs of the time and the power and reach of information science. Given the huge mobile phone penetration in rural India, the National Mission on Libraries plans to provide knowledge related to agriculture, animal husbandry, traditional medicine, and similar subjects in an audio-visual format and have a roadmap for creating a National Virtual Library of India, which will serve as a comprehensive database on digital resources on information about India. Under the mission, the plan is to develop six libraries under the Ministry of Culture, 35 state/central libraries and 35 district libraries, and 629 sub-district libraries across all states will be given Wi-Fi connectivity.

The 17000 ft Foundation, based in Ladakh has been working to promote reading in the trans-Himalayan region, by setting up libraries across hundreds of schools in remote areas. Recently, the organization partnered with Pratham Books and Scholastic Publishers to translate 10 of their titles into the local language, Bhoti. Across 300 schools of Ladakh, 40,000 copies of these books were distributed.

Q: Private reading movements have also started in India. Though still in their infancy, they can go a long way in encouraging the reading habit. Please share your views on how this trend can be developed further.

Himanshu: Many bookstores are now becoming hubs of not just books but author interactions, events, and more. They are vital in encouraging the reading habit of children across India. Many of these stores are well-curated spaces which host a diversity of books—across ages, genres, topics and languages.

Independent bookstores that focus on children's books are fostering the reading movement. Kahani Tree in Mumbai and Lightroom Bookstore in Bengaluru are warm, inviting spaces that are run by people who understand and care about children's books. Both bookstores stock independent publishers from across India as well as a range of international books for young bibliophiles. Readers can choose from bilingual books as well as multilingual ones.

Most of the exciting developments are currently happening in big cities. But Walking Bookfairs changed this plot when they ventured into promoting books across Odisha and then India. Another group that is constantly talking about books is the Reading Raccoons group. Started on Facebook, the group now has 15,000+ members—all passionately discussing books, sourcing book recommendations and more. The group also occasionally hosts contests and crowdsources books for libraries in need.

In Arunachal Pradesh, with its difficult terrain and connectivity, the one hope for promoting reading is the school system. Sathyanarayanan Mundayoor, fondly known as Uncle Moosa has set up more than a dozen libraries, called Bamboosa Libraries, in the villages of Arunachal Pradesh through the Lohit Youth Libraries programme. Volunteers from tribal villages work with reading-deprived children. Books are accessible and kept in open cupboards.

With a nation as diverse as ours, movements and collectives like these can not only increase access to books but provide templates for different types of reading models that can work for varied readers.

Q: Share the various programmes undertaken by Pratham Books for the same. What has been the response?

Himanshu: In 2012, Pratham Books started the 'One Day, One Story' event to engage with our growing community. This is an annual nationwide storytelling event that takes place on International Literacy Day. The main aim of this initiative has been to create environments that foster reading and make reading fun. The programme mobilizes a community of volunteers called Pratham Books' Reading Champions to conduct interactive reading/storytelling sessions in their own communities to spread the joy of reading. These sessions are conducted free of cost and mostly with children from underserved communities. In just six years, the event has grown from 250+ volunteers to 5,700+ volunteers.

Pratham Books's online repository of multilingual books for children, StoryWeaver, has opened digital vistas for disseminating multilingual books to children in various formats. We have been openly licensing most of our content under the CC–BY 4.0 licence which allows anyone to use, reuse or remix the stories as long as due attribution is given.

In 2015–16, our partner organizations took StoryWeaver into 3,900 classrooms across 22 Indian states and worked with us towards making classrooms more engaging, and libraries more diverse. With more stories to capture their imagination, we believe that many more children will discover the joy of reading.

Users can read, download and even print the stories; they can translate or version them into new languages or even create new stories using the large bank of images. This has helped significantly scale the creation of joyful reading material in mother tongue languages. StoryWeaver was launched with 800 stories in 24 languages on

International Literacy Day 2015. Today, the platform is a digital treasure house of over 6,300+ stories in 100+ languages of the world, many of which have been added at the request of our community.

Schools like Tamarind Tree in Dahanu and partner organisations like Mantra4Change are using StoryWeaver to create digital libraries. These can consist of pen drives pre-loaded with an appropriate selection of free books from StoryWeaver, and many schools and learning centres download and distribute books to build their students' comprehension skills. For instance, Bohra Bai, a teacher in a Zilla Parishad school in Phaltan, Maharashtra, uses our books by projecting them in her classroom. While she reads the story aloud, she prompts the children to think, predict the next action, and draw connections with their real lives. She uses Marathi stories to build their vocabulary. In Bangalore, Meghshala uses many of our books in 'teach kits' that teachers use to complement their lessons for the state syllabus. Several other organizations use our stories as part of assessment tools, lesson plans for teachers, and for English-reading programmes. The circulation of memory cards and pen drives, as well as the existence of a digital infrastructure within schools, has helped us reach more children, in more ways than we imagined.

We do believe that mobile phones and the audio medium can, and must be used to reach more children, especially those who have little or no access to having stories read out to them. Following an extremely successful pilot, we opened the Missed Call Do, Kahaani Suno campaign to everyone in April 2016. All one had to do was give a missed call to a phone number, and would receive a free call back with a Pratham Books story in English or Hindi. At the end of the story, the caller could choose to have the story repeated, or find another story to listen to. Callers also received a free SMS with an online link to the story on StoryWeaver.

Mirchi Cares, the CSR wing of Radio Mirchi, recorded the stories for us, while our cloud telephony partner, Exotel, helped us develop and execute this campaign for two whole days across India. Publicized solely through Pratham Books and StoryWeaver social media platforms, our phenomenal online community helped spread the word about the campaign far and wide. The Missed Call Do, Kahaani Suno project was also a winner of the Mobile for Good Awards 2016. Through the grant received by Vodafone Foundation, we were able to extend the reach of this campaign to more organizations and regions across the country. In a period of six months, million minutes worth of stories have been consumed and 300,000 stories have been delivered to 50,000 unique children.

Over the years, our innovative and compact classroom library, known as the Library-in-a-Classroom (LIC), has become hugely popular among schools and organizations. Designed in response to the needs of schools and organizations which are, typically, infrastructure- and resource-scarce, the LIC, is literally a library on the wall. It contains over a hundred books for children to enjoy—displayed attractively in a dispenser that can be locked at the end of the school day for safe-keeping. The library adds colour and provides a print-rich environment for children within their classroom itself.

The classroom library model has proven to be a resounding success in getting more books to children across India, even in the remotest of locations. With support from our donors, collaborators and partners, this year, we are happy to have set up 1,280 classroom libraries with 1,54,000 books across 18+ Indian states.

Besides, Pratham Books has also been instrumental in running the outreach component of literature festivals like the Jaipur Literature Festival. During the outreach programme, visiting festival authors, illustrators, and resource people conduct sessions in schools and NGOs in cities where the fest is organized—thus providing young students a chance to meet the people behind the books!

Q: Why are these initiatives important in the context of the wider 'reading' trends?

Himanshu: In India, and across many parts of the developing world, there are critical supply shortages in reading resources for children—not enough books, in not enough languages, compounded by poor access and issues of affordability. As most publishers cater to middle- and upper-income urban audiences, demand-based economics dominates, to the detriment of creating books for economically weaker groups, where the profit motive is low. Keeping these ground realities as the pain points, Pratham Books created an alternate model to address these inequities to provide quality reading books for children in mother tongue languages with 'reading for joy' as the prime focus.

In 13 years, Pratham Books has published over 375+ titles in 20 Indian languages and distributed over 14 million books and 16 million story cards. However, we realized there was still a long way to go before achieving our mission of 'a book in every child's hand'.

HIMANSHU GIRI is CEO of Pratham Books, India's largest non-profit children's book publishing house. He has 20 years of experience in publishing and has worked on many public and private educational projects for setting up libraries for underserved children in India. He was one of the key team associates that set up Scholastic in India and was associated with the company for more than a decade.

PART

4

The Bigger Picture: Trends and Opportunities

PART IV • THE BIGGER PICTURE: TRENDS AND OPPORTUNITIES

THE BIGGER PICTURE: TRENDS AND OPPORTUNITIES

English language publishing in India stands at 50 per cent of total publishing, 35 per cent is Hindi publishing, and all other Indian languages make up the remaining 15 per cent. The Sahitya Akademi (SA) has played a seminal role in the preservation and dissemination of Indian Language (IL)literature. The first two contributors speak from a vast experience at the SA and other government bodies that have supported the outreach of IL and its translation, even when it was not as popular as it has become today.

Next, four IL publishers discuss their first-hand experiences of working with, and in three cases running, Hindi, Bangla, Malayalam and Marathi publishing concerns. The mood is upbeat and the growth of IL publishing with the entry of multinationals into this arena is welcomed.

Translations from Indian languages have never had it so good as these lists seem to be growing and thriving with both mainstream English language publishers and early pioneers. We have two veterans in the translation landscape share their experiences and views on the bright future of this genre.

Independent publishers have always enlivened the Indian publishing scene, pushing the boundaries in terms of both breadth and attention to detail in their publishing. Three founding publishers, share their journeys and challenges, in lively and candid conversations.

Alongside the Independents we now have a new kind of disruptor in Indian publishing. These are the startups who are marrying content and technology to bring about new kinds of publishing. Be it fiction for mobile phones or testing and chapter apps, the use of AI (artificial intelligence) in illustrated books or a range of applications and value additions to conventional publishing, the contributors in this segment engage and amaze. The last piece here points to another sort of innovation that sees increasing tie-ups and collaborations between English-language and IL publishers and local and multinational players, resulting in benefits for both readers and publishers.

31

THE ROLE OF SAHITYA AKADEMI

'Translations unite us, preserve ancient literature and are a part of our life"

Dr K. Sreenivasarao

Sahitya Akademi, India's National Academy of Letters, is the central institution for literary dialogue, publication and promotion in the country and the only institution that undertakes literary activities in 24 Indian languages, including English.

Q: What is the current scenario in the Indian-language publishing market and what are the prevailing trends?

KS: If we talk about Indian literature in general, it is again on a rising curve. We are regaining in the last four to five years and also getting good exposure. Indian literature is flourishing. Of all the genres, fiction is always a hit and key players are always English publishers. But when we talk about Indian literature, we have great works in local languages and very fine writers, who are nowhere less than any bestselling authors on the national or international front.

However, regional writers are not getting exposure because of lack of good translations and translators. India is very vast country; so private players should also come forward for translations. Mostly, regional literature is available in Hindi and English; it should also be translated into foreign languages, so that it can reach international platforms. Dalit writing and women's writing are getting very focused now and are the latest movement in Indian literature.

Q: How is Sahitya Akademi promoting Indian languages?

KS: Sahitya Akademi promotes Indian writings in all the 24 Indian languages recognized by it. It:

- Confers awards in 5 different categories and Fellowships, which is the Akademi's highest honour;
- Annually organizes more than 600 literary programmes in all the languages and regions of the country including translation workshops;
- Issues travel grants to young writers;
- Publishes more than 500 titles in all the languages every year; and
- Promotes Indian literature in the country and abroad through its several projects and schemes.

Q: What are the challenges in translations?
KS: As we have a scarcity of translators, good translations are not coming. For example, there is not a single translator from Marathi to Manipuri or from Manipuri to Malayalam. Within India we are facing this. Forget about international languages, even our own languages are not getting exposure. And the sad thing is that because of this great works of literature are getting lost. We have only one translator in India from Malayalam to Nepali. In such a situation, how much work can we do? Besides, sometimes in English translations, we lose the Indian essence. So scarcity of good translators is the main problem.

Q: Is it a profitable venture?
KS: Marketing literature is not easy. We are not getting any kind of encouragement. English and Hindi are two languages which are selling really well. Other popular languages are Tamil, Malayalam and Bengali. But at the same time in other languages like Dogri, Kashmiri, Punjabi and Konkani we have very low sales, even though good literature is being published in these languages. Maybe readership is not there in these languages. At Sahitya Akademi, we cannot restrict ourselves to the popular languages; we are giving same treatment to all the 24 languages.

Q: Tell us about the journey of Sahitya Akademi's journal *Indian Literature:* its evolution, readership and content.
KS: *Indian Literature*, Sahitya Akademi's bimonthly journal, is India's oldest and the only journal of its kind featuring translations of poetry,

fiction, drama and criticism from twenty-three Indian languages to English, besides original writing in English. It has been coming out for 60 years now and it has gained immense readership. It has been going to all major universities and even individual readership is there. We have given lot of focus on young writings; we have brought out special issues in Bengali and Assamese, besides Telugu and Marathi. In addition, we are giving importance to tribal and oral literature. So such special issues will also come.

We are getting material from all over, and recently I got to know that we have almost two to three years' publishing material with us. That itself is a kind of testimony to how it has gained popularity amongst litterateurs.

We strive to feature some of the best literature and writers in our journal, old as well as new. There is hardly any significant Indian author who has not been featured in the pages of this journal that has completed 60 years of service to the cause of Indian literature.

Our journal offers a feast of literature with unique sections, such as 'Heritage' and 'Classics'. Our other special features include novel excerpts, travelogues, autobiographical writings, book reviews, author interviews and tributes to writers. *Indian Literature* is also highly valued as a source of reference in India and abroad and is an essential for libraries and for discriminating readers, researchers, and students of creative and critical literature.

Q: What are the future projects and schemes Sahitya Akademi is focusing on?

KS: We need to encourage youth because they are the future. We have some new kinds of schemes for youth, under which if any young first-time writer is unable to print his or her book, Sahitya Akademi will do it for them. Poetry, short stories, fiction, we will publish their work and also take care of marketing. We also give travel grants of Rs 15,000 each to five writers in each language, which means more than 100 writers can avail this. A Marathi writer can go to some other place like Karnataka or

Andhra Pradesh or Assam to acquaint himself/herself with what kind of writing is happening in other parts of India. It also makes them aware of other cultures. In addition to that, we have different platforms for them like Mulakat and Yuva Sahiti.

We also confer Yuva Puraskar on young writers. It's very interesting to know that the young awardees are very mature writers. Recently, in Santhali (a very new tribal language), an awardee saw his own poetry in the Class 12 syllabus, which means his writing is of that calibre. They are not compromising on quality, that is one positive signal.

We never sell our rights, but we are trying to get Indian literature translated into foreign languages and the project is lying with Government of India. Once it is approved, Indian literature will get acclaim on the international platform. We are looking at translations, particularly in six UNESCO-recognized languages—Arabic, Chinese, English, French, Russian and Spanish.

Q: How can we promote reading habit in children?
KS: It's strange but true that youth is the biggest boon as well as bane of Indian literature. So we have to encourage children from school level to read books and appreciate Indian literature. Schools only have library period, which is not enough. Unless we start reading good literature from childhood, we cannot appreciate words in future also.

Besides, we started a programme series called GRAMALOK on October 2, 2017, in which we have started holding reading sessions in villages and as per the interest level and requirement, we provide them literature. We have around 6 lakh villages in India and we want to reach to each and every village, as they are important to mainstream literature.

We have to target youth and bring them back to reading. We participate in almost all major book fairs organized in India. Last year, we participated in 180 book fairs and 200 programmes related to book fair. Now we are trying to organize our book fairs at village and taluka levels. We are also planning to increase our number of shops and open public reading rooms and small libraries in transit metro stations in Delhi.

Q: Is there anything else you would like to add?

KS: We organized 681 programmes last year; that means almost every 14 hours we have one programme. We published 680 books last year, which is also one book every 14 hours. Our workshops and literary gathering, under various heads like Meet the Author, Samvad, Kavisandhi, Kathasandhi, Loka: The Many Voices, People and Books, Through My Window, Mulakat, Asmita, Antaral, Avishkar, Nari Chetna, Yuva Sahiti, Bal Sahiti, Purvottari, and Literary Forum meetings, are attracting huge industry participation.

In India, translation activities have been going on since ancient times. It's not a new thing, but now it is flourishing. And I feel it's only because of translations that India is united even today and, being a multilingual society, translations are part of our day-to-day lives.

DR. K. SREENIVASARAO is Secretary of Sahitya Akademi and has worked with the organization for more than two-and-a-half decades. He is a sitting member of the Press Council of India, Rashtrapati Bhavan Literary Committee, General Assembly of the Indian Council for Cultural Relations, Raja Rammohun Roy Library Foundation, and Doordarshan's Preview Committee, and is on the Council of Sangeet Natak Akademi. He has translated a children's dictionary from English to Telugu, and received the Delhi Telugu Akademi Award for 2011.

32

INDIAN LITERATURE THROUGH SAHITYA AKADEMI

"We can win many more Nobel Prizes if we translate and present our books well"

Nirmal Kanti Bhattacharjee

Q: What is your overview of regional literature in general? Explain with emphasis on Bengali literature.

NKB: The future of regional-languages publishing is very vibrant. Hindi, Malayalam and Marathi are three specific languages in which publishing activities are very bright. A lot of books are coming in; a lot of translations are happening from foreign languages and Indian languages and, most importantly, readership is increasing. As far as Bangla is concerned, contents and readership both are constantly growing. Moreover, the number of publishing houses is also growing; a lot of new niche publishing houses have come up now. Apart from bigger one like Ananda Publishers, Dey's Publication, Patra Bharati, and Mitra & Ghosh, new and smaller publishing houses are also making their mark. Topics, which are not run-of-the-mill, are being published now; a lot of non-fiction is happening and it's finding a lot of readership. Besides, the number of glossy magazines, newspapers and tabloid has also gone up.

Q: You were editor of *Indian Literature* (*IL*) for five years; tell us about its readership profile and how it has sustained. What are the reasons for its success?

NKB: *IL* as a journal has evolved a lot in terms of its readership, circulation and most importantly outlook. Published in English by an autonomous organization under the government, *IL* has its own limitations, but these limitations can be overcome if there is determination backed by innovative ideas. If we take a closer look at *IL*, it is not just a compendium of poems, stories essays and reviews translated into English. There is lot of creativity in it and when we innovate, the journal becomes interesting, readership increases, and, at the same time, it acts as a platform for the younger writers to experiment.

When I started editing the journal, I found out that some of my predecessors used to bring out some special issues, devoted to a particular language, for example Tamil. It would contain some glimpses of ancient, contemporary and modern Tamil literature and writings apart from poems, making it a treasured volume. So I maintained that and also started bringing out occasional special language issues. But we thought of bringing out something new. So we started genres-specific issues: biographical writing in Indian languages, autobiographical writing in Indian languages, travel writing, etc. All these issues attracted the interest of readers. Interestingly, we found that circulation went up.

And then we thought we should include marginal languages as well. We collected some oral literature and scripts from Tripura and brought out a special issue on Tripura, for which we organized a workshop in Agartala and started translation work. Once the issue was out, it was loved by everyone. Not just Tripura, the whole country liked it. It caught the attention of the people of Tripura so much that the then Chief Minister organized a special function, invited us there, and launched the journal and we had to reprint 1,000 more copies to supply to them. Think innovatively, out of the box to add new life to the journal.

Q: What does the future hold for *Indian Literature?*

NKB: Future is very strong as long as freedom of expression is safeguarded. I have no hesitation in saying that during my time as editor, I never had any interference from the authorities. *IL* will grow from strength to strength, as it is the only journal which showcases the entire gamut of Indian languages.

Q: You are currently working on translations publishing; so in your opinion, what is its current status and how does its future look?

NKB: I have always worked with translations. I would go to the extent of saying that translations have survived mainly because of Sahitya Akademi (SA) and National Book Trust, India (NBT). Thirty years back, private publishers were not much interested in translations. Any book to be translated had to go to NBT or SA. I have a mooring in translations and I have also myself translated from Bengali to English and vice versa. My English translations of Mahasweta Devi's *Armenian Champa Tree*, Sunil Gangopadhyay's *The Dreadful Beauty*, Shirshendu Mukhopadhyay's *The Ghost of Gosain Bagan,* and the Bengali translation of U.R. Anantamurthy's short-story collection *Suryer Ghora O Anyanya Galpo* have been critically acclaimed. Translation is the next big thing in publishing, not just in India, but world over.

Just a few years ago, multinational houses never thought much about Indian languages and they had no agenda for translation publishing. But suddenly there is a boom; now all the big MNCs have come into Indian publishing. I think the tremendous success of Indian writers, winning prestigious awards like Arundhati Roy, *The God of Small Things* (1997); Kiran Desai, *The Inheritance of Loss* (2006); and Aravind Adiga, *The White Tiger* (2008) is the main reason. Now international publishers have also started giving consideration to Indian writings.

Q: What are the challenges involved in translations?
NKB: When we have so much of good literature available, the crux is to get good translations. But unfortunately there is a dearth of good translators. No academic courses are being offered by universities and institutions. I have no problem in learning English. But it should not be done at the cost of the mother tongue. I find that our youngsters are not well versed in their mother languages, due to mushrooming of English school education. Youngsters are very good in English, especially conversation. But they have no knowledge of their mother tongue. This is an alarming situation. Earlier things were good; mostly people were bilingual, which was our strength. So we have to preserve it.

Translation is one weapon through which the unity of India as a nation can be preserved. It is about national integration. We need to take Indian literary fiction to other languages of the world. I would be happy for our works to be translated into foreign languages like French, German, Spanish, Italian. For that we need very good English translations. International publishers can only evaluate English version. They have good understanding of English but we need to preserve our essence as well.

If we select say 20 of our best literature marvels in the last 30 years, translate them beautifully to English, and present professionally to international publishers, our Indian literature will be on top. I feel we are capable of winning more Nobel Prizes in literature.

Q: What are the efforts being put in by you and your organization to support translations?

NKB: Translations are very close to me. Whenever I read good Bengali literature or a good author, I feel it can be projected to the national level. I translate it for that reason. When Niyogi Books was planning to diversify, we all were involved in it. I thought surviving only on coffee table books and illustrated books is not enough for publishers. Some diversification is needed. So translation is rejuvenated in a big way. We have three imprints—one for original English fiction; second for translations; and a third for semi-academic non-fiction—which was launched during the New Delhi World Book Fair 2018. We are already publishing in Marathi, Tamil, Oriya, Assamese and Urdu. My intention and ambition is to create own library of Indian literature in Niyogi Books. We are trying to showcase the best of Indian literature.

NIRMAL KANTI BHATTACHARJEE has been Editorial Director of Niyogi Books since 2013. In his previous roles, he was Editor of Sahitya Akademi's bi-monthly journal *Indian Literature* and Director of National Book Trust. He entered the publishing industry as a member of the editorial team for the Encyclopaedia of Indian Literature Project undertaken by Sahitya Akademi, and later took charge of the Akademi's Eastern Regional Office at Kolkata. He has also been Director of K.K. Birla Foundation, a private trust devoted to the cause of art, literature and education.

33

PUBLISHING IN HINDI

"Reinvent and renovate for newer heights"

Aditi Maheshwari-Goyal

Q: Please tell us about the current landscape and key players in the Hindi-language market.

Aditi: Eminent Hindi publishing houses are mostly located in Delhi, and there are a few in Uttar Pradesh, Bihar, Punjab, Madhya Pradesh, Maharashtra, Orissa, Kerala and West Bengal as well. The global big-5 of Hindi publishing are Vani Prakashan, Rajkamal Prakashan Group, Rajpal and Sons, Prabhat Prakashan and Bharatiya Jnanpith. In addition, there is Kitabghar Prakashan, Prakashan Sansthan, Aadhar Prakashan and Samayik Prakashan. Besides, National Book Trust (NBT) and Sahitya Akademi (SA) are the government-funded publishing houses producing Hindi books. All of them have done noteworthy work in Hindi literature. The relatively newer ones like Hind Yugm and Nayi Kitab Prakashan are catering to specific readership. The latest trend is Hindi imprints of English publishing conglomerates like Harper Hindi, Penguin Random House's Hindi imprint, Westland and now Oxford University Press.

The Indian publishing sector is data-starved and experiences lack of analysis and meaningful insights. The only data available for reference is that provided by *The Nielsen India Book Market Report*, published in October 2015 by the market research firm Nielsen. According to the report, India's print book market—which grew at a rate of 20.4 per cent, compounded annually between 2012 and 2015—is worth Rs 26,060 crore. The release of Nielsen's report provides us with an opportune moment to take stock of the industry as a whole. We are still trying to estimate the size of Hindi publishing in this gamut, with more than nine states in India using it as their dominant language of communication, and with 650 million speakers globally and 450 million who use it as their mother tongue. To give estimated figure of its sales, it could be a Rs 1.5 billion (150 crore) market. And the number of new books published every year in Hindi, might be about 5,000–6,000 books, in addition to about 1,000 translations from over 25 national and international languages.

Q: Why are there so few new publishers in Hindi?

Aditi: Because it is a low returns on investment profession. The balance sheets are always under immense pressure for any new business strategy or operation to take off in this field. Sometimes, commissioned publishing takes care of the cash flow for the new ventures, otherwise they find it very difficult to sustain. The Hindi publishing market has a tendency to grow by the x-axis, which is by the number of books each publishing house publishes each year, and not by the y-axis or the number of copies sold. This assertion holds true for most publishing ventures.

It requires a lot of patience, perseverance, and, most importantly, passion to manage a Hindi publishing house. It is probably for this reason that most Hindi publishing houses are family-managed businesses.

Q: What are the genres and range of topics Hindi publishing is embracing? What are the latest trends?

Aditi: The range of topics that Hindi publishing is embracing has widened post liberalization in the last three decades. From the traditional *kavita, kahani* and *upanyas,* the Hindi readership is switching to popular and academic non-fiction, graphic books, travel writing, environment, self-help and ethnographies. With this, even the use of language has undergone a systematic socio-linguistic metamorphosis. The *Shaharnama* series is an attempt to talk about our cities and their histories in a new way. The *Kavi ne Kaha* series brought together Hindi poets. *Dastan Kehte-Kehte* is a series that brings most *ustads* of *shayari* under one roof. The 'nayi wali Hindi' campaign has created a buzz among youth. Also, it is after 12 long years that the National Film Award or Swarn Kamal has been conferred on the writer and publisher of a Hindi book *Lata: Sur Gatha.*

There are important literary magazines like *Gyanoday*, *Alochna*, *Vak*, and *Sahitya Amrit* along with several *laghu-patrikas* that underline the active debating culture of the Hindi public sphere. The latest addition to Hindi journals is *Pratiman*: world's only peer- and blind-reviewed journal of social and political sciences in Hindi.

Q: What is the impact of traditional, online and retail bookselling mediums on Hindi publishing?

Aditi: All of them co-exist in Hindi. I would identify traditional bookselling with the word 'passion', online with 'new-age' and retail stores with 'marketing'. The public library system buys books from publishers and makes them available to the masses in the country. The largest one being the Raja Rammohun Roy Library based in Kolkata.

The traditional book distribution channels have been working with very low operational turnaround cost. The new Goods and Services Tax (GST) has made it difficult for this category to remain self-sustained. The new-age commercial chains changed the financial ecosystem, which most Hindi publishers are finding difficult to adapt to. Hindi publishers do not find themselves comfortable buying bookshelf spaces, organizing expensive book-launch programmes or writing-off discounts that are bordering on the cost price of the books. These marketing activities never get justified against the production figures. Online retail, however, is a boon as it makes books available 24 hours for the readership.

While most Hindi publishers exist simultaneously in the dual world of traditional publishing and digital operations, the ripples of transition are being experienced far and wide in this ecosystem. The online bookstores, one of the most comprehensive innovations of the digital revolution to hit the banks of global publishing industry in the new millennium, brought with them an enhanced lifespan for books. They created fertile contexts for rethinking about making a book travel and find its readers globally. With it, however, came the biggest bane for the traditional bookselling business. The online booksellers bargain for heavy discounts with the publishers that get transferred to the readers largely due to online retail's low operational costs.

In addition, e-books and audio books are also catching up.

Q: What is your take on recent trends like tie-ups with English-language publishers?

Aditi: I find them very interesting because it marries world-class intellectual property with local treatment in operations. Penguin Random House has tied up with independent Indian publishing company Manjul Publications to produce, market and distribute their Hindi publications. This has happened after they received lukewarm response in the first decade of the 21st century due to the complicated distribution system. The relationship has worked out well for the author, publisher and readers. The Hindi originals and translation list of HarperCollins Publications has also brought forth interesting titles but faces similar distribution problems. Yatra Books produces Indian-languages translations for Westland Books Pvt. Ltd., now taken over by Amazon and has seen bigger sales in recent times.

Q: What is the role of social media in Hindi publishing?

Aditi: The publishers are actively using their own websites, blogs, Facebook, Twitter, Pinterest and Instagram handles to cater to Hindi readership globally. Google AdWords and investment in digital marketing is finding a space in the annual budgets of Hindi publishing firms.

Social media has tremendously changed the face of Hindi book marketing. Earlier Hindi was marred by politics of criticism and handicapped by ever-rising advertising costs in mainstream media. With the advent of social media, every reader became a critic and there is an upsurge of democracy of thought at relatively low cost. Therefore, publishers have also refined their role in a very dramatic way from being the traditional printing facilitator to a public thinker responding to the changes in the socio-intellectual climate.

Q: How do you see the future of Hindi publishing?

Aditi: With 48 spots in the country that are important centres of Hindi readership, which is the largest for any language in India, I foresee a great future for Hindi. The selection of books that are getting translated in Hindi has also widened in the last three decades. The language has attracted major global corporations to set up editorial and operational offices in India. The market is very attractive and the recent announcement by the world's oldest publisher, Oxford University Press, about entering the Indian-languages market and having Hindi as one of its focuses underlines its scope.

Demographically Hindi is the fourth-largest-spoken language globally. The international readership has improved in the last decade because of online sales and digital books. Hindi literature has become more vibrant and diverse with even more authors choosing to write their first books in Hindi. Also, the demand for quality books in terms of printing and operations has shot up. We find more and more people aspiring to resources in Indian languages as they lead the cultural, socio-political and economic growth engines of our country. This, along with logical solutions to pitfalls like lack of distribution channels and dependence on institutional sales, will amount to a glorious future for Hindi publishing.

ADITI MAHESHWARI-GOYAL is Director, Copyrights and Translation Department at Vani Prakashan. She is Managing Trustee at the Vani Foundation and Advisor to Jaipur BookMark, Mumbai Lit-o-Fest and Indore Literature Festival. Aditi is also Curator of India's first Hindi literary festival 'Hindi Mahotsav', and teaches publishing and editing at University of Delhi.

34

PUBLISHING IN BENGALI

"Bengali publishers still rely on traditional ways of distribution"

Tridib Kumar Chatterjee

Q: What is the current landscape and who are the key players in the Bengali-language market?

Tridib: The current landscape of Bengali publications is very bright. New, young and educated people are joining in this field with bright ideas and new authors. Many of them have left their lucrative jobs and started Bengali publications not only from West Bengal but also from other parts of the country like Assam, Tripura, Bengaluru, Delhi. Hopefully, within a couple of years, these new publication houses will achieve success.

At present, some of the key players who focus on conventional book publishing are Ananda Publishers, Deys Publishing, Mitra & Ghosh Publishers, Patra Bharati, Sishu Sahitya Samsad, Deb Sahitya Kutir, Karuna Prakashani, and Sahityam. Some upcoming publishers are Gangchil, Karigar, Cafe Table, Lalmati, Pata Bahar Publications, Parampora, Atmoja Publishers, Osomoy Prakashan, Reekal Books, Feriwala, Dhansiri and Sristisukh Publishers.

Q: Are these family businesses?

Tridib: Bengalis have always had an inclination towards literature and culture. This is because of a 200-year heritage of rich literature. The great social reformer in the 19th-century Bengal Renaissance, Pandit Ishwar Chandra Vidyasagar, was the key founder of Bengali prose. He was also a pioneer publisher of Bengal. The great Rabindranath Tagore also founded his own publishing house, Visva Bharati. Many of the modern Bengali

Publishing houses are not family businesses. But interestingly, it has been seen that often the grandfather started a book publishing which couldn't survive, beyond two generations. The third generation again started a publishing house with a new name and style and the fourth generation diversified the business by starting another new publishing house. Patra Bharati, my publishing house, is a good example of this. My grandfather started Vidyodaya Library in 1934 which came to an end in 1980 due to family partition. I started Patra Bharati in 1981 and my daughter Esha, after completing her MBA, joined me in 2014 and she not only took forward my business but also started BEE Books—an English publishing house. Mitra & Ghosh Publishers was founded by Gajendranath Mitra and Sumatha Nath Ghosh, both eminent authors of their time. After their departure, this private limited company was carried forward by the shareholders like Sabitendra Nath Roy and Manish Chakraborti. The majority of the key players in present Bengali publishing houses are either controlled by new generations who may be the heirs or new people or the entire house was taken over by another bigger publishing house. Apart from these examples, there are a few other names like Subarnarekha, Signet Press, Chuckervertty Chatterjee & Company, taken over by New Central Book Agency, Ananda Publishers and Deb Sahitya Kutir.

Q: How have marketing and outreach changed in recent times?
Tridib: Most of the conventional Bengali Publishers are dependent on traditional offline distribution channels through rural and semi-urban booksellers of various districts and participation in hundreds of book fairs happening in West Bengal, Assam and Tripura. Online business is not possible in many remote places where internet and courier service is not available.

On the contrary, new-generation publishers who don't have distribution strength all over the states and are mainly concentrated in metro cities are trying to avail of the online platform. But this is merely not more than 5 per cent of the total turnover.

Q: What are the geographies and customer demographics for Bengali books?

Tridib: In general, Bengalis have unparalleled love for books. This is the reason why the International Kolkata Book Fair has grown to an unbelievable figure of 2.2 million people and Rs 25 crore direct bookselling in 12 days. Apart from this mega event, as I mentioned, there are profound customer bases in districts, Bengali-dominated Assam and Tripura. Further, a huge literate and cultured Bengali population of the high-income group stays in the metro cities of India—Delhi, Mumbai, Bengaluru, Pune, Chennai, Hyderabad—which the Publishers & Booksellers Guild caters to every year with books of all eminent authors and publishers during special Bengali events like Durga Puja, Bengali New Year, Tagore Jayanti, and it always gets very good results.

Q: What are the key creative trends and author base?

Tridib: Bengali has a very strong author base; every year special big volumes of Puja issues of magazines sell thousands of copies. The authors contributing to those volumes have their fiction come out in book form within a couple of months. Most of these fictional books sell well.

As a regional publisher, I have noticed the increasing interest of readers in the following categories of fiction: historical, religious, political, crime and dark fantasy.

Q: Are you selling translation rights of the books to other regional-language publishers? How do you view the potential of this?

Tridib: Among the Indian languages, the number of books translated into English is the highest for Bengali. But as far as other neighbouring languages are concerned, the sales of translated Bengali books are not so encouraging.

Q: What is your view on big multinationals getting into regional-language publishing including Bengali?

Tridib: We welcome it, but before getting into Bengali-language publishing, multinationals must feel the pulse of Bengali publications. Already, many multinationals have started translations of their books written by eminent Indian English authors into Bengali. So far as my knowledge goes, success has not been achieved.

TRIDIB KUMAR CHATTERJEE is Managing Director of Patra Bharati Group of Publications, a major player in the Bengali-language publishing industry. He is also Chief Editor of *Kishore Bharati*, a children's periodical. Tridib writes regularly in various Bengali newspapers and periodicals.

35

PUBLISHING IN MALAYALAM

"Experimenting with new ways of writing"

Ravi Deecee

Q: What is the current landscape of Malayalam-language publishing?

Ravi: In general and trade publishing, the market for Malayalam-language publishing would be Rs 75–100 crore with almost 3,000 titles published in Malayalam every year. They are mostly family-run businesses, traditionally handed over from father to son; one or two are public limited companies.

Q: Marketing and outreach: how have these changed in recent times?

Ravi: Publishers now use two to three things actually. This is because with so many books in the market, the bookshelf space is shrinking. Traditionally, we share information about the book, along with book launches. Currently, social media has also become very important for promoting books. For example, teaser of a book can be sent via WhatsApp. Facebook has become a big tool for marketing and books can be promoted on various groups and forums. Publishers also use optimazation through Google AdWords. Publishers now have dedicated people who only look after social media.

Q: What are the distribution channels?

Ravi: Mostly, we rely on traditional distribution channels. We have more than 100 major bookshops in Kerala and we also reach out to 1,000 small shops at railway platforms and bus stands. We are also active online and we rely on major online stores like Amazon for distributing our books. Almost 80 per cent of our sales are within the state and 20 per cent is elsewhere. There is a huge market in the Middle East as well.

Q: What are the key creative trends in this segment?

Ravi: In fiction, formats are changing; publishers are experimenting with new ways of writing, new genres of fiction and a new breed of writers. This is very popular as many new writers are on the top sellers list. People who are above 35–40 years of age also like to read the new breed of writers. For example, there is one author whose book is published by Penguin and Hamilton in English and Malayalam by us—the book has sold more than 1 lakh copies in the last three years which is a good number.

Q: Are you selling translation rights of books to other regional-language publishers? How do you view the potential of this?

Ravi: We do sell translation rights, especially for translations into Tamil and Hindi. We as an organization have a policy on translations and do 60 books a year. There are other publishers who focus on translations. Translations are also happening in other languages like English, French, German, Tamil and Oriya as well. There has been a very significant development in the last two to three years, where Malayalam University, which has a translations department, now funds publishers in India and abroad for translations from Malayalam.

RAVI DEECEE is Managing Partner of DC Books, a leading book publisher in Malayalam. He is also Managing Director of the bookshop chain Current Books (India) Pvt. Ltd. Ravi serves as President of the All Kerala Publishers and Booksellers Association.

36

PUBLISHING IN MARATHI

"The future is bright"

Devayani Devesh Abhyankar

Q: Tell us about the current landscape and key players in the Marathi-language market.

Devayani: On an average, about 2,500 titles are published every year in Marathi. This number does not include titles published by ephemeral publishers.

The list of key players is long: Continental Prakashan, Dilipraj, Majestic, Mouj, Manovikas, Mehta Publishing House, Saket are a few which may be mentioned. There are institutional publishers such as Sadhana and Rajya Bhasha Vikas Sanstha too.

The major genres include fiction (novels, short stories collection, poetry) and non-fiction (travelogues, academic books). Translations and children's literature include both fiction and non-fiction.

Q: How have marketing and outreach changed in recent times?

Devayani: The techniques of marketing and outreach have undergone colossal change. From traditional promotion through marketing executives, advertisements, release functions, marketing is now also done online through events such as 'Meet the Author', besides release functions in meets of Maharashtra Mandals abroad.

Q: What are the geographies and customer demographics for Marathi books?

Devayani: Though Maharashtra and pockets of Marathi population in India are important focuses, with increasing e-publishing, geographical barriers seem to be crumbling.

Children and adolescents generally read what their elders recommend. Youth go in for what helps to develop their personal and professional skills. The 40+ like to read fiction, though some may prefer academic books. This age group is also interested in books on health, cookery, yoga. Some reread historical novels they may have read in their youth.

Q: Are you selling translation rights of books to other regional-language publishers? How do you view the potential of this?
Devayani: Sale of translation rights to other regional language publishers is highly recommended. Mehta Publishing House has been successful in bringing out translations of titles from Gujarati, Kannada and Bangla. Periodicals such as *Maimavshi*, or *Kelyane Bhashantar*, that are devoted to translation (theory and literature), are gradually becoming popular. Translation needs to be direct, not through English or Hindi.

Q: What do you feel about recent trends like tie-ups with English-language publishers?
Devayani: Sunidhi Publishers has been regularly publishing academic books in collaboration with SAGE Publications for the last five years. Generating translations for higher academic reading, particularly where the content becomes dated faster, is easier than commissioning titles in Marathi.

Q: What is your view on big multinationals getting into regional-language publishing including Marathi?
Devayani: Multinationals are always welcome. They will get quality products in terms of content and production. But they will have to operate in the local language and in local environment. Trying to reach remote areas in Maharashtra with communication in English may not be fruitful.

Q: Do you think they will be successful? How different is this market from the English market?
Devayani: The multinationals will be successful: for one their names carry weight and, for another, they deliver quality products which are welcomed by the local population. The multinationals will, however, have

to follow the saying, 'When in Rome, do as the Romans do' to set up dialogue with the locals for their business.

Q: How do you see the future of Marathi publishing in the next five years?

Devayani: The future is bright. Digital publishing may give a setback but it will be temporary. Books have survived not only those who burnt them but also theatre, films and other media. In fact all media forms are complementary and face no competition from one another.

DEVAYANI DEVESH ABHYANKAR has been Director and Partner at Marathi-language publishers Continental Prakashan since 1994. She is a member of the Federation of Indian Publishers (FIP), and has won nine national awards from FIP for excellence in book production. For her contributions to publishing, Devayani won the Parvati Bhooshan Puraskar in 2013 and was feted by Lions Club Pune in 2014.

37

INDIAN-LANGUAGE PUBLISHING BY GLOBAL PLAYERS

"Changing the way Indian-language publishing is viewed globally"

Shalini Singh

Q: What was the motivation for getting into translations/Indian-language (IL) publishing?

Shalini: Indian languages form the bulk of publishing in India. There is very little commitment to quality in the academic and serious non-fiction space. This is the void that we wish to fill. SAGE remains committed to dissemination of knowledge; publishing directly in Indian languages is an extension of this mission.

Q: How have translations helped to increase the reach of academic titles? Share some facts about new commissioning.

Shalini: Since the launch of the SAGE Bhasha imprint in 2015, we have published 110 titles—65 in Hindi and 45 in Marathi. All these are translations from our own academic English-language programme, majority being from our Indian authors. Although we have not actively started commissioning for original titles, we have received quite a few original manuscript proposals that we are evaluating currently. In addition to this, we are also receiving requests to translate titles that have been published by other academic publishers. Each year, we plan to add at least 50–60 titles to our Bhasha programme.

While our current programme is focusing on the first pillar, that is, translations, we remain committed to publishing original authoritative research that serves academic needs in each language we choose to publish in. We are targeting to publish 5–10 original manuscripts in 2018.

Q: Which languages have you chosen to start with and why?

Shalini: Currently we are focussing on two languages only—Hindi and Marathi. Hindi because it is the most widely spoken language in India—it's the official language of 10 states in India. The market is large and has great potential even though it is populated with a lot of players. There are no global publishers focusing on this space and hence we see a definite business opportunity and synergy with our mission to disseminate knowledge as much as we can. This is further fuelled by the demand for quality social sciences academic research work in Hindi.

There wasn't any particular reason for selecting Marathi; it was the first language we experimented with in IL publishing in 2008. Marathi, although dominated by local players, has a large academic market fuelled by the state's focus on education.

Q: How does the economics work, especially given the low levels of pricing in IL publications and the high costs of translations?

Shalini: We understand the needs of this market and also remain sensitive to the pricing requirements of the regional market. Quality translations come at a cost and time, which is the backbone of our regional publishing programme. Yes, maintaining the price point in translations is challenging. But we remain focused on our long-term vision and totally invested in this programme.

SAGE is backed by 50 years of publishing in social sciences, with over 35 years of publishing in India. As a global publisher of repute, we have sufficient bandwidth to invest in a new product line and wait for investments to reach a point when they start becoming self-sustaining.

Q: How is quality managed and controlled? Is there a separate team for different purposes?

Shalini: SAGE takes pride in managing most of the work in-house. While we have tied up with passionate individuals and companies for translations, we have an in-house production team in each language. We take feedback seriously and constantly encourage our readers and academic communities to share their thoughts with us. We have a dedicated sales team for SAGE Bhasha, each is managing a distinct language. This team eats-breathes-lives SAGE Bhasha.

Q: How is your programme different from those of Penguin, Oxford University Press (OUP), etc.?

Shalini: Our USP remains what we are best at doing—catering to academic publishing. SAGE remains committed to dissemination of knowledge. To the best of my knowledge Penguin's programme is heavily focused on fiction. As of this interview date, OUP's programme is yet to hit the market even though they had announced their entry in April 2015. We have been in the space since 2008 with our co-publishing arrangements that led to our direct entry into this space in March 2015. We are in this for the long haul. We remain focused on the needs of our authors, customers and market. This, along with our commitment to disseminating knowledge in the academic space, makes us different from other publishers.

Q: What about the local language publishers? How do they view these developments and do you see them as competition?

Shalini: There are established players in each of the languages we are currently focusing on. They have been in this space long before we entered. However, the market has grown and there is clearly a demand and supply gap. Our entry will enrich the overall publishing environment by bringing in transparency, rigour and quality standards that have perhaps not been seen earlier in this side of publishing.

In addition, SAGE is uniquely placed to take all of this content global. With one contract (whether original or translated works), we ensure that the IL publication will be displayed and sold globally. All SAGE Bhasha books will also be available globally as e-books. We believe all these factors will clearly set us apart from any real or perceived competition.

Q: What are the opportunities and challenges you see in this arena?

Shalini: We believe that our customers and our authors are our biggest strengths. The academic world's—researchers and academics—response to SAGE's entering IL publishing is very encouraging. We are aware of the type of market we choose to cater to. All these factors add up to a serious opportunity.

Being a global publisher of repute, we don't compromise on ethics and values. This is leading to supply-chain management issues that we are still working through. We remain convinced that there is a demand for our products and it is logical that supply will follow.

Q: What are the prospects?

Shalini: Publishing in Indian languages has been more challenging than we had anticipated. It is a territory that is dominated by regional players with very little transparency. Authors and customers are not served at levels we believe they should be. Our entry into this space should change the way IL publishing is viewed not just in India but also globally.

But we are here for the long haul. Hence our strategy will be to penetrate the market in each of the languages we are publishing in—that is Hindi and Marathi. We are already receiving publishing requests for Hindi journals and the first one is scheduled to launch in 2018. We will continue to explore how we can support academic institutions in publishing quality content.

Our first translation in Bangla was launched in the New Delhi World Book Fair and Kolkata Book Fair 2018. We would like to introduce another language in the next year or two.

SHALINI SINGH is Director, Publishing Services, SAGE India. After many years of spearheading multiple roles in advertising, she shifted gears and joined publishing at an entry level in 2005. She established the Publishing Services division at SAGE India and is now responsible for SAGE Bhasha commissioning and production. Her other core responsibilities are managing India Editorial Production (Books and Journals) and SAGE Global (Publishing Services).

38

TRANSLATIONS: A PUBLISHER'S VIEW

"In translations lie our histories, identity and belonging"

Mini Krishnan

Q: Your work and experiments in translations are noteworthy. Please share your experience.

Mini: I publish translations of Indian writing because in them lie our own histories, our sense of identity and belonging; because we need to breathe our native breath; because it is our historical duty in a largely illiterate country to preserve our word worlds and slow their disappearance. In the indigenous writing of the subcontinent lay the memories and history of a people who were rapidly losing their languages. What better service than to retrieve and reinterpret in a link language creating a body of work which is emotionally important for India?

Q: Tell us about your first translations project.

Mini: The first project I handled at Macmillan India was a 4,000-page typescript called *Comparative Indian Literature* (two volumes). It included a survey of all the literary forms from the recognized languages of the country, managing 200 contributors, 17 language editors. I went from harbour to the high seas in a month! As I helped our editor for that particular project to write up synopses of work after work in all the languages and polished the mangled drafts the editors sent up, I kept asking him where I might read the works. 'You can't. There are no translations,' was his unvarying response. By the time both volumes were published in 1985, I had made up my mind to try to publish at least modern Indian fiction in English translation.

My grandiose dreams to publish English translations of modern Indian fiction took flight, but not before they met with a few big dips. I experimented with V. Abdulla's translation of Malayattoor Ramakrishnan's *Verukal* (Roots, 1982) and failed. Not a single salesman showed interest in promoting it. Macmillan made it quite clear that there was no money for translations. So I set about looking for funding which, after seven years and many 'nos' from others, came from the MRAR Educational Society . If ever a low-key group influenced trends and shaped tastes, it was this trust in 1992 when it decided to sponsor the Modern Indian Novels in Translation project out of Macmillan India. Luckily, we got a grant of Rs 50 lakh for five novels each from Tamil, Kannada, Telugu, Hindi, Malayalam, Bengali, Urdu, Punjabi, Gujarati, Oriya and Marathi. No one setting out to publish translations today will ever know how difficult the terrain was 20 years ago.

From 1992 to 2000, when I left Macmillan, the unquestioned support of a few people helped me to source and edit 37 works of fiction and one autobiography. The publications were prepared both for the Indian market and for Macmillan's overseas market in the UK, which absorbed 200 copies of each of the titles. When I realized very painfully that Macmillan was no longer interested, I moved the project to Oxford University Press (OUP) in 2001, where the writers, translators and I were welcomed.

Q: How was your experience of translating Dalit writing?
Mini: I edited numerous translations from Malayalam and Tamil literature into English that primarily engage with the problem of caste and untouchability. A mega two-volume publication called *The Oxford India Anthology of Modern Malayalam Literature* could not be finalized without a healthy representation of Dalit writers and that happened after the *Oxford Anthology of Malayalam Dalit Writing* was published (OUP 2012). Secondly all Bama's works in translation have been prescribed for study so, since academia is the last to change, I think we can tell ourselves that there is some hope. There was a general awakening of interest. People grasped the potential, the field suddenly opened up. By the time the Navayana list was launched in Oct 2003, I had published *Outcaste* (Marathi Dalit) and *Stepchild* (Gujarati Dalit) through OUP. The Gujarati work was the first Dalit novel

ever. It was published in 1965 but had found a translator only in 1998 when I was still with Macmillan. Sharan Kumar Limbale's *Akkarmashi* (Outcaste) had gone into two editions at the time I commissioned the translation from Macmillan in 1999. I left Macmillan because when I published the translation of then unknown writer Bama's autobiographical work, *Karukku,* the upper-caste management in the Madras Branch turned hostile to my proposed plans for Dalit writers. The only support I had was my Managing Director who agreed that if a list of Indian works was being planned, it would be incomplete without Dalit voices. Macmillan was not interested in promoting translations. By a fluke of history, a Branch Manager in Delhi submitted *Karukku* for the Crossword Awards and it won. Strange twist. It is an autobiography but it won a prize for fiction.

Q: What is your view on indigenous literature finding its way to readerships outside the country?

Mini: I think India, which was once captured by the British, has now captured English, and opened up a parallel universe for its writers and translators to travel in. Having said that, both serious studies and hastily cobbled articles based on interviews with writers and publishers over the last two years reveal that outside India, very little of our huge literary output—contemporary or otherwise—is being read anywhere in the world. We are a literary supercontinent but as dark as Krishna and as difficult to reach. Yet one half of the literary brigade of India—in which I include myself—loves to daydream that its indigenous literature simply has to find its way to readerships outside the country. Should we worry so much about exporting our writings? Right here in our midst there are readers who could enjoy Indian writing—except that they do not know what is available out there. Millions of Indians can read, but know nothing or very little about Indian writers simply because they have not been introduced to them or trained to admire them: great, not so great, old, modern, and very new and nearly all of them unheard of outside their regional-language islands. Well, the picture of us with our Indian-language writers shows that the rest of the globe is fairly safe from us: our writers have not penetrated any other culture's consciousness deeply.

Indian Literature Abroad (ILA) was a Government of India venture supported by the Ministry of Culture and the brainchild of U.R. Ananthamurthy and Ashok Vajpeyi. I was on the advisory and working panel along with Namita Gokhale and other luminaries. We even prepared an exhaustive catalogue for it. But the programme was shifted to Sahitya Akademi. We do have a marvellous machinery in place: the Sahitya Akademi and the regional Academies. If they could collaborate with private publishers, it would be a wonderful thing.

Q: What tips would you like to give to translators today?
Mini: According to me, three things a translator might keep in mind. First, patience: listen carefully to what the author is saying. Listen to how it is being said. Don't exaggerate either the substance or the tone. Then, translation is about a reader becoming a writer and offering a strong phantom voice to someone on the other side of the wall. Remember that you are translating both for someone who might be functioning well in the source language without being able to read it, as well as for someone who has never even visited the linguistic state where the source language originates. And third is to take care to use not just accurate echoes and recasts but keeps an eye on appropriate registers. You cannot use elevated Latinized English when you are translating the speech of say domestics or unlettered characters or a young child. 'Desist' and 'enumerate' are not words that a vegetable seller or rag-picker would use in their language. So use your imagination!

Q: What is the future of translations in India?
Mini: I would say that the future of translations is very vibrant. In academia, it is a gold mine for research. In the trade market, it is like Aladdin's Cave full of treasures—national treasures. Translation holds hands with other disciplines: women's studies, caste studies, rural histories and political biographies. Personal histories in the form of autobiographies are an archive waiting to be discovered. Then there is drama and poetry, the performing arts, which comes back with double strength when translated for an audience which does not share the original language of the work.

In future, I look forward to more translations, more memoirs through OUP. I'm the consulting editor of a prestigious and ambitious project of Malayalam–English translations planned by the Thunchath Ezhuthachan Malayalam University, Calicut, which plans to hold hands with multiple publishers like Orient BlackSwan, Penguin Random House, Yoda Books, Navayana, Women Unlimited, Juggernaut and OUP to support the publication of translated texts. Rs 50,00,000 has been earmarked in the current budget of the university for this project.

MINI KRISHNAN is Translations Editor at Oxford University Press India. She is involved in sourcing fiction, plays, travelogues, autobiographies and biographies from sixteen Indian languages. She consults for Thunchath Ezhuthachan Malayalam University's translation programme, and writes two monthly columns for *The Hindu*. Mini also selects short fiction in translation for *Frontline*.

39

CHILDREN'S PUBLISHING AND TRANSLATIONS

"Creating culture links within our country"

Geeta Dharmarajan

Q: Trace the history of Katha. How, when and why did you start?
GD: I happened to walk into the UNICEF office one day and found that 400 children in India are dying of diarrhoea every day, which made me think how important it is to maintain hygiene. In 1988, I conceptualized and launched *Tamasha!* the health and environment magazine for first-generation schoolgoers, taking big ideas to small kids in a fun way through stories. *Tamasha!* is a friendly elephant who has set the tone, pace and culture of everything we do since then. In an effort to keep the magazine alive, I designed, edited and wrote most of the stories for nearly a decade. *Tamasha!* reached out to over 800,000 children across India, in six languages with a print run of 100,000 copies.

This was the precursor to the 'profit-for-all' social organization, Katha, that we got registered in 1989. *Tamasha!* is still the teaching tool par excellence in Katha schools, and the inspiration behind our inclusive work with children and communities. Today, Katha schools are centres of community activism and resurgence, fun and laughter. We are a very philosophical organization and we want to see children as the masters of their own futures.

Q: *Tamasha!* also became an important tool for introducing children to India's diverse languages and cultures. Tell us how this came about.
GD: From the first issue, we started introducing different languages and literatures in *Tamasha!* The first issue had a poem by Sukumar Ray, illustrated by Atanu Roy. The constant effort was to take translation to

children and to introduce other cultures to them. We wanted them to celebrate heterogeneity, linguistic diversity, diversity in culture, thinking, food and faith. We want our children to be tolerant and celebrate the diversity that India has.

Q: Katha's byline is 'Translating Stories, Transforming Lives'. Tell us something about it.

GD: At the other end of the spectrum, our work in Indian culture and literature stems from our strong belief in translation as an important tool to understand ourselves and as a culture link within the country—horizontally, vertically and historically. In the beginning, when we started translating stories, we took them to women and youth who were undertrials in Tihar Jail. There were a few children also, who were allowed to stay with their mothers till the age of 10. We wanted to inculcate kindness and empathy in them. We also wanted to grow their imagination and make them realize their sense of being. We handed them stories that gave them strength and made them believe they could be what they wanted to be. We were able to put dreams into their eyes which seemed very blank. On the other hand, we also talked to them and they shared their stories, which translated into verbal expression. So we were translating stories, transforming lives in a true sense.

Q: Tell us about the translations done at Katha? How are the texts and languages chosen?

GD: Known as one of the top ten publishers in the country with a strong pan-Indian community of writers, translators, academics and editors, Katha works from a base of 21 languages for the 21st century, and has published more than 350 of India's best language writers. The 21st language is a tribal language and we started translations with adult literature. We found translation was not just about words and sentences. We wanted the reader of the translation to feel the pull of emotion the characters in the stories are going through. We wanted to maintain the earthy tone of the language. The translation process begins with a feeling that it is a great story and we need to bring it to a pan-Indian audience and that's what happens at Katha.

We have been the springboard for many young writers and top literary translators today. In order to unearth the rich talent in the various Indian languages, we conceptualized and launched the Katha Awards for Short Fiction in 1990. These are now recognized as one of the leading national-level awards for writers, translators and editors.

Q: What is the role of translations? Why are translations important?
GD: In a multi-cultural country like India, translation is a very important thing. It helps to culture-link. With stories, we get to know about other cultures, heritage and traditions. We need to change the stereotypes existing for various regions. We need to change our mindset and we want to see ourselves as people of India, and not as majority or minority community. Translations help us to do so.

Q: How has the translations landscape changed over time? With so many big English-language publishers entering the arena, would you agree that translations have become mainstream and are no longer a niche?
GD: Even with English-language publishers entering the translation arena, it is still a niche segment. When Katha started in 1988 with translations, Penguin had also started its translations imprint in 1987 but it was for a different audience. When we look at India, we are in a very unique position. We write, translate, publish and critique for ourselves. That's not the case elsewhere. Very little of our work was reaching outside of India as there was, and still is, a huge population of readers in the country. That clarity was always there at Katha and we knew there are certain words which can be understood by all and so we were able to retain the essence in translations.

I am happy with mainstream publishers getting into translations. With the kind of translations coming now, I am happy to see the diversity and richness.

Q: What do you think this means for translations in the next few years?

GD: There are two concerns for translations. One is that that whatever rules or parameters are there are for adult translations. Then, there is a big gap in the practice of translation in the world of academia. The amount of translation writings in magazines, newspapers or review journals has gone down greatly. Translated books are not reviewed much. So, as translators, there is nothing with which we can hone the art and craft of translation.

The second concern is in children's translations as there is no academic field for it. There are no transmission laws, terms of endearment, terms of abuse, etc.

Q: What is Katha's focus, in this context, for the next few years?

GD: Katha's focus for the next few years would be to get an academic field for children's translations. We want academia to think about it. We wish to do a lot more translations for children and we want literary culture-linking to happen. Old writers are still relevant in India and we want our children to know more about their writings.

Q: Given the decline in the reading habit and equally the need to provide access to reading and materials to more and more of our younger population, what is Katha's role?

GD: When we generally talk about decline in reading habits amongst children, we talk of children sitting in big schools in metropolitan cities, but that's just 20 per cent of children in India. Almost 80 per cent children have a great hunger for reading; even if they can't read, they appreciate a book, right from children in Bihar to Uttar Pradesh to Tamil Nadu to tribal villages.

We have 300 million children in school, of whom, studies indicate, 50 per cent can read and 50 per cent cannot. If each one of us can make a child read, then the problem is solved. That's what Katha aims at! Reading is a basic skill; we can't talk about upskilling our younger population until they know how to read. If you want upward mobility, reading is a crucial skill.

Q: Tell us about your programme for educating 300 million children and spreading the reading habit.

GD: The 300 Million Challenge or the 300 M Challenge as we call it, comes from that fact that there are 300 million children in India. If all 5 to10-year-old children read for fun and for meaning, they will be prepared to bring change to themselves and society. With its firm roots, Katha has forged 120 strategic alliances and partnerships that will help tackle this massive challenge and bring reading to all children of India.

Q: What is your take on e-books?

GD: I believe in e-books and technology. Physical books are important for a large number of children, but we have to be future-ready when we will have good connectivity and mobile phones in India. We are working on e-books and there is a lot of experimentation and innovation happening at our end. Katha Digital Lab is working very hard as we need to catch up with the changing times.

Q: Tell us something about your reading campaign and writers' workshops.

GD: Katha was started in 1988 to enhance the joy of reading. We realized that unless children know how to read, we cannot give them the joy of reading. So we started the first Katha Lab School or 'deschool' in 1990 with five children in Govindpuri, one of the largest slum clusters in Delhi. Over 191,190 children have been in Katha schools since then. The special 'Story Pedagogy' centred on story has been in use in Katha learning centres since 1992. This curriculum and pedagogy has helped increase attendance and retention levels in the schools to over 80 per cent. Learning happens with stories. We have our own assessment systems. It is skill-based learning.

Writers' workshops are organized to celebrate the writing capacity of children in our country. It is about writing and expressing oneself better. When we write, we understand ourselves. We are not looking at great writers but at the act of writing. India is blessed with lot of not-for-profits looking at children who are underprivileged, and opening doors for them into the future. We are not only conducting writers' workshops in schools but also in 700 different slums. We have tied up with Amazon and we will publish stories of slum children.

Q: What do you aim for in the next five years?

GD: I want every child to read and I am optimistic that if all of us can join in, we can do it. We have one lakh volunteers with us and there are 600 volunteers on LinkedIn wanting to join. Together, we can make the world a kinder place for everyone. I think we all are compassionate and have empathy for others and we can create a world which is more peaceful and fun-loving. If this happens, I will be the happiest person on this earth.

GEETA DHARMARAJAN is Founder and Editor-in-Chief of Katha. A writer, editor and educationist, Geeta is interested in learning across boundaries. Her work has focused on education, especially for children from economically poor families, and on linking India's diverse cultures, values and traditions through translations. Her interests have shaped the inclusive and integrated work of Katha and its various activities in the fields of literature and literary translation, community activism and education.

40

THE TULIKA BOOKS STORY

"Giving direction to niche publishing"

Indira (Indu) Chandrasekhar

Q: Trace the history of Tulika: how, why and when did you start, the initial days, and the growing pains and struggles of Indie publishing.

Indu: Tulika started in the late 1980s as a DTP unit, a company that exists till date, as Tulika Print Communication Services. This venture was started by Radhika Menon and me—but always with the intention of moving into book publishing ourselves. Radhika later moved to Chennai and set up Tulika Publishers in 1996, publishing children's books, while I started Tulika Books, publishing academic books, in 1995.

So, Tulika Books has been in the academic books segment of Indian publishing for more than 22 years now. My own training was in academic publishing as I started my career in the higher education division of Macmillan India in 1980. I have been associated with academia from the very beginning of my working days as several close friends including my husband teach at universities, and I have had teaching stints at colleges in Bangalore and Delhi myself. So you could say that my training in publishing, as well as natural surroundings and personal interests led me towards academic publishing, as it were, and to set up Tulika Books, which is one of the early small and independent publishing houses in India. The path of independent publishing, of course, was laid by the first independent publishing house in India—Kali for Women, founded in the mid/late 1980s, which published feminist books, and which is now represented by two publishing houses, Women Unlimited and Zubaan, set up by the co-founders of Kali. Independent publishing started proliferating and flourished in the 1990s. And today, the publishing scene in India is marked by several independent publishing houses.

Q: Why do you call yourself independents?
Indu: We call ourselves independents because most of us are professionals who came out of the world of book publishing to set up our own publishing houses, giving direction to lists with focused political content as well as niche publishing.

Q: How does independent publishing continue to thrive and grow in spite of the challenges?
Indu: I believe that we actually have an advantage as independents in today's publishing environment. We have remained small and concentrated on bringing out books in our particular areas, which cater to a defined readership—we are not generalist publishers like most of the large publishing houses, is what I mean. Because of the kind of content we develop and since our lists have a defined focus, we are able to gain visibility for the kind of work we do. Many of us have remained small by design, and this helps us to add value to the books we publish. Independents have fairly rigorous editorial processes in place; out-of-the-box thinking where formats and production values are concerned; we seek out and nurture new authors; we take risks by publishing in areas where large publishing houses, especially multinationals and corporates, shy away due to higher visibility and the play-safe attitude that often comes with that.

Another advantage with Tulika and most independents is that we have a strong backlist that we do not allow to die. One practical reason for this has been that smaller publishers are able to keep stocks of books for longer periods of time since the problem of warehousing is relatively small as compared to that of bigger publishers. Further, speaking for Tulika, the strong content we offer in many of the academic disciplinary areas ensures that successive generations of students come back to our books—and so we ensure that they are always in print. For example, *Essays in Indian History: Towards a Marxist Perception*, a collection of essays by the historian Irfan Habib of Aligarh Muslim University, which was Tulika's first book, published in 1995—we reprint this every alternate year if not every year, on average, and it has now entered its 13th edition.

Q: What have been the challenges of costs, staff, quality, and of distribution and collections?

Indu: But the flip side is that having spent a lot of time and energy in developing and nurturing new authors, once they become established names, they often abandon indie publishers and opt for the 'brand' of bigger publishers. I must, however, say that this is not a problem that has affected Tulika. In fact, most of our authors come back to us with their new books.

The major problem independents face is sales and distribution, which affects liquidity and our ability to publish an optimum number of books every year. Our business model is such that we rely exclusively on returns from sales of our books in order to invest in publishing new books. At Tulika we bring out 10–15 new titles every year plus reprints, which totals to approximately 20–25 titles in any given year. If the sales revenue comes in as it used to, even in the not very distant past, then it would be a viable project. But that is not happening now, with credit periods in the market having extended to 12 months in many instances despite agreements that specify 4 to 6 months.

Another major problem we have been facing at Tulika in recent years is that funds to college/university libraries and research institutions seem to have dried up—which is part of the general crisis in which institutions of higher education find themselves in our country. Similarly, bulk purchases by public agencies like the Raja Rammohun Roy Library Foundation, which supplies books in turn to public libraries across India, have taken a hit. For academic publishers like us, such institutional sales have been traditionally very important, with sales to individuals from retail outlets being mostly add-ons.

Moreover, older distribution houses of academic books have either become publishers themselves or changed their focus of distribution to trade books—fiction and non-fiction. Also, the multinationals that have entered the Indian market, besides a couple of them, are mostly trade book publishers.

Visibility is also a big challenge in terms of the distribution options open to independents, as the bigger publishing houses, like Taylor &

Francis or Oxford University Press or SAGE, bring out 100–150 titles a year, which means their visibility is obviously higher in the market in terms of sheer numbers.

Q: How was Independent Publishers' Distribution Alternatives (IPDA) formed? How does it work, and what is its future?
Indu: In 2006, 8 independent publishers came together to establish IPDA, which is primarily a distribution house for independents. The 8 partner-publishers of IPDA are: Leftword Books, Navayana Publishing, Samskriti, Stree Samya, Three Essays Collective, Tulika Books, Tulika Publishers and Women Unlimited. The bulk of the distribution of the lists of several of these eight publishers is done by IPDA, while it also distributes books of other small and independent publishers of a certain quality.

IPDA has a resourceful and dedicated sales and marketing team, but it must be admitted that while it has managed to survive against odds for more than 10 years now, it has been a struggle for it to grow, especially in the last 3 to 4 years.

Q: Why are independents still going strong?
Indu: Independents seem to be going forward with none of us having had to fold up yet—despite adverse conditions at least for some of us. I think this is because every independent publisher, one way or the other, is motivated to continue for reasons other than just making money. The returns may not be great but most of us are willing to 'carry on regardless' if we break even and have enough money to put into future books.

Also, since many of us have our own means and tactics of survival and of subsidizing our individual publishing programmes—some of us are writers/authors besides being publishers and editors, some provide consultancy services, etc., to take care of financial needs—we manage to keep the flag flying. Many of my publishing colleagues and I myself belong to the first generation of independents, and we are confident that younger independents will chart newer paths and carry this forward.

Q: What are the prospects?

Indu: One of the lessons we have learnt as small, independent publishers is that sharing experiences and evolving alternative strategies, which includes coming together in collective solidarity, is one way of achieving visibility and recognition, and carving out a place for ourselves, amid the larger scenario of publishing in India. Especially in an environment of competitiveness and rivalry where trade secrets and poaching rather than sharing and pooling of talents is the order of the day, generally speaking.

Some of us also share and pool resources like editorial and typesetting services, which makes it more affordable than if we had to hire professionals in these areas as individual publishers. Similarly, there have been attempts at co-publishing within the same market, on an equal sharing of costs and revenues principle. This kind of sharing of resources is in the nature of baby steps as yet, but perhaps this direction is really the way forward for independents.

In terms of publishing networks and collectives, Tulika Books is one of two independent publishers from India, the other being Women Unlimited, who are members of the English-language network of the International Alliance of Independent Publishers (IAIP), based out of Paris. This is an alliance of indie publishers from across the world that supports the efforts of member-publishers to both initiate publishing projects and share existing projects with each other in co-publishing arrangements.

Q: What do you think about the survival of Indie publishing, given the global tendency towards mergers and consolidation amongst publishers?

Indu: Of late, independents in India have started to co-publish or collaborate with other players in the industry, but they have managed to keep their own identity alive in most cases—unlike the global trend of acquisitions and mergers which often result in a compromise of content and identity, and a certain uniformity that sets in with the loss of the spark of independent publishing.

Collaborations that do not compromise their editorial autonomy can be beneficial to independents and be welcomed, but not editorial mergers or take-overs. Publishing under joint imprints has been happening on a small but significant scale in recent years: Zubaan with Penguin, Yoda Press with SAGE, Stree-Samya with SAGE, and Social Science Press with Routledge. This is an emerging trend and it might grow.

Q: What is the roadmap for the future of Tulika?
Indu: I hope Tulika will continue to grow, strengthen and expand our list in the directions we set for ourselves—and for as long we can. Talking about the future, there is a sense of mortality that affects us—just as it does most professionally run independent publishers that are not family businesses—especially among the first generation indies. We can't really say what will happen after our time—five years on, I will be still be around; ten years on, I hope I will still be around; for the rest I do not know. Personally speaking, it would be great if younger colleagues or a like-minded publisher took over and ran Tulika after my time. But of this I'm sure: I would rather see Tulika shut down than see it go the way of a merger-and-acquisition that would retain its name but erase its identity.

INDIRA (INDU) CHANDRASEKHAR is Publisher and Managing Editor of Tulika Books, New Delhi and has been associated with the book publishing industry in India since the early 1980s. She is a founding partner of the Independent Publishers' Distribution Alternatives, a distribution network set up by eight independent publishers to promote alternative/independent publishing in India. Indu is also a member of the Paris-based International Alliance of Independent Publishers, and a trustee of the Sher-Gil Sundaram Arts Foundation.

41

FEMINIST PUBLISHING: THE JOURNEY AND WAY AHEAD

"The perspective is feminist, but the literature is not niche"

Ritu Menon

Women Unlimited, a non-profit trust, is an associate of Kali for Women, India's first and oldest feminist press, established in 1984. We explore new issues, anticipate trends, develop new perspectives and offer the best of feminist scholarship, activist material and creative writing, in India and South Asia, at affordable prices.

Q: How has feminist publishing evolved over time?

Ritu: Across the world, feminist publishing has declined. There are only about half a dozen independent feminist publishers in the world. In the North and West, the pioneers like Virago have been absorbed into larger corporate publishing, whereas others like The Women's Press and Pandora have ceased to exist.

In India, feminist publishing is still quite active as there are three presses in India which continue to function and produce a steady number of books in English every year. These are Stree in Kolkata, and Zubaan and Women Unlimited in Delhi; all three are run by women and are independent in terms of financial control and ownership.

How long it will continue is very difficult to say as feminist publishing has been very very successful around the world and that was the reason why it has been taken over by bigger publishers. The entire initial spadework—the risk-taking, the development of this market and readership, finding authors, identifying issues—all this was done when the publishers were independent. When they become economically viable and successful and they are no longer a risk, they become a part of mainstream publishing. That has been a trend across many parts of the world. Many have just closed down, for example, feminist publishers in Thailand, South Africa, Zimbabwe, Arab, Indonesia, which were very successful in the beginning but later closed down or were taken over due to various reasons.

Q: Do you think feminist publishing is a niche segment?
Ritu: No, we are not niche; we are feminist presses dealing with everything, as 50 per cent of the population is women. Our perspective is feminist, but the books we publish are not niche. Because women are marginal does not mean we are niche. Every big publisher now has a list on women's studies because it is acknowledged in its own right.

Q: What is the USP of independent publishers?
Ritu: The quality control in smaller independent presses is much higher than large publishers because we do a smaller number of books and are able to put much more time and effort in them. Because smaller presses are editorially driven, we are selective about the books we do and then we spend a much larger amount of time in interacting with authors, in developing a project, in suggesting ideas in commissioning work, and so on. Very little work is outsourced. The quality of our books is usually to our advantage.

Q: What is the future of feminist publishing in general and of Women Unlimited in particular?
Ritu: The future is a question mark but I think feminist publishers will continue to provide an alternative with regard to perspective and analysis. They are not just economically independent but have a distinct political project, which is social change. So a feminist press is by definition a part of the women's movement and will challenge established orthodoxies, whether in society, in the family, in media, in academia, or in publishing itself.

I foresee that the potential of Women Unlimited is very rich…even after 30 years of its existence.

Q: What are the challenges of being independent?
Ritu: For all independent publishers, the biggest challenge in India is distribution. It is one of the poorest serviced and capitalized sectors in

the book trade. The question I often ask large multinationals is why they haven't gone into distribution. Though they are keen to enter into publishing, they are not at all that invested in developing distribution. It's a very big gap and it's much bigger for language independent publishing. If distribution is inadequate, then impact on publishing is obvious. Independent publishers, unless they have their own distribution channel, have to rely on wholesalers, distributors, vendors, retailers, etc. The nature of discounts being as it is and the very long credit periods, ranging from 180 to 360 days, are almost ruinous. So, before you realize sales, you have already paid royalties for the year, which makes it difficult to finance the publishing.

In short, keeping the publishing going becomes a huge financial challenge for independent publishers bringing out trade books. Moreover, we do not have the funds for promotion and marketing which the larger publishers can afford.

Q: How do you see the market for book exports?

Ritu: Exports are even more difficult. For example, in South Asia, there is no trade as trade between countries is not easy. So we have to go through distributors but realization of money and sending books across are not easy. So, no matter how valuable or useful your books might be, we are still not able to get them to places where we know there is readership.

Q: What do you think of the survival of independent publishing, given the global tendency towards mergers and consolidation amongst publishers?

Ritu: All independent publishing have their own survival capacity. But, in my opinion, there will always be an independent publisher as it is a counter to corporate publishing. It performs a service and develops a need. But, it requires an independent structure to run. For example, Salim Saboowala in Mumbai had a mobile bookshop for independent publishers, and he serviced the whole of Maharashtra. But after he retired, nobody has taken it further.

Another example is Ram Advani Booksellers in Lucknow who serviced generations of publishers. After his death, the bookshop closed down after being operational for 71 years. Independent publishers require networks of independent support like these. Most distributors are independent but they generally service larger publishing houses, because of volume and turnover.

Q: How is Women Unlimited tackling the distribution issues?
Ritu: Women Unlimited is a founding member of a unique experiment in distribution, the Independent Publishers' Distribution Alternatives (IPDA) (Delhi); as well as a member of the International Alliance of Independent Publishers (IAIP) (Paris), an international network publishing in five major languages: English, French, Arabic, Spanish and Portuguese.

But it is not easy to compete in the market as independents in distribution; in fact it requires a very different kind of enterprise. New publishing houses like Aleph Publishing have distribution arrangements with Rupa & Co. All the experience independents have in publishing, which is considerable, has not found a response in distribution.

Q: What are the prospects?
Ritu: A lot of younger publishers, who started out as professionals in big publishing houses, have set up their own independent publishing units. They will continue to thrive as they are willing to take risks which bigger publishers do not want to take. So they have come up with new areas in publishing like gender equality, transgenders, third gender, cultural studies and even graphic novels. They encounter a lot of problems but they are willing to do it, as this is the creative path of publishing. They are the path-breakers. The future for this kind of publishing is enormous as independent publishing is small in size but its impact is enormous. Feminist publishing is a shining example of this phenomenon.

RITU MENON is Publisher at Women Unlimited. A writer and publisher who has been active in the South Asian women's movement for over 20 years, Ritu is the co-founder of Kali for Women, India's first and oldest feminist press, as well as the founder of Women Unlimited, an associate of Kali for Women.

42

NAVAYANA

"Bold, innovative and experimental"

S. Anand

Q: What is your opinion of the current publishing ecosystem, and what drives you to innovate and experiment?

Anand: In fact, one finds that in trade and commercial publishing, risk-taking has drastically come down. Most mainstream publishers want to do 'safe' titles that do not incur financial, political or intellectual risks. The sad part, as the pioneering American publisher of Pantheon and founder of The New Press, Andre Schiffrin, says is that publishing was for the longest time not seen as a 'business' as such. People were happy with 4 per cent profits—what you got from a savings bank account. Suddenly with conglomerates entering the market, with holdings companies treating books like any other 'investment', books came to be treated like FMCG products; expectations of profit went up to an unreasonable 20 to 25 per cent.

A friend who returned from the last London Book Fair says the most interesting titles in the UK are being done by small- and medium-sized independents like Saqi, Serpent's Tail, Comma Press, etc. The same holds true for India where presses like Yoda, Blaft, and Navayana have shown that you can do cutting-edge books. Older players like Seagull and Zubaan have fortified themselves. Seagull has in fact gone seriously international; they have a Nobel laureate like Mo Yan in their list; they have all of Mahasweta Devi. So all this gives me courage to be bold, innovative and experimental at Navayana.

Q: Share your experience of annotating Dr Bhimrao Ramji Ambedkar's *Annihilation of Caste (AoC)*.

Anand: I had tried my hand at annotating *AoC* on and off since 2005 since I felt no one seemed keen to pick up the gauntlet. But I felt intimidated by the kind of work it required. Was I even qualified? Was passion enough? When I commissioned the Ambedkar Readers, I spelt out why and how clearly. I had carefully read Anthony Parel's scholarly annotations of *Hind Swaraj* written in 1909 when he was on a ship back from England to South Africa.

Irrespective of my problems with *Hind Swaraj*, I found the annotations excellent. In 1999, along with Ambedkar, I also read the Wendy Doniger/Brian Smith edition of the annotated *Manusmriti*, a work that was undoubtedly a little more backward than *Hind Swaraj*. I felt Ambedkar's pivotal text too needed a similar effort to make it reach a wider and newer audience today.

Basically I undertook this task to address my own ignorance of many crucial matters. In 1936, the Jat-Pat-Todak Mandal (the Forum for the Break-up of Caste) invited Ambedkar to deliver their presidential lecture, and on seeing a copy of his address, they disinvited him, for in this work he asked them to 'apply the dynamite to the Vedas and the Shastras'. Now, what was Jat-Pat-Todak Mandal? Who founded it and when? Why did they branch out of the Arya Samaj? Whom did they invite before and after Ambedkar? What was the connection between Ambedkar's famous 1935 announcement that he'd not die a Hindu and this invitation? Who was Sant Ram who stood up against the mostly upper caste Mandal members who opposed Ambedkar? Why did all this happen in Lahore? What happened to Sant Ram after the 1947 Partition? Each page of *AoC* threw up implicit and explicit questions—to which I attempted to provide answers through extensive notes.

Q: What was your reaction to critiques, after getting the introduction done by Booker prize-winning author and activist Arundhati Roy?

Anand: To come back to the critiques on Navayana's edition of *AoC*—back then, it upset me hugely that those who attacked the book had not even laid their eyes or hands on it. It took me a while—and some distance—to realize such a reading need not be of the book at all; it could be a reading of the entire act or gesture involved in the Navayana edition with Arundhati's Introduction, the annotations, the endorsements, the magazine placements, etc., for this edition—a parade of entitlements at one level—was presented as an event, as a totality. They were reading and reacting to a situation that had imposed itself on the world; consequently, it was a reading of the world and not a reading of our reading of *AoC*. I was also initially disturbed because some of those attacking had been friends who knew of this project, friends who though sceptical of me, seemed to have guarded regard for the work Navayana did. Now they said, after Arundhati whom will Anand ask to introduce the next Ambedkar book? Sachin Tendulkar? Chetan Bhagat? I was shocked, but soon came to understand the resentment as being historical and not merely particular and personal. The time was ripe for such an attack, it appears. It's also a question of purchase—attacking someone like Roy will get you eyeballs. Not, however, Sharmila Rege, not that a critique of such 'lesser' mortals is not valid.

Q: How are language and caste related in India, and what impact does it have on vernacular literature?

Anand: Language becomes another site of exercising power and maintaining hierarchy. Almost all languages in India carry the baggage of caste. We forget that the various 'official' languages—there are 22 listed in the official schedule of the Constitution—themselves are contested terrains. Take Telugu, for instance, the language I grew up with (though I am a native Tamil speaker). What's called 'literary' Telugu has been mostly a brahmanical variation spoken by less than 5 per cent of the coastal population of the state of Andhra Pradesh. And classical literature invariably deals with epics, gods and brahmanic religion. Prosody, meter, 'suitable' subject matter, etc. are all dictated by the elite few.

By default, the language spoken by ordinary people—the leather-workers, weavers, masons, fisher folk, etc.—is rendered unsuited for literary production. Which is why when a Dalit woman like Gogu Shyamala wrote short stories in Telugu, her work did not find a publisher in Telugu—because the Dalit Telugu she wrote in did not have an audience, and it was a region-specific, caste-specific 'dialect', it was argued! Her work was first published in English translation by Navayana in 2013. And such were the problems posed by her Telugu that nine translators were deployed to translate her eleven stories.

The same holds for Marathi or Hindi. This is why when Tukaram in the 17th century writes the way he does in Marathi—not shying from using words like fuck even when he is talking of his god Vithoba—it is a revolution. But those who sing, rather perform, his Abhangs—verses—on stage, avoid the Abhangs in which he swears. The same holds for Kabir, the 16th century weaver-poet of Benares. Again, these radical poets got assimilated or appropriated through sanitization and nationalization. This is the linguistic tradition from which Namdeo Dhasal (1949–2014), one of India's finest poets and one of the founders of Dalit Panther (modeled on the American Black Panther), comes.

Whenever language becomes a site of power, you have to apply the dynamite of love to it and raze it down. Good poetry does that.

Q: In your opinion, what is the future for publishers?

Anand: I feel it has good future as well. Do not forget that the guesstimate for per capita spending on books in India is an abysmal Rs 80 per person per year. Even if only 20 million of the 1.2 billion have the luxury of reading for pleasure in India, that's a huge market. And they don't seem to be reading as much as they ought to, notwithstanding the mind-numbing sales of authors like Chetan Bhagat and Amish Tripathi.

Q: What are the challenges being faced today?

Anand: Money! And most small publishers would give you the same answer likely. I do not seem to have a good head for the business end of things. *Bhimayana* has been our only funded project, but otherwise it is quite hand-to-mouth. Navayana survives primarily on the generosity of friends, though since 2010, after Slavoj Zizek's first annual Navayana lecture, our market presence matches the best. We do make sure all our titles are well reviewed. In terms of profits, I doubt if even the bigger presses really make any profits with all the heavy overheads they have.

The real profit-earners in Indian publishing are textbook publishers. Ratna Sagar's turnover could well be more than HarperCollins or Penguin's, but the overall visibility of a Ratna Sagar will be poor.

[Excerpts from an interview in Cordite Publishing Inc., *Cordite Poetry Review 55*.]

S. ANAND is Publisher at Navayana. He co-founded Navayana in 2003 along with Ravikumar, and in 2007 won the International Young Publisher of the Year award instituted by the British Council and London Book Fair. He has annotated Dr B.R. Ambedkar's *Annihilation of Caste* and *Riddles in Hinduism*, and curated and co-authored *Bhimayana*, the graphic biography of Ambedkar that has been translated into nine languages.

43

BRINGING BOOKS TO PHONES

"Readers have loved it; some genres are working better than others"

Chiki Sarkar

Juggernaut aims to create a world-class Indian publishing company that redefines reading and writing for the digital age. Their mobile app has created waves in the industry.

Q: Please tell us how an innovative publishing venture grew out of many years of working with a giant mainstream publisher.

Chiki: Having worked with the country's largest publisher, I became very aware of the problems facing the industry (low sales, fewer bookshops, etc.). At the same time I looked at the world of growing digital readers and the rise of Wattpad, China literature (valued today at US$1 billion). Alongside this, I just looked everywhere around me and saw people constantly on their phones. India is the world's second-highest user of smartphones. All these came together to make Juggernaut.

Q: What has been the experience so far: in terms of variety of books and formats, author base and reception among readers?

Chiki: We have a wide range of formats and genres—so all the usual genres and then works of varying lengths from 5,000 to 100,000 words. Readers have loved it, of course some genres working better than others. Our free classics, non-fiction and erotica are the three big genres. But we are also finding growing readers for our writing platform where amateur writers upload their stories and we showcase them in the same way as our curated authors.

Q: How does the economics work?
Chiki: It's very simple...we charge per book. Authors are paid fees with bonus fees built-in when they have reached a certain level of downloads. We will be introducing a subscription service shortly.

Q: Tell us about the mobile short-format books. How many has Juggernaut done and how has that worked both from the authorship and readership viewpoint?
Chiki: We have about 3,000 own titles, which combines our own digital originals, out-of-copyright classics and writing platform.

We've broken our new writers like Mayur Didolkar who writes a lot for us and found new spaces for a writer like Andaleeb Wajid—both of whom are becoming very popular. We also have favourites among the erotica writers who write regularly for us.

Q: We notice that a lot of mainstream, even academic, authors have published with you; for example, the sociologist Nandini Sundar with the book on Bastar. How did that happen?
Chiki: We have a boutique list of books that we do in physical along with digital—that list will mostly have names of authors who are well known. Nandini Sundar on Bastar, Rajdeep Sardesai, Sagarika Ghose, Meena Kandasamy, William Dalrymple, Twinkle Khanna and Rujuta Diwekar are just some of these names.

Q: Who, if anyone, is the competition for Juggernaut?
Chiki: We are at the intersection of a range of spaces—so traditional publishers, self-publishing platforms like Wattpad, and Amazon which sells e-books—all are our competitors.

Q: Do you know of other creative ventures in Indian publishing?
Chiki: There are loads. In India, there are wonderful self-publishing platforms like Pratilipi; while Pratham seems to be doing fun stuff around the kids' space.

Q: What is your forward plan?

Chiki: We will build more on Hindi. Eventually, we will give Hindi a different home page, introducing subscriptions, enabling the writing feature within the app (currently you can upload only on desktop). Besides, we also plan to go international.

CHIKI SARKAR is Publisher and Co-Founder of Juggernaut Books. She started her career in publishing with Bloomsbury Publishing in London, and after seven years moved to Delhi and joined Random House in 2006. In 2011 she took over at Penguin Books India, and following the merger of Penguin Books and Random House in 2013 she was made the India head of the new company. She set up her own publication house, Juggernaut, thereafter.

44

OFFERING CHAPTER-LEVEL CONTENT

"Many people don't have time to read a full book"

Rohit Kumar

Q: From mainstream publishing to your own venture Chapter Apps, what prompted you to go in for it?

Rohit: We all have multiple books on our bookshelves...most of the time we never read the entire book ever; we read in parts. Whatever information we want, we quickly find it on the internet, rather than referring to a print book. All that now is happening on the phone. That was the fundamental I had in my mind four years ago. It took me one year to plan and leave my job and start Chapter Apps.

Q: What was the idea behind Chapter Apps? What is the USP?

Rohit: The idea behind Chapter Apps is fundamentally that people don't have time to read a full book, especially for professional studies. So, whether it is ongoing learning, lifelong learning, corporate learning—people like to read in chunks. They would like to buy chapters, rather than the whole book. And we thought that most of the consumption of the content would happen primarily on the mobile. That was the fundamental idea behind the venture. I started it three years ago and got the investments for the same.

Our USP is that we have more users on the mobile than our competition…so we understand how to make things work better on mobile, better than the others. We understand how to give people a proper integrated solution, which includes content at users' experience, because we built the product. We integrated the company in Silicon Valley; we have actually built it through a product software company—so we are able to take on more clients live in a matter of hours. It's a robust system and we have several thousand users a month now from different companies using it, and every company is growing in its usage dramatically.

Q: What about the content?

Rohit: We are very selective with content. For the insurance sector, we are developing content and taking it to multiple organizations, customizing it to their requirements. So we offer both content and technology. When the platform is established in more places, then it becomes easier to sell more content. We believe that the first problem to solve is the technology adoption, content adoption follows.

Q: How has the journey so far been?

Rohit: It's been a very fulfilling and fun-filled one, because what I love is discovering how people will actually use it...and that process of discovery is actually most fascinating, because as you start understanding what they like and don't like...then you make that change. You start connecting with people and when more people start doing it, that's when you get the real satisfaction. That's part of starting your own venture, you can experiment in so many different ways. Intellectually, it is very fulfilling as well.

Originally, when I started, I thought I would publish content on my platform and it would be content from multiple authors. It would have to be new content, as for the mobile format, content needs to be small. When we started taking the content to the masses on mobile, it was still early days. We got feedback from people saying that they require content which their company/ professor is using or approves. That led to a very interesting journey, faced by the choice of whether we should focus on content adoption or technology adoption and what we realized was that content adoption is a longer sales cycle as people took time to decide whether they wanted our content or not, but for technology adoption there was greater willingness, especially in the corporate market. Two years ago, we started with corporate pilots. It took us one year to build the product and take it forward...and then we did the first few pilots and 1.5 years ago, we got our first long-term contract with an insurance company. Since then, there is no looking back. We have more than 20 corporate clients now and the list is growing. Our biggest concentration is on financial services as of now.

Q: What about competition?
Rohit: The competition has started increasing rapidly, because mobile as a mechanism is starting to take off; there are a lot more companies coming into mobile apps. Most of our competition is coming from very different spheres—trading companies, HR consulting companies, LMS companies. But, the actual requirement is to have a fully-integrated platform, with a complete solution. Content—upload or edit—that would be the real challenge. Eventually the best platform with the easiest usability will win.

Q: What is the forward plan? How do you foresee the future market?
Rohit: The future is very clear: there will be more usage on the mobile and the demand is exploding now. Two years ago, people would say that it is an interesting concept but were not sure who would pay for the data; now people know mobile is cost-effective. And every user has a mobile, but every user does not have a laptop. There is going to be a shift in terms of how to make content more engaging, how to engage more users, and how to reach out to them in small interventions, every day and every week. I think in the future, there would be chatbots—that would happen in the next two years or even earlier.

The future of the publishing industry is digital and to have a platform like this. Now the question is if all the publishers put their content on our platform...then we will actually see a huge amount of success coming. If every company builds its own app, that may not work. If a mobile platform for textbooks existed where content from all publishers is there—that is where I believe the future is and that is going to happen.

ROHIT KUMAR is Managing Partner of Guiding Star Digital Publishers LLP and its subsidiary Chapter Apps Inc, where he is building and leveraging mobile technology platforms to improve productivity for professionals and students. Prior to starting his entrepreneurial ventures, Rohit was Managing Director, South Asia, Health Science Division, Reed Elsevier India. He was President of the Association of Publishers in India during 2013-15, and Co-Chair of the FICCI Publishing Committee during 2013-16.

45

ILLUSTRATED BOOKS IN THE DIGITAL AGE

"Is augmented reality the future?"

Bipin Shah

The emergence of augmented reality in illustrated-book publishing may offer a ray of hope to keep readers falling off the curve by offering them print books and digital components rolled into one. But are we ready to forego the touch and feel of a book—the smell of a fresh book, feeling the textured paper and seeing the vast expanse of an image, which is almost like a sensual experience that could never be replicated digitally?

Q: How has illustrated-book publishing evolved over the years?

Bipin: The classic model for illustrated-book publishing was established by Paul Hamlyn, followed by many others, which saw high overall pre-press and print costs for illustrated titles offset by large print runs, traditionally including one or more co-editions with foreign-language publishers. This was several decades ago and the torch has been carried forward by the likes of Thames & Hudson, Harry Abrams, Prestel Publishing, and exceptionally talented teams at Phaidon and Taschen. Today, most—but certainly not all—illustrated publishing has modest print runs, produced mainly—but not exclusively—in the Far East, as printing costs are lower than in India. Museum publishing growth has slowed down considerably in the last several years, yet they continue to publish some of the best art books.

Q: What have been the challenges in this segment?

Bipin: Publishers of illustrated books have been put in a state of high alert for several years. The first shock I got was about six years back when I was waiting for a meeting at the booth of an American art book publisher at Frankfurt Book Fair. The display did not reflect what I had become familiar with over the years. The number of art books on display had declined by half, replaced with popular picture books and illustrated trade books. On another occasion, I was sitting with an editor of a highly respected art book publisher discussing co-edition options for a forthcoming book. He liked the idea very much but wanted the manuscript to be reduced from 48,000 words down to 25,000 words!

Over recent years, print runs have been falling in line with reduced demand from retailers, and disappearing bookstores. Although colour digital printing has become a mature technology, it is still expensive compared to traditional offset printing.

Shelf space for illustrated books has been reducing year after year. What I saw on a recent visit to the showroom of one of the largest distributors of illustrated books in India, revealed the current state of the illustrated-books market in India. As recently as five years ago, there were three large tables piled with new and recent titles. This has now fallen to just 25 per cent of that volume.

Q: What are the creative trends in this segment?

Bipin: It is a great pleasure to develop a new concept with a talented author who is able to write art history, an editor who is able to maintain the flow and enrich it, and a designer who can enhance the content where the art book itself becomes an object of desire. I realize that we can't keep publishing the way we have been doing. The combined stress factors of sales going online and offshore on consignment, with fewer bookstores available to display books, and declining sales, we have to get real about the fact that business models need to change as more and more readers want to read in digital formats rather than print. There is a lot of scope for creativity—and admittedly rather a large demand for sensitivity and diplomacy as well—which appeals to readers whom we are constantly struggling to retain. As a publisher of books on the visual arts of India, we have the special challenge of trying to make sound business decisions when the technology isn't quite there yet to produce digital products that are genuinely satisfying. Digital publishing guru Mike Shatzkin made the point that the digital future is set for those who publish 'immersive reading', but for illustrated books it is still somewhat of a mystery.

Q: Does digital printing technology have the potential to transform the illustrated-book industry?

Bipin: The problem with art books is that we still haven't figured out what a digital art book wants to be. We need to have a creative spark to figure this out. Digital platforms for trade books have matured, where we just take content and dump it into a programme. But we can't just simply import the content of an art book on to a digital device. The big question is whether there is a market for art books and a market that wants the book to be enhanced. This creates an argument to be made for print, as opposed to digital enhancements. The technology doesn't exist to use digital art books in the same way that scholars, designers, artists use them—spread out a dozen books on a table and get an overview of all of them at the same time. Another stumbling block is getting the licensing rights to images or to put backlist titles on to a digital platform is still a huge and expensive issue. There are many unanswered questions. For example, what if a digital book has a link to an image on a site? Who pays royalties for that image? How much? A prolific illustrated book publisher said he would be happy if 20 per cent of his business was digital by 2020.

Digital printing technology has the potential to transform the illustrated-book industry. But has anyone seen the future? A story in *The Bookseller* acknowledged that e-books just haven't worked for illustrated books. It appears that the publishers of illustrated books they spoke to think that situation is temporary. One Managing Director said, 'You have to make a very clear distinction between the situation now and the situation in five years' time.' And another CEO emphasized that his team is being kept up-to-date with digital workflows and innovations, so they can 'be there with the right product at the right time'. But maybe, except for an opportunity that will arise here and there, for illustrated book publishers trying to exploit the same creative development across both print and digital, there won't ever be a 'right time'. There certainly is no guarantee there will be.

Q: How are publishers in this segment poised for the change?
Bipin: Illustrated books in print form depend on bookstores more than fiction, non-fiction and biographies do. If the value in a book is in its visual presentation, then you might want to look at it before buying it, and the view you'd get of it online might not be doing justice to what you'd see if you held the book in your hands.

For the publisher of fiction and non-fiction, this means the book is competing with other media that would accomplish a *different* purpose. For the publisher of illustrated books, the book also must compete with *similar* visual material on the net, with the *same* purpose (bombarded with new videos posted on YouTube every day). But they can't do it for the same price, because that material is free.

So illustrated-book publishers not only have to learn how to make videos—a new skill to be acquired—or expect the author to provide video and audio, they also have to come up with a new business model that enables their videos/audios to be part of a priced commercial product as part of augmented reality, competing with a plethora of those that are free. And they have to finance a substantial creative component that isn't contributing value to the print version at all. Or is it?

Q: Tell us something about the scope of augmented reality in illustrated books.
Bipin: The lines between books and enhanced books and book apps will continue to blur, but the human need to *see* stories existed long before the invention of writing.

The **BooksPlus** app introduced by Mapin last month, in collaboration with a technology firm, Ignite Solutions, allows readers through image recognition to see video and listen to audio from those books which are embedded with such digital variants, thus enhancing the book and enticing readers to experience the magic of print books coming alive.

There are a lot of very smart people working on delivering illustrated books ('books' is too limiting a term; 'narrative experiences' is better) to the digitally enabled reading public. While there have been some notable successes for what are known as 'enhanced e-books' and book apps, and some publishers are doing well with these products, it's a market that hasn't yet taken off compared to what's called 'immersive' e-reading.

The challenge—very specifically—for 'general illustrated book publishing' seems much more severe. Nobody is so sure about it, but it seems like they can see a profitable path in the future to navigate the digital change in immersive reading books but not in illustrated art books.

From my interaction with mostly illustrated publishers, I gather the mindset for change is very slow. The general consensus is let's wait and see. Others have a different, practical approach, emphasizing market forces need be addressed too. The unwritten editorial policy in several major publishing houses is that no illustrated books would have more than 25,000 words—with of course some exceptions—in most cases, still lower. Most admit that they see the problem but haven't yet figured out a solution.

A digital expert at a German Book Office seminar in Delhi several years back cited the example of a record label in the late 1980s when audio cassettes dominated the market by nearly 90 per cent. Then came the digital revolution. It took several years of denial before Sony accepted the challenge that CDs were the way forward. The expert warns the illustrated book publishers that the future is here and now!

Q: What do you see as the future of the illustrated-book business?
Bipin: As with all media, innovation and uptake will happen over time. But to suggest there is no future in illustrated e-books is like the stage-play producer who walked into a Nickelodeon in 1910 and said there was no future in moving pictures. Those who refused to embrace moving pictures disappeared into oblivion.

Richard Stephenson, founder of Yudu, a not-so-new start-up from the UK has an interesting point of view on the future of illustrated digital titles. Stephenson believes that illustrated digital titles will take off with consumers when publishers build several of the same type and sell them through a proprietary app.

The disadvantages? Well, for one, the products are still expensive, time-consuming and labour-intensive to create, and without a defined market to sell to may not be worth the risk.

'There will be cul-de-sacs, roads where people go down and don't lead to anything,' said Yudu's Stephenson. 'But you've just gotta keep trying things until you hit the spot.'

BIPIN SHAH is Publisher and Managing Director of Mapin Publishing, publishers of illustrated books on the art and culture of India. Mapin offers packaging services to international publishers and museums and custom publishing solutions to corporate clients in India, and has expansion plans involving the development of educational content in the art, architecture and design, and children's segments. Bipin has recently led Mapin's introduction of BooksPlus Augmented Reality for illustrated-book publishers.

46

TIE-UPS AND COLLABORATIONS

"Staying the course"

Aarti David

In 2015, SAGE India entered into partnerships with independent publishers to form new imprints, namely SAGE Stree, SAGE Samya, SAGE Popular Prakashan and SAGE YODA Press. This initiative takes forward the tradition of developing dynamic lists, both academic as well as popular, which will open interactive spaces for further discussion, scholarship and writing to effectively capture the non-mainstream and critical reality of contemporary India.

Q: What was the motivation and objective of these collaborations?
Aarti: The idea of engaging in these kinds of tie-ups was to provide a wider reach to the co-partners and to add to or supplement our own existing list of titles. Each partner comes with their unique strength and it is up to SAGE to ensure we retain their originality and individuality. That is the reason why we created a separate logo for each partner to protect their identity within the co-publishing.

Q: Are tie-ups and collaborations part of a wider strategy globally as well?
Aarti: Yes, tie-ups and collaborations are a part of the wider global strategy as well. If it works commercially for both the parties, then it is a win–win situation for all. The idea is to create a bigger brand and yet not lose focus of one's core philosophy/vision/mission. SAGE's mission and vision globally is to disseminate knowledge and we are open to collaborating on this aspect as long as it fits in with our work

ethic and core philosophy. There are local variations when approaching collaborations, while the rationale remains consistent across offices.

Q: How are the work roles between SAGE and each publishing house working?
Aarti: Each co-partner has their unique style of working and is used to managing each aspect differently. We may not always agree on everything, but have worked towards figuring out a path that works for both. However, I would like to add that it is still very much work-in-progress and we continue to grow and evolve this relationship. Partnering with someone is all about mutual respect and collaboration. There can be situations where the partners may feel intimidated by SAGE and feel they are in danger of losing their identity. It is our duty to smoothen things out and strike a balance that works for the benefit of all. At the end of the day, we are all in it together, and for a reason. A common passion 'dissemination of content to a wider audience' drives us.

Q: How many titles have been printed under this arrangement so far?
Aarti: It is still early days, but we have published a total of 22 titles with the co-publishers and we continue to ideate and collaborate on future titles to be published under this arrangement.

Q: How is the tie-up with Popular Prakashan different from that with Stree, Samya and Yoda Press?
Aarti: There are really no significant differences in the tie-ups with any of the partners in terms of the contracts that we may have signed with them. The terms are fair and similar for all and that is the reason why they agreed to partner with SAGE. The authors too had to be brought on board before these tie-ups were done. So we have the validation of the creators of the content too for these partnerships. While each partner may be significantly different from the other, we continue to share a great working relationship with each of the partners we engage with. With Popular Prakashan, the opportunity is to bring back titles that continue to remain relevant; there are no front-list titles in this list.

Q: What benefits does the partnership bring to SAGE and to the other parties?
Aarti: The partnership helps strengthen SAGE's existing list in the social sciences and the co-partners get greater visibility across platforms. Each partner adds their distinct flavour to the programme and in turn SAGE provides them a steady growth path.

Q: How many titles are in the pipeline under these tie-ups?
Aarti: We have monthly/quarterly discussions on projects we can/cannot publish under this arrangement. We hope to publish 15 new titles in 2018 and continue to grow the list.

Q: Are you taking backlists along with front lists?
Aarti: We are only looking at the front lists. However, if the partners need help in selling their backlists, then our sales team does provide them with some leads and support. The exception is Popular Prakashan where we have selected existing bestsellers as we collectively believe that these titles still have potential to sell in large numbers.

Q: Has SAGE achieved the targets anticipated from these tie-ups?
Aarti: When this arrangement began, it was not about meeting any specific targets. It was in fact, as I have mentioned earlier, to provide a wider reach to the partners and to grow our own list. Each partner adds value with their excellent content to further strengthen and grow our list. The target we collectively agreed upon was to learn to work as a team. That I believe we have achieved. Good publishing is about staying the course. A year or two doesn't really tell you if something is working or not, nor should one be looking for an answer to this question.

Q: Are there any plans for more such collaborations in the future?
Aarti: We have recently tied-up with Vitasta and would like to establish the current relationships before we enter into more such partnerships. Publishing is a creative profession and one that is filled with passionate individuals. It does require a lot of careful management/handling when

dealing with so many entities with their own unique strengths. However, we are not averse to the idea of conversations for future collaborations.

Q: There are many other collaborations happening and that have happened in the past; do you see this trend growing, and why?
Aarti: I think it makes perfect business sense if two entities with a common ideology are able to tie up with each other and leverage each other's strengths. It is a very competitive environment and if these kinds of partnerships work, then the end result is there for all to see. It's a mutually beneficial arrangement and not something that is happening in publishing alone. Many smaller firms are tying up with bigger entities in the online/start-up space also.

In a dog-eats-dog world, I'm happy to state that we have been able to carve a space for this unique arrangement where each stakeholder is benefited equally and a much larger purpose is served too; the ability to publish and disseminate quality content without any compromise. We remain committed to making this work. It ensures global practices come to the smallest publishing entity that strives for growth and excellence.

AARTI DAVID is Vice President, Publishing at SAGE India. She heads marketing and leads books commissioning across all subject streams. She is also responsible for managing joint imprints with Yoda, Popular Prakashan, Stree, Samya and Vitasta.

PART

5

Genres: Enduring and Emerging

PART V • GENRES: ENDURING AND EMERGING

GENRES: ENDURING AND EMERGING

The final section looks at English-language publishing in its core genre. Within educational publishing which forms the overwhelming bulk in India, school publishing is predominant. In the first part, four private school publishers, two Indian and two multinational, tell us about the astounding growth and innovation this genre is seeing. All the publishers are upbeat and believe there is much to do, to grow and thrive, in this market.

The next cluster has four academic publishers look at higher education publishing landscape from their vantage points of S&T (science and technology), HSS (humanities and social sciences), medical publishing and textbook publishing. As can be seen from the responses, each segment has its own distinct trends and trajectories.

General books publishing is 6 per cent of total publishing in India and the subsequent protagonists take us through the glamour and the economics of general non-fiction and fiction, the difficulties and opportunities of bringing out illustrated books and the incredible sustaining power of comics.

While readership may be in jeopardy, authorship in India is growing in leaps and bounds, as is amply clear from the experiences of our final three contributors all running thriving self-publishing business.

47

PUBLISHING FOR CHILDREN

"The more you read, The better reader you are"

Neeraj Jain

Q: What are the recent trends, opportunities and challenges in the children's publishing segment?

NJ: The recent trends we have observed are all about making books fun and engaging. If you look at Scholastic's *Kids and Family Reading Report*, the main things that came out are that kids are looking for books that make them laugh and books that make them think and take them into the imaginary world. They look for books where the characters are strong and brave.

The biggest opportunity in this segment is that 35 per cent of our population is 0to14 years of age, and this figure is ever growing. So the Indian population is an opportunity for us.

The biggest challenge is that the concept of read aloud and picture books has still not taken shape in this market. We are working closely with parents and schools to make them understand the value of reading aloud and the value that a picture book brings to the child. Even our Report says that one of the things which determines whether the child will become a frequent reader or not is whether their parents read aloud to them or not. We are trying to educate young parents on the importance of reading aloud to their child to inculcate the habit of reading and to nurture overall growth as an individual. If all parents knew why reading aloud is so important and critical, I think they would find those 20 minutes for it.

Q: How has been the journey of Scholastic in India? Is it in line with the global objectives?

NJ: Scholastic is 20 years old in India. As we are known globally, in India too we are known as a reading-promotion company much more than a children's publishing company, though we are a big name in children's publishing too. For us, the whole endeavour is to promote the habit of reading. We work closely with schools to promote the habit of reading. While doing this, we not only promote our own books, but also books in general, across the globe.

Q: How does Scholastic promote the reading habit in India?
NJ: We reach 7,000+ schools with our reading-promotion activities across the country, right from Kargil to Lakshwadeep to Gangtok to Gandhinagar. We are present in every possible market and we try and take books to every kid. We believe that if you have to build a strong reading habit, it has to stand on four strong pillars—access, choice for kids, involvement from parents and teachers, and practice. So the more you read, the better reader you are. We have brought out new programmes that can enhance the skillsets of Indian kids. Scholastic News Kids Press Corps is a group of talented Kid Reporters, aged 10 to14, from across the country and around the world. We are very happy that three kids from India were selected and now they are on the panel of Kid Reporters. Our corporate communication team interacts directly with the kids, and they would be reporting on certain important matters. This will be very good exposure.

Besides, we have been organizing Scholastic Writing Awards where the kids write their stories and the top ten stories get published in the form of a book. What could be more encouraging for a 10 to 12-year-old child than to see his/her story published?

Q: What is the road ahead? How do you see the next five years?
NJ: We would like to carry on doing what we are doing, improvise on it and do it in a much better way. One of the things we are going to focus on is how to reach more kids. We would also like to share our research and learning with others, so that we equip them with the right ammunition. We are also doing curriculum publishing. There, we try to bring all the best things that are practised across the globe to the Indian classroom, in a way that it is organically connected to the Indian curriculum. Again the pedagogy, the methodology, the spiral progression

are all taken care of, as in the global environment. Our focus remains pre-school to grade 5, though we also have series for Classes 6-8.

Q: How has the CBSE (Central Board of Secondary Education) directive to use NCERT (National Council of Educational Research and Training) books impacted school publishers and how does your organization plan to handle this development?
NJ: Any directive that the CBSE or NCERT comes out with, will always have an impact on all publishers but there is enough space for everybody. One has to see what comes through and strategize accordingly. It does impact us, but we are trying to create the best, so that our schools get the best.

Q: How have teaching resources/aids evolved over time?
NJ: Scholastic is one of the companies which creates maximum amount of teachers resources. Also, on the curriculum side, we have a lot of professional development for teachers when we engage with schools. We also offer teaching guides, which help them deliver content in the best possible way. We have digital resources, webinars, videos, etc., to equip teachers with the resources they need.

Q: What is your take on e-books?
NJ: Even if you look at the broader global perspective, where e-books have become more popular than in India, especially in the children's segment and in the younger section, e-books have never been too big a component. We are still in the initial stages. According to our *Kids and Family Reading Report*, 80 per cent of kids who were exposed to an e-book, now prefer a print book. Though it is very difficult to predict which way it will go, we at Scholastic feel that the medium is not important, what is important is that they consume the content. It is important that they read. That is what our focus is.

Q: What are your views on declining readership?
NJ: In comparson with earlier times, today's kids have got many options and they tend to choose one of the options. So today we are competing

with screen time. People also say kids' attention time is declining. Rather than focusing on the reading habit going down, we should focus on how to improve reading, so that it becomes the most important activity among the other activities. For this, in India, we introduced a method for schools to measure a student reader's ability, called Lexile level or Lexile measure. Lexile measure is a valuable tool for teachers, parents and students. It serves two unique functions: it is a measure of how difficult a text is as well as a student's reading ability level. The Lexile Framework was developed by MetaMetrics, an educational assessment and research team, funded originally by the National Institute of Child Health and Human Development. We took it a step further and introduced LitPro through which any individual can log on and get to know what her reading level is. This helps in reading the right books of your choice within your reading level and thereby improving it. Currently, we are offering this to schools but we are also looking at it to take it to individuals as a retail model.

Q: Tell us about your experience as a publishing professional?
NJ: I have learnt a lot about how books play a critical role and how reading is so deeply connected with academic success too. I have been reading aloud to my daughter since she was 9 months old and today she is an avid reader. I was privy to all the research that goes on at Scholastic and I was fortunate to share these books and my learning with her. Besides, I get to read a lot of children books which keep the child in me alive. We should all remember we are catering to a segment which changes and evolves very fast. Every 2 to 3 years, there is a generation gap. We have to ensure we are on top of the latest development so that we can provide material that resonates with today's kids. The biggest satisfaction is that we are always giving back to society.

NEERAJ JAIN is Managing Director of Scholastic India. Before joining the publishing industry, he worked with media and direct marketing companies and has been in the Steering Committee of 'Excellence in School Education', an initiative by IIT Delhi. He is a member of CII and the American Chamber of Commerce.

48

GEARING UP FOR THE 21ST CENTURY

"Putting new wine in old bottles "

Atiya Zaidi

Q: How big is the K-12 publishing segment?

Atiya: There is huge opportunity in the K-12 publishing segment. As the population keeps increasing, the number of schools increases as well. Every parent is aspirational now and wants her/his children to study in 'English-medium' schools. With this, publishers in this segment are increasing and all feel that the more there are, the better. Competition is increasing but quality is what sets us apart. We take great pride in the quality and pedagogy of our books and I am not talking about just quality in content, but also visuals, designing, printing, binding, etc. Besides, we use CFP (chlorine-free paper) to do our bit for the environment.

Q: Tell us something about the journey of Ratna Sagar.

Atiya: Ratna Sagar started 35 years ago with just five people. Now we have 600 plus people. Ratna Sagar means an Ocean of Gems. The name has been taken from Nalanda University, where the library building, which housed valuable manuscripts, was named Ratna Sagar. So it is a 3,000-year-old tradition we are carrying forward.

The first series we brought out was *Living Science* in 1984, which has become a legendary series, and is still going strong. It was the first four-colour science book at that time and was readily accepted. People did not believe it was printed in India!

Another series which furbished our image was *My Big Book of Social Studies* for Classes 1–5. This is a bestseller till date. It was launched in 1990 and has become invincible. Later, we also published for Classes 6–8.

Teachers and principals have appreciated our books and the journey has brought us more appreciation than challenges.

Q: What are the recent trends, opportunities and challenges in the K-12 publishing segment?

Atiya: In our country, things change slowly; there are no visible trends as such. Almost 25 years ago when the Central Board of Secondary Education (CBSE) introduced the communicative pattern of learning in English, all publishers followed it. It is interesting to note that Orient Longman (now Orient BlackSwan) had introduced this kind of a book called *Onward English* long back, but even though a very good series, it was not very successful because people were not open to change. However, when CBSE introduced the pattern, it was mass adopted and schools accepted it readily.

Since the past two decades, most of our ELT courses have been based on LSRW (listening, speaking, reading, writing) skills. A few years ago, on the HRD minister's suggestion, the HRD Ministry introduced the CCE (Continuous and Comprehensive Evaluation) pattern of learning. It was a useful concept but it did not work because the implementation was not effective, as schools were not prepared for it. Many private schools, where teachers were trained and qualified enough to handle the new system, could implement it properly. But schools in smaller cities were not able to implement it fully. The system was revolutionary and the books were more learning-oriented and less exam-oriented. Here, the role of teachers became more important and so did their accountability. But it did not work the way it should have. As a result, the pattern was dropped.

Q: How has the CBSE directive to use NCERT (National Council of Educational Research and Training) books impacted school publishers? How is your publishing house taking this new directive?

Atiya: Last year, there was a confusion that schools affiliated to CBSE were asked by the board to use only NCERT books for all classes. But, there has been no directive from NCERT and publishers are not affected. This year, we brought out 317 books, the highest number we have ever done. This is also due to the fact that the Council for the Indian School Certificate Examinations (CISCE) changed the syllabus and we revised all the books. We have not dropped a single book from our publishing plan.

Q: What makes a good textbook?

Atiya: Publishing textbooks is a big social responsibility as you are moulding the minds of future citizens. On an average, a textbook has a shelf life of 6 to 7 years and a successful book sells 50,000–60,000 copies a year. Some of the bestselling books even sell 1-lakh plus copies!

A textbook should be easy for an average teacher to use and should be student-friendly for the child to feel interested. If a science teacher is not in school on a particular day, the book should be such that an English or social science teacher can take it up and teach the class, at least upto Class 8. That is one of the guidelines for our editors!

We are blessed to be in this culture-rich country. But, the more plural a country, more the scope for stereotyping. Thus, books should also have universal values likes caring for the environment, mainstreaming the differently-abled, knowing the extended family, gender equality respect for other castes, religions, classes, regions etc.

Q: What specific things does Ratna Sagar do to face up to the competition and other challenges?

Atiya: It has become imperative for publishers to provide teacher resource material along with textbooks. At Ratna Sagar, we provide a Teacher Companion with detailed lesson plans so that teachers can plan their lessons accordingly. The lesson plans are detailed and technical, designed by practising teachers. There are a few articles on pedagogy as well, besides guidelines for activities, worksheets, etc.

We also provide digital support for teachers in the form of e-books, more activities for smart boards, games, assessments, test generators for different lessons, apps, virtual reality, 3D, etc.

Moreover, we do a lot of teacher training. Every year, we conduct around 14,00 to 15,00 workshops across the country, which are free for teachers. We do it as a service as we believe that we cannot expect the government to do everything. If we can take even a small initiative, it will make a difference somewhere.

Q: How has e-learning impacted K-12 publishing in general and your publishing house in particular?

Atiya: E-learning is an additional resource; the print book is still the king (or queen!) and will remain so. E-learning aids teaching; it goes a long way in explaining abstract concepts like various body systems and concepts like rotation and revolution.

However, it has not reached many schools due to issues like lack of proper infrastructure, low connectivity and inadequate teacher training. Maybe, it will take another 5 to10 years to become a part of classroom teaching. However, e-learning material does help publishers in getting their books prescribed as schools feel it is a value-addition.

Q: What are the creative challenges you have faced in your career?

Atiya: In mainstream educational publishing, if you are too creative, it does not work. It is important to keep your dreams and creativity under control and create a book, that is suitable for one and all. I think keeping a balance between acceptability, conformity and non-conformity is a challenge.

We did a path-breaking series of English readers, based on the concept of language across the curriculum, as we believe in holistic education and not teaching in compartments. For example, one chapter of the *English Reader* was linked to the science curriculum and another with maths. The series did not succeed because it was far ahead of its time.

Another series, which also did not get much success, was *Hindi Reader*, which had a Mickey Patel painting on the cover and lots of funny stories inside, and even a few English words here and there. It was created by a well-known educationist and linguist, an expert in elementary education. One teacher from an elite school remarked that it was too interesting and looked like a magazine rather than a book!

So, we learnt the trade secret that instead of putting old wine in new bottles, we should put new wine in old bottles. We have to give good content in the way teachers or children want. For example, instead of putting all literary works in one reader, we put one story from the likes of Ranjit Lal or Ruskin Bond in the reader. The same story in a book of stories might reach 2,000 children but in a textbook, almost 200,000 children get to read it. Thus, we found the formula of reaching the acceptance point, which is to keep 80 per cent of the content conventional and 20 per cent new. Most of our books work on this formula of acceptability.

Q: What are the other challenges you face?

Atiya: There is a very small pool of editors and content creators to draw upon. For content writers, we prefer practising teachers as they know the problems and needs of children and they understand what a teacher can handle in a 40-minute class.

The other challenges in the industry include rising paper costs, returns going up, and the problem of long credit cycles, which has increased from 60 days to 180 days to as much as 360 days now.

Q: Where do you see the industry five years from now?

Atiya: K-12 publishing will grow more content will be created and disseminated, though the platform may be different. Traditional classroom teaching will be around and remote learning will still take time to be mass adopted. We are geared for the 22nd century and will always keep a step ahead of others in technology or pedagogy. We are on solid ground and our company is aligned to the vision of the future of education.

ATIYA ZAIDI is Publisher at Ratna Sagar. She has 26 years of experience in writing and preparing books for children. She specializes in ELT, and creates course material for the social sciences, maths and science as well. She is on the faculty of two major publishing courses and is a founder member of the FICCI Publishing Cell.

49

TECHNOLOGY IN EDUCATION

"Technology is an enabler in K-12 publishing"

Himanshu Gupta

Q: How big is the K-12 publishing segment and who are the key players in India?

HG: According to the Nielsen 2015 report, the K-12 segment is close to US$3.5 billion in India, which would be around Rs 22,000-23,000 crores, of which 65–70 per cent would be with private publishers. This segment is growing at the rate of 8–10 per cent annually and it will continue to grow as India has a very specific school market. According to the latest reports, we have 270 million students of whom 40 per cent go to private schools. By 2030, there will be approximately 350 million students going to school, of whom 65 per cent will be private-school students. This is because both the students and the parents feel that the quality of education, teaching faculty, learning materials and infrastructure at private schools is much better than in government schools in most cases. So, even low-income group parents feel that putting their children in private schools will not only enhance their careers but also give them the same opportunities as children from higher-income groups. They want their children to become doctors, engineers or management graduates, which they feel is more attainable if their children study in English-medium private schools. Else, they will remain stuck in the lower income strata.

So we believe there is a transformation and evolution happening in the education segment, which will give a whole lot of opportunities to players like us in the future. There are a lot of players in the industry and in time consolidation will happen in the industry, with only limited players who offer quality content and services able to survive. This will be good for the industry as well as for customers as it will grow in size but the number of players will be fewer and they will be more quality conscious.

The key players operating in the Indian school market today are Oxford University Press, Macmillan, Cambridge University Press, Pearson, Orient BlackSwan, Ratna Sagar and Encyclopedia Britannica. According to industry estimates there are around 20 to 25 players who control 70–75 per cent of the total CBSE (Central Board of Secondary Education)/ ICSE (Indian Certificate of Secondary Education) market worth Rs 4,000–4,500 crore.

Q: What are the recent trends, opportunities and challenges in the K-12 publishing segment?

HG: The major trend is that schools do not want just books, they want a complete solution with digital products, web support material, teacher resources, assessments, worksheets, etc. There are lots of opportunities for players who can provide these kinds of products and services. But the environment is definitely challenging. The market is becoming more and more competitive but we believe only players with long-term vision and focus on customer satisfaction will have the best chance of surviving in the coming years.

Q: How has the technology interface evolved over the last five years?

HG: In the education space, technology has evolved a lot in the last five years. There are new app developments. In the S. Chand Group also, we have a smartclass by our group company DS Digital, which offers a digital classroom solutions with a rich portfolio of interactive K-12 curriculum-based technology products and services in all subject areas. Based on modern educational research and established educational practices, it uses the latest and easy-to-use technological framework for an enriching teaching–learning environment. The solution presents a holistic educational programme with digital and print materials, student-tracking and report-generating facilities, professional development services, and technical maintenance provisions.

We also offer MyStudyGear, which is an innovative app which makes education and guidance available to students at their fingertips. It is a free model now and we hope to convert it into a freemium model.

We are also launching first-ever books with virtual reality content for 9th and 10th standards for the school market. These would be available in six books of science (physics/chemistry/biology) by Lakhmir Singh. Students can have a 360° immersive view of the topics. We will also provide a free VR glass which the student can use to have the virtual reality experience.

We think technology is an enabler and not a disruptor in education. S. Chand has most of its schoolbooks coming with some or the other digital or web support material for learners or teachers. That is what we believe has made books a hybrid solution with print and digital combined into one.

Q: How do you maintain the balance between content and platform/technology?

HG: Content and technology are inter-related and we have to first create quality content and then comes technology development for deployment of that content in the best possible manner. For technology development, we depend mostly on outsourced vendors who are experts in their field, with strong internal quality checks and controls to ensure quality standards are met. I believe content and technology go hand-in-hand. Pure content is not saleable anymore; it has to be supported with some kind of technology interface.

Q: What is the future of technology in K-12 publishing?

HG: Augmented Reality (AR) is also happening in books now. Our basic aim is not to be pure print publishers but more of complete education solutions providers who can deliver quality content in accordance with the changing needs of the customer. We want to be more of content and service players, who can deliver on any platform. Today, we are delivering through books; tomorrow we may deliver through web, digital, tablets, mobiles, etc. One thing is certain, a learner or teacher would require some kind of intervention of quality content to teach or learn better.

Q: What would your focus areas be?
HG: Our company will always look for new technological development for learners and teachers. Early this year, by the second quarter, we will launch a new product for pre-schools. For this, we have tied up with one of the best education companies in South Korea, which is the largest education technology company. They have a product called NuriNori, which provides state-of-the-art quality teaching materials and tools on- / off-line for teachers. It aims to contribute to the healthy development and growth of kids by enhancing teachers' capacity and improving the early childhood education environment. In addition, it reduces teachers' activity preparation time; they can share more time communicating with kids.

Besides, we are also creating our own TestPrep platform, where we will put lots of our products which are already bestsellers. Children can take tests and improve their learning and performance.

Q: How would technology have an impact on learning in schools?
HG: Schools now have various options like smartclasses, tablets and other solutions. It solely depends on the infrastructure of school and its willingness to adopt technology, on how it can integrate print with digital solution. At S. Chand, we are helping them adopt it in a much better fashion.

Q: How would it square up with the government focus on using NCERT (National Council for Educational Research and Training) books?
HG: The NCERT has been selling books for many decades and has also started e-basta. But technology is not about offering PDFs of the book, it is much more. Children need much more interaction in the learning experience, which is not there in PDF content.

Q: What is the value and volume of K-12 publishing for the S. Chand Group?

HG: S. Chand has become the second publishing company in India to be listed on the Indian stock exchanges. Today, we sell anything between 40 and 45 million books a year in this segment. The target value will be close to Rs 700–750 crore for the upcoming school season.

Q: Tell us about acquisitions, focus and potential in the regional market?

HG: We believe S. Chand has made significant acquisitions in the publishing segment in the last four to five years, the recent one being that of Chhaya Prakashani. We believe there are more opportunities for acquisitions in the regional market, especially in the western and southern markets. We are also talking to a player outside India, which specializes in international schools all over the world, specifically in the International General Certificate of Secondary Education (IGCSE) Board.

Q: What are the steps taken to stay ahead of competition?

HG: As a company, we have to be very competitive and aggressive and nimble on our feet. We have to take decisions and make sure our actions are faster and better than others. So, we do more and more marketing activities to connect with our customers, like teacher workshops, more interactions with teachers in schools, making sure that all our customers are serviced properly. We are also conducting a lot of ground-level activities that very few players are doing, like teacher conclaves and educational tours outside India. We believe these things are helping us get more ground coverage and improve our relationship with schools, which will help us get more business.

Q: How is the CBSE directive to use NCERT books impacting school publishers and how does your organization plan to handle this development?

HG: There is no directive that says that schools can use only NCERT books. It was more of a media scare. Schools are free to choose their books as they always have been. Some schools prefer NCERT books. Most of the publishers provide support materials with their books, which are right now not available with NCERT books.

Q: What will be your strategy in the next three to five years?
HG: We want to give good quality content and service to our customers and make sure we increase our market share in the school segment organically at the rate of 18–20 per cent per year. We are also looking at acquisitions; whenever we find a perfect fit, we might go in for another acquisition.

HIMANSHU GUPTA has been Managing Director of S. Chand Publishing since 2007. He has over 15 years of experience in the knowledge products and services industry. He was Vice President (South) of the Federation of Indian Publishers in 2012-13, and received the Young Publisher Award from the Federation of Educational Publishers in India for 2011.

50

CLASSROOM LEARNING AND TEACHER SUPPORT

"Need to develop PPP model-based solutions"

Sivaramakrishnan V. (Siva)

Q: What are the biggest challenges to school publishing today and what are the ways of dealing with it?

Siva: We would like to call out three challenges that the present education system must address quickly. Foremost being the ability of schools/parents to sift through tons of education content and select only quality learning material. This is also pertinent given the easy availability of uncurated content on the internet. The second challenge pertains to the integration of digital with print—this must be seamless and completely aligned to benefit the learner. It is not uncommon to see disparate content being delivered to the learner via different mediums, which does more harm than good. The third challenge is the need to offer continued professional development to teachers, who are the principle pivot in the teaching–learning process. The K-12 community must come together to respond to these challenges and at some stage also engage the government/regulators to develop public–private-partnership model-based solutions.

Q: Who according to you are the key stakeholders in school publishing?

Siva: The government, educational institutions, authors, teachers, students and parents, privation education players are all stakeholders in the school-publishing system. There are interdependencies, synergies and opportunities to collaborate with one other for the benefit of the learner. The contribution of each of them is crucial to the further development of the school-education ecosystem.

Q: What does the Oxford University Press (OUP) brand stand for in school publishing in India and how has that changed over time?

Siva: The OUP's longstanding presence of over a century in India is testimony to the acceptance of its education products and solutions by generations of learners. Its school education publishing programme in India draws from its vast experience of working with schools, students, teachers, authors and others in the education ecosystem. The OUP brand today is synonymous with pedagogically superior content packaged to produce quality and trusted education products and solutions that impact the learner profoundly. It has remained innovative in its approach to product development in order to better respond to the needs of the new-age learners.

Q: What is the focus of your publishing programme today?

Siva: Our present-day school publishing programme is focused on producing classroom learning outcomes. This has entailed packaging content differently, often giving prominence to illustrations and design given that children nowadays are visual learners. There's also a focus on summative assessments which are neatly integrated with our courses to enable teachers and students to have a 'measure of learning' in the course of instruction.

One of OUP's strong focuses in recent times has been the development of teacher support material, both print and electronic. This we believe empowers the teacher immensely in a classroom setting, especially if they are trained by experts to effectively deploy these resources in the course of teaching. Our direct engagement with several thousand teachers every year, through training workshops, brings us deep insights into the needs of the new-age learner, allowing us to continuously improve our products for the better.

Q: Tell us about e-books uptake in schools. How do you respond to this?

Siva: Digital uptake is fast catching on and its adoption is taking place in multiple ways, e-books being one of them. The regular use of e-readers and devices in classrooms is still a very metro-city phenomenon, and there also, limited to a small percentage of schools. Print books continue to be the primary medium of instruction in classrooms, of course supported by digitized content played out on LCDs or digitized boards. OUP has a vast and growing repository of e-books, as also capabilities to digitize content on demand for varied platforms.

SIVARAMAKRISHNAN V. is Managing Director of Oxford University Press India, with regional responsibilities including Bangladesh, Sri Lanka and Nepal. He has extensive experience in the education services, e-commerce, automobiles and FMCG domains. In his previous assignment, Siva was Executive President, Education Services at Manipal Global Education Services. He worked for nearly ten years with the Ford Motor Company and has held various consumer branding roles within Procter & Gamble.

51

SCIENCE AND TECHNOLOGY

"Challenges and opportunities coexist"

N.K. Mehra

Q: Given the promising landscape for higher-education (HE) publishing in India, how do you approach the Indian market? What is the current and ongoing strategy for growth?

NKM: A lot of higher education is linked with publishing. S&T publishing suffers from lack of quality authorship. We don't have the kind of authors we would like to see. There is a lot of plagiarism existing which is a big problem. Indian-authored books are not being cited as frequently as we would like to see, though there is an increasing trend. Research work is not being published in books, though it is published in local journals, however these are too few and far between, compared to international publishers. So local research publishing is suffering to a great extent.

On the other hand, overseas publishers pick up this research because they are used to publishing research, but then the Indian publishers suffer. Authors would like their books to be published by international publishers rather than Indian publishers, because they get higher grades for their promotion when they produce books under the imprints of foreign publishers.

But there is a silver lining too. Many overseas-based Indian authors are keen to publish books in India, to reach Indian students and also wish to give something back to the country. But it's not philanthropic; they do expect royalties. Even so it is a tendency which we need to encourage.

E-books are constantly used in libraries which have a separate budget to buy e-books. Indian publishers don't have so many such books, so most e-books are purchased from foreign publishers. Indian publishers are working with aggregators to make their books more popular. But returns will take time.

Indian books are not being co-published, primarily because Indian, American as well as British publishers publish in English, and they would choose their own authors unless the book is so good it strikes the eye of the editor. Besides, if you opt for French, Spanish publishers, it is not cost-effective. Even then, co-publishing goes on. At Narosa, we have books translated in Chinese, Russian, etc., and we have sold rights to American and Arabic publishers. Our mathematics books are being reviewed in international journals, which is good for both the publisher as well as author. These things are happening and if things are not bright, they are not bleak either.

We have the Notebooks of Ramanujan (Srinivasa Ramanujan) in two volumes, which brought us into the mathematics world globally. The books were published in 1988 and are still in demand today.

Q: What is your pricing strategy and how do you deal with the photocopier competition?

NKM: We cannot keep reducing price, that's not the solution. It's not the pricing but the attitude of people that has to be changed. If attitudinal change is there, then the books are sold. When the books are sold and the quantity printed is higher, prices automatically come down.

But students still do not buy books, although they get grants. They make packages from different publishers and that becomes their book.

Q: What is your take on e-books?

NKM: I was looking at a British Publishers Association report, which clearly states that e-book sales have reached a certain level and are not increasing any more in academic/scientific publishing. In fact, e-book sales are going down. Physical books are still considered important.

Q: What are the priorities for your publishing house in the next few years?

NKM: I think the next five years will be a difficult period for finding financing, authors, sales, etc. But it could be bright also, given the fact that we are not only publishing textbooks but reference books as well, with certain books which we sell more of abroad than in India. In that sense, we are in a good situation. When you look at the research work, the print runs are going down, almost one-fourth of what they used to be.

N.K. MEHRA is Managing Director, Narosa Publishing House and President, Federation of Indian Publishers (FIP). He started his publishing career in 1959 and set up two companies, Narosa Book Distributors and Narosa Publishing House. Nandi, as he is popularly known, has been on FIP's Executive Committee for over ten years, and has also served on the Executive Committee of the Federation of Publishers' and Booksellers' Association in India where he was President for two terms.

52

HUMANITIES AND SOCIAL SCIENCES

"Think of a topic and Routledge will have a book on it"

Pankaj Bhardwaj

Q. Routledge is an old and strong HSS (humanities and social science) presence in India. Could you tell us how this is a strength in the current market? Can it also be a liability in a traditionally S&T (science and technology) market?

Pankaj: In 2017, Routledge published 8,500 books covering 1,250 unique topics including unconventional ones such as disability sport, music theory, Egyptian archaeology, guerrilla filmmaking, dance movement therapy, ethnomusicology, trauma and dissociation, global slavery, rap and hip-hop, ship operations, quality of life, bullying and truancy, animals and ethics.

As evident here, the width and breadth of the Routledge publishing programme is such that it not only covers current trends of academic disciplines, but also emerging academic areas. That's what makes it a strong HSS brand in India and other world markets. Often, in conversations with academics, I say 'You think of a topic and Routledge will have a book on it.'

I don't think that India is traditionally an S&T market. It has an equally strong HSS market which has grown stronger in recent years with the emergence of institutions like South Asian University, Azim Premji University, Indian National Defence University, Shiv Nadar University, Ashoka University, and O.P. Jindal Global University, where the primary academic focus is HSS. HSS publishing enjoys a unique edge over S&T, namely 'the older the better' and this characteristic makes HSS publishing commercially viable where the backlist can sometimes contribute higher revenues than the front list.

Q: Taylor & Francis (T&F) is the largest social sciences publisher in the world. How do you promote and sell such a wide range of books, given that globally you publish more than 5,000 books each year?
Pankaj: The mantra of handling such a wide range of publishing is that we see it as an opportunity rather than a challenge. Wider range offers scope for catering to an institution's needs in its entirety. Of course, it requires meticulous working before approaching the customer. We believe in bespoke selling and put in great effort in researching customers' needs to cull out the most relevant cluster of books to suit their teaching needs. A large backlist gives us the opportunity to scoop out topic-specific clusters and series-matching current academic trends. That enables us to bring them out at affordable prices for students. So, in a nutshell, 'Big is Best'.

Q: Academic publishing is dependent on library grants and these are shrinking consistently, so what are the strategies being adopted to sustain growth?
Pankaj: I agree that library grants are shrinking but institutions are still keen to invest in the books specific to their needs, and for this they have the capacity to provision special funds. In most cases, the funding agencies don't in fact specify the library fund allocation to an institution; it is the prerogative of the Vice Chancellor and senior administration. Given that academic excellence is the foremost priority of a university, investment in good and relevant books for any library comes foremost. Hence, one just needs to pitch it right.

Q: Selling academic books, especially in the HSS domain is a specialist skill, as a market often must be created. Would you agree? If so, please share some insights from your experience of selling these books?
Pankaj: I think the biggest skill to be a successful academic-books sales professional is to possess the ability to sense the need of the customer and to work hard yet passionately to match the product basket as well as the offer to the needs and pocket of the customer. The advantage of academic-book selling is that it has a definite captive market in the

form of libraries that are growing in numbers, have constant need, and a perennial flow of funds to upgrade their content to cater to the diverse and emerging requirements of researchers.

Q: What role do local authors and researchers play in this context?
Pankaj: Authors and researchers are well placed as decision-makers for procurement of books in their respective institutions and play a vital role in creating opportunities and platforms for you to showcase the strength of your publishing. In the publishing profession, good author and researcher relationships are of prime importance. I have personal experience of maintaining long-term rapport with teachers and professors who eventually rose in the ranks in the academic world, paving the way for me to reach higher platforms to promote my products.

Q: Can you tell us a bit about your key customers? What are their key requirements and how do you meet them?
Pankaj: Our key customers comprise central universities, institutions of national importance, private universities, and government-funded and private research organizations. This customer base focuses on higher levels of learning with good affordability to invest in reference and research monographs which are the key strengths of our publishing.

Q: How does T&F support the academic community of institutions, librarians, researchers and students?
Pankaj: Each year T&F conducts a large number of editorial workshops, author talks, and orientation programmes on e-resource usage, open access publishing, publishing ethics, etc., for the benefit of librarians, the academic community, and budding scholars. T&F India's South Asian reprint programme helps young scholars access world-class research in the forms of monographs, handbooks, and companions.

Q: T&F is known to keep adding new imprints via acquisitions Tell us a bit about some recent acquisitions and your plans for them in the Indian market.

Pankaj: T&F has a good eye for quality publishing and aspiration to grow as an academic publisher; hence it is continually investing in new imprints via acquisition. T&F has recently acquired reputed publishing brands such as Ashgate, Westview Press Karnac Publishing, Greenleaf, Baywood, Leftcost Press, and Speechmark. We plan to reintroduce the books of these imprints into the South Asian market in market-friendly ways.

Q: Are you reaching out to non-academic markets as well with your list?

Pankaj: By virtue of a diverse publishing range and acumen to invest in new publishing verticals, T&F now has a wide variety of products suiting the non-library markets. We are offering customized content to our non-academic customers, helping them prepare teaching material from across range of our globally acclaimed content. We have set up focused teams of sales and editorial professionals to understand and cater to the needs of these markets.

Q: T&F is unusual in that it has built digital books sales alongside print. Could you tell us how that came about and has sustained, especially in markets like India?

Pankaj: T&F is aware of the fact that despite rampant growth of demand for digital books the market share of print publishing sales still stands strong at 70 per cent of the global publishing market and our sales strategy is to balance the focus between both forms of products. India continues to be a large consumer of print books and hence T&F will try to remain a predominantly print publisher with a sharp eye on the opportunities to sell its digital content alongside.

PANKAJ BHARDWAJ is General Manager, Sales Operations at Taylor & Francis India. A publishing professional with over 20 years of experience, he looks after the company's HSS publishing business across the South Asia region, and has worked with leading international publishing houses in the past.

53

MEDICINE

"Still predominantly print in India"

Ajit Kohli

Q: If you had to introduce the medical-publishing genre to the uninitiated, how would you describe it in a few words?

Ajit: Medical publishing for a lay person is making available information and data produced through medical research, aiming at providing the best-possible treatment and care to patients. Medical publishing fills the gap between research and practice. By publishing the results of medical studies in a credible and trustworthy way, this vetted information can then be accessed by students and practitioners who turn to these publications for the most up-to-date, high-quality information when treating patients and to enhance their knowledge.

Q: How has the landscape of medical publishing changed in India?

Ajit: I joined publishing 10 years back—it was a quantum shift from the world of advertising to a relatively unorganized industry, the size of which was not known, an industry dominated by old players who worked for their own cause, an industry bitterly divided among booksellers, distributors, and publishers, and within publishers, Indian publishers and the so-called foreign publishers. Ten years later, the situation hasn't changed much—the volumes may have increased but we are still as unorganized as we were 10 years back.

Q: How is it different from the other professional publishing in your view?

Ajit: Each publishing segment has characteristics which differentiate it from the others and medical publishing is no exception in this regard. The difference lies in the kind of people who are associated with this industry—the authors, the specialized distributors, the readers are all associated with healthcare and want to keep abreast of developments in medical science, research and other related scientific developments. The size of the medical publishing industry is, thus, limited to such people. However, with the rapid expansion of the pharmaceutical industry, healthcare, and medical education and research, the industry has tremendous potential for growth. That said, content creation from a publisher's perspective is expensive and limits growth opportunities in a price-sensitive market like India, and so, any medical publisher's growth plan here has to negotiate this challenge.

Q: The medical market in India is considered very large and most global publishers plan print runs for this market. What is your take on India and how is it different from international markets?
Ajit: With a population of 1.32 billion, the market is large. The per capita amount spent on healthcare is US$267 per annum in India compared to the international average of over US$4000. India spends just 4 per cent of its gross domestic product (GDP) on healthcare compared to an international average of 10 per cent; the government spend is only 30 per cent of the total, the remaining being done by private players. With the government aiming to improve the quality of healthcare in India, the investments in this sector and in medical education and research are steadily increasing. Global publishers have therefore started considering India as a high potential growth market and are increasing investment in India. The market, however, is volume driven as selling prices need to be kept at a level the market can afford. Global publishers, thus, either plan special low-priced editions for the Indian market or publish reprints in India in larger quantities and at lower prices. Being in a predominantly distributor-dominated market, high discounts play a role in driving sales. Thus publishers tend to mark up the list prices and offer higher discounts to distributors to push the sales of their products. The levels of returns are increasing and the credit cycle is high, with payments being made to publishers in an average of 180 to 210 days. The discounts are showing a tendency to rise under pressure from distributors and the margins for publishers are diminishing.

Q: What are the challenges and specificities of medical publishing and selling in India?

Ajit: Medical publishing in India, be it books or journals, is still predominantly print, despite the rapid spread of the internet, and the sale of digital products has not threatened the existence of books as it has in the American and European markets. Publishers are, therefore, to a very large extent dependent on print books and journals for the growth of their business. The print-book market comprises the student education segment and clinical reference. The student market is dominated by local Indian publishers selling low-priced books, the quality of which still has scope for improvement. Foreign publishers have now made an entry into this market with some degree of success but price sensitivity remains a major area of concern. The clinical reference market continues to be dominated by foreign publishers selling original editions and low-priced special reprints for the Indian subcontinent. Publishing quality content at reasonable prices and still making a profit remains a challenge in medical publishing in India.

Q: Is the medical market still largely print? If so, why?

Ajit: The Indian medical publishing market is still predominantly print. Even though publishers are gradually venturing into the digital and online markets, the demand for print books continues to grow. While e-products are growing, the investments in this space are still not high enough to make a dent in the print space. As a result, while the number of titles published each year has been rising in the last three to four years, the online space, though growing, is far below international growth rates. Print-versus-e-book is not yet a topic of debate in the book industry and publishers in India have realized that print and digital formats are likely to coexist for some time, and in the future, lead to a hybrid publishing model that taps the strengths of both. The primary reason of the predominance of the print book over online content in India is the inadequate infrastructure for access to online and digital products in most parts of the country, as well as for the promotion of online and digital products. Digital India is still a distant dream. Internet penetration and average bandwidth availability in India are still one of the lowest in the world. Medical colleges, hospitals and educational institutions still lack basic infrastructure. Handheld devices and internet are still not widely affordable for the primary means of access for the average Indian customer/student/researcher. Pedagogy, especially medical pedagogy using digital tools, has still not caught on in India. Meanwhile, local Indian books are still available at affordable prices and are, thus, the preferred means of information and knowledge sharing.

Q: Is online/e-books and medical content picking up, in India or globally? What about supplementary tools like videos and tutorials for practical work in hospitals?

Ajit: Globally there has been a major shift of focus to online publishing in medical content. Publishing companies have invested heavily in the development of online content. The print- book market has shrunk rapidly in the last 4 to 5 years and some product lines are struggling for survival. Publishers who did not anticipate the market shift have lost out on their market share. The Indian scenario, however, is still print dominated. Supplementary tools like videos and phone apps are used only by a very small minority of institutions, not large enough to have a significant impact on the market.

Q: Content originated in India: is it growing and does it have a global reach? What are the numbers and growth plans for this going forward? Do elaborate on this programme and how it competes with local players like Jaypee and CBS.

Ajit: Establishing 'Indian Originals' in the Indian market has been a long and tough journey. The need for quality content, both in education and clinical reference, was recognized by Thieme right from the beginning. The decision to venture into this market was not without risks. The market was cluttered with local and regional publishers who had been in the business for over 30 years and reading their low-priced books had become a 'part of life' for the medical community. Dominant amongst these were Jaypee and CBS. With print runs of some titles of over 50,000–75,000 and low unit costs, competition with them was not so much on quality but on price. Thieme has been successful in making inroads in this market with quality and the reputation of its authors as its USP, but we still have a long way to go.

'Indian Originals' are primarily published for the Indian market and their reach in the international market is still limited.

Q: How does the Indian market fit into the global strategy of Thieme?

Ajit: The Indian operations of Thieme started in December 2007, thus we have completed 10 years of existence in India as an independent company. Starting with six employees in a 600 sq. ft business centre to over 70 employees, with office space of over 10,000 sq. ft, offices in Delhi and Mumbai, and sales representation in Kolkata, Lucknow, Hyderabad, Bangalore, Chennai and Kochi, the operations have grown from a sales office into a full publishing services company having its own publishing programme. The journey has been a satisfying one. The Thieme brand is now recognized in India and known for its quality content in medical publishing.

The Indian office of Thieme has been given the freedom to evolve its own publishing strategy, develop its own local publishing programme, and adopt a pricing strategy which suits the local market. The Indian company continues to sell the original books, journals and e-products of the group companies at Indian prices, publish locally commissioned books on education and clinical reference, and develop its own journals acquisitions programme. The Indian company also offers expansive editorial support services for journals and books for the group companies. The Indian operations are, thus, a significant part of the company's global growth strategy.

AJIT KOHLI is Managing Director and CEO, India and South Asia, Thieme Medical and Scientific Publishers. He joined Thieme in 2007 and was responsible for setting up operations in the Indian subcontinent. He has an over 30 years of experience in managing start-ups, profit-centre operations, business expansion, foreign collaborations and equity dilutions. He has worked extensively in the advertising industry as well.

54

HIGHER EDUCATION

"Teaching and learning services underpinned by technology"

Vikas Singh

Q: Given the promising landscape for higher-education publishing in India, what is your current and ongoing strategy for growth?

Vikas: India's higher-education sector is the largest in the world, with 30.1 million students enrolled across 48,116 universities and colleges. The annual enrolments are estimated to be 21.5 million per year, making it the third largest higher-education sector in the world by annual enrolments. However, at present, India has a low GER (gross enrolment ratio) of 18 per cent in higher education when compared with China (26 per cent) and Brazil (36 per cent) and the Indian government aims to increase this to 30 per cent by 2020. This would mean an additional 14 million students to the higher-education space would be inducted.

Given the potential the segment offers, as the world's learning company, Pearson, we are devoted to preparing students to compete in an ever-changing, global economy by using technology more effectively and by making learning personal. We create a complete learning experience through textual pedagogy, digital learning solutions, CD and web-based supplements, and instructor support.

We provide:

- High-quality college textbooks, plus new digital interactive tools that work alongside existing materials;
- Digital resources providing flexible access to online courses; and
- Implementation and training for instructors at higher-education institutions;

We also publish customized editions of academic book titles for universities and institutions, to cater even more specifically to the requirements of Indian students. Therefore, our strategy is to combine content and assessment, powered by services and technology, which will enable us to reach our goal of helping more learners learn more.

Q: What levels and areas are you focused on? Is it print or online; technology or content?

Vikas: We are focused on providing an engaging, interactive learning experience focused on academic achievement. Respected educators and practitioners author Pearson's long-trusted course content in a variety of formats—digital and print—so students can access them however they like.

We have launched a ground-breaking suite of new digital products that will change the way students learn and teachers teach, with rich content accessible online and offline in any environment. We have also introduced Pearson Digital Learning Solutions that are customized for teachers or colleges to provide low-cost programme solutions that meet the needs of both the students and faculty.

Q: What is your pricing strategy and how do you deal with the photocopier competition?

Vikas: We started our operations in India by offering the 'Low Price Editions' of our bestselling titles from across the globe. For example, a typical book in the US costs US$150; however, it is made available to the Indian readers at around US$12. Hence we continue to provide the best-in-class products at highly competitively price points. To answer the second part of the question, learning is moving beyond books and is becoming hybrid, hence photocopying the book would have limited benefits to the photocopier.

Q: What about local publishers? Are they competing in your markets or are their markets different?

Vikas: The higher-education landscape in India is overfilled with local publishers but with the advent of digital learning, the competitive landscape has transformed quite substantially. The new push is coming from technology companies who are working in the digital-learning space. However, Pearson is focused on how to shift the brand to become more experience-led, as increasingly the power is sitting with the learners who are influencing purchasing decisions, and increasingly we go directly to them. The company's ambition is to become more simplified and efficient and it is driven by the recognition that digital disruption in the education sector is heavily under way, with students now expecting new, predominantly digital, ways of teaching.

Q: Can you tell us a bit about your primary customers? What are their key requirements and how do you meet them?
Vikas: Our primary customers are those who seek to upskill or specialize themselves in any given subject area after completing K-12 or class 12. The current generation of learners is keen to adopt learning solutions which are tailor-made to individual requirements, are interactive in nature, convenient to use/access, and which provide continuous feedback/progress-check. As a result of which, we have adopted the strategy of providing personalized content and assessments backed by technology.

Q: What are the priorities for your publishing house, specifically in the next few years?
Vikas: Our mission is to help people make progress in their lives through learning—because we believe that learning opens up opportunities, creating fulfilling careers and better lives. We are building a more digital and sustainable business through our three strategic priorities:

- Investing in our fast-growing market segments, such as Online Programme Management, virtual and blended schooling and English-language learning.
- Growing market share through the digital transformation of our educational content and assessment businesses.
- Working to simplify our processes and operating model to drive efficiency and a better customer experience. Together, these three priorities will help drive the future growth of Pearson.

At Pearson, our commitment to efficacy and research is a true differentiator: rather than simply delivering on operational support, this engagement is leading to programmatic enhancements and improved student outcomes—a win for students and our higher-education customers.

VIKAS SINGH is Managing Director, Pearson India. He is responsible for spearheading the overall growth of the company in the Indian education sector by driving a robust business strategy and guiding excellence to strengthen the diversifying business. He has played a crucial role in making the region emerge as one of the most significant contributors to Pearson's global growth strategy.

55

BALANCING CREATIVITY AND COMMERCE

"A thriving market will see both bestseller and midlist working well"

Thomas Abraham

Q: How does the economics of trade book publishing work in India, given the low price base, large numbers of books and problems with piracy?

Thomas: Like it works anywhere else…it's just that the margins here are relatively lower. In the West you'll have a mark-up of 10 to 12 times the cost, and here you'll be between 2.5 and 5 times. Hence, within the margins left, we don't have as much to spend on marketing and promotions as they do in the West. The number of bookstores to people and even towns is very few. Piracy is another issue that is a constant spoiler.

Q: How does the value and volumes game work in trade publishing? Are print runs still large in the era of print-on-demand (POD)?

Thomas: POD has merely ensured the survival of the long tail and that very few books need to go out of print. But the fundamental thrust of trade business has to come from bestsellers, which more often than not do mean large print runs.

Q: What proportion of books tends to be bestselling? How do you deal with less successful books?

Thomas: The 80:20 rule applies here too…or perhaps the 90:10 in India. Less successful books are not to be confused with books with smaller print runs. A successful book is that which achieves its sales forecast. So, a 20,000 forecasted title that sells just 40 per cent of its run is a bigger failure than a 2,000-copy seller that sells out. The marker of a healthy market is bibliodiversity—something we had a decade ago and are slowly losing out on. A market cannot live by bestsellers alone. A thriving market will see both bestseller and midlist working well, and different segments working well.

Q: How do you find the bestselling books/authors? Has the role of literary agents evolved in this context?
Thomas: Yes and no. Whether offered by a literary agent, or picked from the slush pile, or commissioned, a bestseller is first an idea approved in-house, which has the particular editor's hunch and passion behind it. That is backed by the sales and marketing teams supporting the book and doing what it takes to build the first tailwind. After that it is almost always word of mouth.

Q: How does the resurgence of print impact general-books publishing? Are e-books and online content being developed as well?
Thomas: No particular impact because India never saw the e-book boom at all. It was always print and continues to be print. In between, for a couple of years, there was some buzz around e-books but unlike the West (where it peaked to being a 30 per cent contributor), in India the average stayed at being below 7 per cent.

Q: New growth areas like short-format mobile books and audio books are emerging. Could you tell us a bit about this evolving landscape?
Thomas: It's still early days. These are interesting times as publishers try to anticipate the next big thing. Short-format books so far have not worked in general; largely I suspect because those wanting that sort of content also want it free.

Q: English-language publishers are foraying into Indian languages. How do you see this development?
Thomas: There are Indian-language publishers who are very good at

what they do. I'm sceptical about English-language trade publishers trying to publish in Hindi, but am happy to be proved wrong. I've seen attempts at this but it is too fragmented a market and in general too low-priced a market to effectively engage with. So, sure, one will see many people trying this out but in the last 10 years, outside a couple of aberrant bestsellers, I've not seen any real traction anywhere where a single list has been built to being any sort of significant contributor.

Q. How does India fit in the global market game and is it a market of the future as well?
Thomas: India was and will remain a significant market simply because of that much-abused phrase 'demographic dividend'. The market is in a state of churn because of a lot of disruptions, but what can't be denied are the demographics of age, and market size, and gradually growing spending power. What is key, and something the industry is paying no attention to, is the building of readership.

Q: What are the challenges here, and how are trade publishers dealing with them?
Thomas: There are three main challenges, which are not being dealt with at all.

Readership: This has to be built outside just the next buzzy bestseller. This is critical not just for the market but for the intellectual and socio-cultural health of the country. The levels of reading that we achieve are going to have a far-reaching impact on the skilling levels of a young populace—the country's biggest challenge.

Piracy: As we compete with China, this is one area we have to get better on. We cannot have the absolute flagrant disdain we have for intellectual property rights (IPRs). The goverment cannot just wash its hands of any sort of enforcement because it thinks it has done enough by making books tax free. We need a separate IPR cell just as we have a separate cybercrime cell.

Low price market: Allied to all this is the fact that prices absolutely need to go up. I am not talking about textbooks or educational reference books which have a socio-economic angle to them and, yes, must be kept low priced. But all other segments need a gradual price increase.

THOMAS ABRAHAM is Managing Director, Hachette India. He was CEO and President of Penguin India during 2003-07, before he started at Hachette. He joined the publishing industry in 1994 as an editor with Oxford University Press India. He thereafter moved to marketing and left OUP to join Dorling Kindersley as Marketing Director in 2000. He joined Penguin Books in the same position following the buyout of DK by Penguin.

56

COMICS AND GRAPHIC BOOKS

"Comics are the best medium to communicate with children"

Gulshan Rai and Arpit Bhargav

Q: What is the need for comics and graphic books?

GR: The idea of Diamond Comics was to introduce comics at reasonable price to reach Indian children as we believe that comics are the best medium for communicating messages to children of any age/ any profile. We brought high-quality entertainment to Indian readers through the creation of original Indian comic characters like Chacha Chaudhary, Billoo, Pinki and Motu Patlu. The company also started publishing foreign comic books such as Phantom, Mandrake, Superman, Batman, Spider-Man, He-man and James Bond in Hindi. Our dedicated and creative team of publishing professionals is committed to producing high-quality multilingual books to both entertain and educate.

Q: How has digitization changed the comics scenario?

GR: Besides publishing, we have also ventured into the field of 2D and 3D animation and digitization of comic books. Fun-filled popular television serials and cartoon programmes based on our characters continue to entertain viewers of all age groups. We are also planning to launch an exclusive TV channel for kids in the near future.

Q: What have been the challenges in this industry?

GR: Diamond Comics faced a lot of challenges with more than 100 competitors and fast changes in the environment because of TV, digital and social media. But Diamond Comics maintained the quality of its publications in spite of all the challenges and performed changes in the stories and artwork in accordance with changing times and also entered electronic media in 1990. We released eight telefilms of 60 minutes each on Doordarshan based on Diamond Comics Super Heroes and after that a series of 500 episodes of Chacha Chaudhary on Sahara TV, followed by 500 episodes of Shaktimaan on Doordarshan and now Motu Paltu on Nick TV and Chacha Bhatija on Hungama TV.

At present we are working on a digital platform for mobile and web, where we are planning to launch all the comics (over 5,000) published by Diamond Comics in Hindi, English, and all the regional languages available on one platform and that too at a reasonable price, affordable for all. Also, digital animated comics (voice comic) of all the characters are available on YouTube.

Q: How has the market for comics changed over time?
GR: Diamond Comics was able to generate a very big market from 1978 to 1995 in print and thereafter, from 1995 to 2002, there was a great fall in print due to electronic media. But, after 2002, Diamond Comics was able to re-establish its print, electronic, and the digital markets and maintained number one position in the country.

Q: What future do you foresee for comics?
GR: We hope to maintain the continuity in print, digital, social and electronic media according to the changes in the environment.

Q: What are your views on digital publishing in India?
AB: Technology advancements continue all the time. But in the entertainment industry, content is the most important aspect. We, at Diamond Comics, aim to entertain the world with incredible content using new technologies. The growth possibilities are endless, because the digital era has just started in India. We feel the entertainment industry in India has potential for becoming a leading industry player across the globe; all we need is the right team and focus.

Q: What are the new areas of expansion in this segment?
AB: There are many big surprises coming up soon from the house of Diamond Comics. For example, we are coming up with a special animation series with one of the leading online players. Plus, we are also developing one short, animated film, which we'll submit in international film festivals. Besides, we have also launched our online reading app.

Q: How did Chacha Chaudhary comics start?
GR: Earlier, Chacha Chaudhary used to be printed in the *Lotpot* magazine. In our trading shop that time, *Lotpot* was very popular. Another character, who was very popular amongst children, was Cheeku, who appeared in the *Champak* magazine. Later, *Champak* compiled and published Cheeku books and they saw tremendous sales. That was the time, in 1978, when we started Diamond Comics. I called up Pran (the creator of Chacha Chaudhary), and told him that I wanted to make a collection of Chacha Chaudhary. In 1981, the first collection was out and we promoted it on popular radio channel Vividh Bharti. It was an instant hit. At that time, we sold 5–10 lakh copies, which was a big achievement. We published it in three languages—Hindi, English and Bengali and the price was Rs 8 only.

Q: How has the journey been and what were the main highlights?
GR: We kept the size of the comic unique, a size nobody else has ever adopted. Then the comic is different—it is not a magazine, nor a comic, nor is it a book. Our objective was to ensure that if a reader spends Rs 10, he must get readable material for 48 pages. Our size allowed us to give more pages at cost equal to a 32-page book.

Q: How did you manage to sustain and grow the brand?
GR: We later combined two comics and brought out a digest and named it *Diamond Comics Digest*. The price was kept at Rs 25. As time went by, we combined four comics to make a double digest. Today, a 48-page comic sells for Rs 30, a 100-page comic sells for Rs 100 and a 400-page comic sells for Rs 250.

The look has changed…we now print on better paper and we get the cover laminated. We also have talking comics on YouTube. Earlier, the readers used to take comics on rent, now people buy and read as the purchasing capacity has increased and parents like to buy books for their kids.

Q: How did you connect with your reader?
GR: The beauty of our comics is the positivity of all our characters. The reason for the popularity of Chacha Chaudhary is that the characters represent a family, just like our own. There are always good values to be learnt and the grandfathers always love their grandchildren. Chacha Chaudhary is just an ordinary old man, who adores his grandchildren. We made Billoo a naughty child, Pinki the darling daughter of the house, who is naughty too and loves to trouble her grandparents. I have developed all these characters and even the stories are so much a part of me. By the grace of God, we are still maintaining the quality of this publication.

Q: What are the different areas you ventured into to keep the brand alive with the reader?
GR: We are now in the digital domain too. In this, we have 5000 comics for children in different languages—Hindi, English, Bangla, Gujarati, and Marathi. Children can access them through the website and mobile app too. The beauty of our comics is that young parents, who have read the comics when they were children, are my promoters.

Our availability is very strong; our comics are available at news stands, railway bookstalls, magazine shops, online shops, etc.

We are also working on options for merchandizing of different characters. We have 40 characters and we wish to build around these only. We might add new characters to the prevailing ones.

Q: How do you continue and what are your plans ahead?
GR: A lot of our readers also help in the promotion of our comics... there are some doctors who order the comics for their clinics. Besides, we also do customized comics for corporates like ACC Cement and SBI.

We are selling 1.5 lakh copies in Hindi and English every month and sales have started in Bangladesh as well. We are also present in a mall in Dubai. We hope to increase our market in future.

GULSHAN RAI is Managing Director of Diamond Comics, the largest comic publishing group in India. In addition to Diamond Comics, he founded Diamond Pocket Books which has published over 2,000 books in Hindi, English, Urdu, Bengali and in other regional languages. Mr Rai has won a number of awards including International Professional of the Year by International Biographical Centre, Cambridge, UK (2005); Bharatiya Udyog Ratna Award by National Education and Human Resource Development Organisation (2005); and World Business Leader Award by World Confederation of Businesses, Houston, USA (2015).

ARPIT BHARGAV is Director, Diamond Comics Digital. He has more than 10 years of experience working on Indian and international TV commercials, entertainment, travel and lifestyle programming, and documentary films. He has worked for production houses such as Endemol, Bunim/Murray Productions, Sony Pictures, TLC, Sun Network, Zoom TV, Star India and Zee Network.

57

ILLUSTRATED BOOKS: A CHANGING WORLD

"Perils and opportunities of today"

Aparna Sharma

For over 40 years, DK (earlier known as Dorling Kindersley) has been publishing illustrated reference books for adults and children that have become staples on bookshelves in homes and libraries the world over—most notably children's reference and family learning. We carry a legacy of immense dedication to this genre, creating products of the highest quality.

But in the last decade or so, rapid development of new technologies and advent of the online world has changed our reading and learning habits entirely. The extent of this disruption has meant that there is a need to rediscover ourselves, break new grounds, and adapt to this ever-shifting landscape.

As publishers of illustrated reference, there are three things we have been asking ourselves:

Demand: Will anyone buy a reference book anymore?

Competition from free online sources is an issue in almost every category of non-fiction, but nowhere more so than in reference. Why buy a 3-kg encyclopaedia when you can get the definition for free? Why sift through pages and pages of information when you can find the answer instantly with the click of a button?

The answer is in winning *back* the book lover. Books as physical objects have to be instantly and incredibly arresting. The look and feel need to be as special as the content, making it an object of desire, of permanence, as opposed to a fleeting source of information.

And the information in them must be curated and rock solid, as opposed to a million entries on Google—who can tell what to read first or if the content is authentic?

There is now a definite blurring of lines between reference and coffee table. Illustrated books of all forms are also a huge percentage of the gift market—and DK book jackets are designed and created with a lot of thought and innovation—dye cuts, metallic foils, luxurious ink finishes and fabrics adding to a special tactile experience. Beautiful reference books that are not just a source of information, but also inspire the reader—to travel, to garden, to cook, to learn something new every day.

Discoverability: With brick-and-mortar retail disappearing, how do we get our books found?

Illustrated books in printed form depend on bookstores more than novels and biographies do. In the west, brick-and-mortar stores are fighting an abyss in cyber space, and here in India, we've never had enough, and space is at a huge premium. The silver lining is that with fiction going online, it could open up more bookstore display space for illustrated books. And as e-books now have a larger share of the fiction pie, booksellers have turned to illustrated non-fiction as a way of offering customers something they can't buy on most digital devices. Discovering them online is a challenge we're still grappling with. Digital marketing and social media play an important role in reaching the reader.

Digital: bane or boon?

We've been deeply committed to digital but it's become clear that the technology isn't quite there as yet to produce illustrated digital products that are genuinely satisfying—be it a cookbook, or kids picture book, or a travel guide. The digital illustrated books business achieves a single-digit percentage for most publishers. Yet, we are looking at a generation of people that consume knowledge visually, through the internet and television. How-to videos fill a need for the participant. We have to work harder at giving the reader what they need in a visual way. With so much content available for free, monetization is the biggest challenge.

What does this mean for DK in India?

India's business is becoming more and more relevant to DK as are the other growth regions across the globe. Traditionally, our children's list has been most popular, and this is where we continue to see maximum potential for growth, as demand for good-quality reference and learning content grows to cater to the aspiring middle class. Much more limited, but exciting nonetheless, is the demand for books on travel, food, sports, health and fitness, and several other lifestyle subjects – as the young and prosperous millennials become more adventurous and indulgent – holidaying, exploring, and learning new things.

We already have a great international list with several titles that appeal to the English-reading reader. Most of them are relevant as they are, with little or no need for adaptation. Besides the children and family-learning list, we do extremely well with books on yoga, pregnancy and childcare, history, science and business, to name a few subjects. In addition to this, introducing some India-centric titles has helped capture more interest in the list, becoming more relevant and reaching a wider audience within India.

We've also taken this opportunity to create some books on Indian subjects that will be sold in other territories, so not just bringing world-class products to India, but creating world-class products on Indian subjects that would appeal to a global audience. Our cultural, historical and geographical diversity offers an abundance of great content, so much of it poorly documented and presented to the lay reader.

This has been the most gratifying aspect of our local publishing, and one that we hope to keep growing. In a market like ours, where print runs can be as small as 1,500 for large-format illustrated books, we've printed 5000 units of our latest local title, and are now going in for a second print run.

As we spent more and more time understanding the market and getting feedback from our readers, I realized that contrary to the way it would have been some years ago, the Indian reader wants books by Indian experts, personalities and authorities they can relate to and identify with. I think this is a hugely positive change and the prospect of discovering and collaborating with local experts is an exciting one. But this has come with its challenges too—finding subject matter experts who can work and deliver to our exacting needs has been a difficult process, as has the task of finding well-archived images and objects to illustrate our books with. Often, there are poor or no records of ownership or inaccurate information about the images themselves. All this and DK's high standards of production and ethical guidelines make the whole business of illustrated publishing an expensive one.

There is also a huge opportunity in online of course, but monetization is not easy. According to a recent study by the telecom company Telenor, around 98.8 per cent of schoolgoing children in India have access to the internet in urban areas. Among them, 49.5 per cent access it from home after school hours, but more than 57 per cent parents said they allow their child to have only 1 to 2 hours of screen time per day, and 21 per cent restrict access to less than one hour a day. Understandably, parents are concerned about internet security and inappropriate topics that their children may encounter online, on social media and various websites.

DK has a free homework help website DK Find Out! that allows a child to search, learn, and explore information on a safe and secure site. It's the perfect site for help with homework, and DK's clear, reliable, and highly visual content covers all curriculum subjects and more. As DK's CEO, Ian Hudson, has pointed out: 'the opportunity for children's non-fiction shouldn't be seen as "a battle between books and the internet". Non-fiction books can be trusted gateways to additional materials on the internet which can enrich the entertainment or learning value that the book itself brings. And, of course, well-constructed e-books can deliver many of the intrinsic values of their physical counterparts.'

APARNA SHARMA is Managing Director of DK India, part of the Penguin Random House Group. She began her career with DK in 1999 as Project Art Editor, and quickly rose to become Head of the General Books division in 2003, gaining valuable exposure and experience handling multi-dimensional projects and teams.

58

ILLUSTRATED BOOKS: AN AFFORDABLE LUXURY

"The art of publishing art books"

Trisha De Niyogi

Despite a long-term decline in the circus industry, Cirque du Soleil profitably reinvented circus by creating a *blue ocean* market for itself. When I first read about this phenomenon, I could somehow relate to Niyogi Books entry point in the Indian publishing industry. At a time when hard market data for the Indian publishing industry was non-existent, acute observations, experts' views, and a gut feeling were essential in taking any major business decision. The decision to publish large-format illustrated books from the Indian subcontinent had its own challenges as well as opportunities.

Till a few decades back when high-quality large-format books on the Indian subcontinent were published primarily by international publishers like Phaidon and Rizzoli and imported to India, the prices of these books was quite high and thus they were inaccessible to most of the Indian readership. But today, many indigenous publishers have picked up the gauntlet effectively.

However, in a country where bestselling books are in the Rs 150 to Rs 500 price range, large-format illustrated books, whose costs of production are higher than the marked price of these bestsellers, are looked upon with trepidation. Despite that, a few publishers like Roli, Mapin, Marg, as well as Niyogi Books have taken up this challenge. I remember, a few days before the launch of *Nainsukh of Guler* by Professor B.N. Goswamy, my father (Bikash De Niyogi, the owner of Niyogi Books) very casually mentioned to me, 'the art of publishing books can be best understood while publishing art books'.

Large-format illustrated books, as against the popular terminology of coffee-table books, are a segment that dovetails two segments of the publishing industry—trade publishing and/or reference books—and is most definitely an existing niche market with discerning readers all across the globe. In fact, with the advent of internet, coffee-table books also shape-shifted and adapted to changing times, technology and demands. The ever-expanding digital libraries of photographs being made available for free, rendered coffee table outdated. And as product innovation continued, large-format researched books with photographs, paintings and other illustrations made their way into the hands of readers. Once considered useful for the casually informed discussion and imparting snob value, these large-format illustrated books have evolved into reference material for many specialized as well as unique subjects.

For example, in 2016, Niyogi Books published a tome on the history of horse racing in india. It is perhaps the only book on that subject in India today and it might come as a surprise that the moderately priced book was eight years in the making. Another coffee-table book, which caught my attention in the last couple of years was *India: Five Senses* published by Roli Books. The crowdsourced photographs, compiled after an online competition, were stitched together and given perspective by celebrated filmmaker Shyam Benegal in his compelling foreword.

Apart from curating content, the Indian publishing industry, pays significant attention to the user–reader interface as well as the user–reader experience. Today, apart from coffee-table books, large-format illustrated books have another avatar, with a fine balance between text and visuals/images/paintings and/or other illustrations. Marg's special edition of the Kochi-Muziris December 2016 Biennale is a splendid example of the balance between researched text and quality visuals. Another book worth a mention in this context, is Mapin's *Gifts of Earth* by Stephen P. Huyler, which was my childhood favourite. *Alluring Kashmir: The Inner Spirit* by Irfan Nabi and Nilosree Biswas, brought out by Niyogi Books, is another such book. As a matter of fact, scientific evidence confirms that visual aids help in creating a better aesthetic experience as well as promote memory and recall. Especially when one is reading a book on paintings and art and architecture or dance, pictures make it easier to grasp and remember.

For a product designed for a niche market, communication and marketing become extremely crucial and niche marketing in this instance is aimed at a specific target audience. In many cases 'niche' many not even exist, it is created by identifying what the consumer wants; thereafter come smart marketing and communication strategies. However, it is imperative to understand each book has its own niche audience. For example, *Crafts Atlas of India* by Jaya Jaitly has a different audience from *Indian Classical Dance* by Leela Venkataraman. To make it simpler, each genre has a different niche target audience. For example, people interested in a recently published Niyogi Books title, *Maps of Delhi,* may include people involved in urban planning, architecture, history, and Delhi enthusiasts. On the other hand, takers for *Food Path: Cuisine Along the Grand Trunk Road, from Kabul to Kolkata* would most likely be different, with of course some overlaps. Similarly, the target audience for the title *Chikankari: A Lucknawi Tradition* is again largely different from that for the other two.

However, the challenge arises not in the identification of the target audience, but in getting the information across to it. For books of this nature, social media may not prove to be the most serious platform for reaching interested readers. The process of reaching target readers is quite labour intensive and is mostly through the traditional distribution channels. While book reviews are one of best ways of reaching desired readers, the space for reviews of such books in Indian newspapers and magazines is shrinking by the day. However, we do see good coverage from time to time. One of our stellar successes was when one of our bestselling titles *Mapping India* by Manosi Lahiri, was featured in *Forbes* magazine as well as reviewed in *The Times.*

Apart from reviews, e-mailers, and other marketing channels prevalent in publishing, each book, which gets personalized attention from our in-house designers, editors, and printers, should also be marketed individually as well as collectively. In this process, we have realized that each of the books we have published serves a purpose of its own. For example, one of our bestselling titles, *The Forgotten Palaces of Calcutta* by Joanne Taylor, published in the year 2006, may have been one of the earliest sparks for the ongoing movement to preserve these great houses of Kolkata from being destroyed or demolished. Another book, which has been instrumental in highlighting cultural harmony, was the title *Historic Temples in Pakistan: A Call to Conscience* by Reema Abbasi.

To conclude, niches exist for discerning readers seeking well-researched and well-produced illustrated books. It is for a marketer to identify these niches and target marketing strategies accordingly. We have to look back as well as forward and develop and define our own niches. The existing niches may evolve in different ways in the future and new and promising ones will surely open up.

TRISHA DE NIYOGI is Business Development and Outreach Officer at Niyogi Books, where she heads business development, strategic planning and marketing. She began her career in publishing with SAGE. She has also worked in various projects in product development, marketing and advertising with multinationals including PepsiCo, Toshiba, EY and Tesco-Trent.

59

ONLINE AUTHOR EDUCATION AND SUPPORT

"Offering the market more choice than before"

Keith Ogorek

The Author Learning Centre (ALC) is a one-of-a-kind online author education community designed to help educate, motivate and support authors at every stage of their writing and publishing journey, including marketing the book.

Q: What is the role of self-publishing in the publishing world today? Has it changed over the last decade or so?

Keith: Self-publishing has created a dramatic shift in power and control of the market. Prior to self-publishing becoming a viable alternative, the power to decide what readers could purchase rested in the hands of agents and publishers. But now authors who self-publish have a say in what is available to readers. So the market offers more choice than ever before. In addition, authors who believe in their books can still make them available to readers even though agents and publishers may reject them. Publishing is now democratic.

This revolution started about 15 years ago, but what has changed in the last decade is that self-published books are better. More authors are taking more time to write a better book and investing in editing so their book is as good as it can be. A second trend is Hollywood is now looking at self-published books for ideas. That would not have happened 10 years ago.

Q: What kind of author services does your company provide? What has been the experience and trends in India?

Keith: If you are looking to self-publish, you have three options. The first is Do-it-Yourself (DIY), where you do everything yourself using a platform like Lulu. The second option is what I call General Contractor, where you hire the people to do the work, but you coordinate the activities. The third option is Supported Self-Publishing, which is one company that offers every service you need to get your book done.

Simply put, there are authors who want the convenience of having a one-stop shop of professional services available to them. That way they don't have to depend on their own talents or take the time to search for what they need. They have one phone number to call to get everything they need to get their book complete.

As for India, our experience has been similar to other countries around the world. There are certain authors who prefer to work with one company rather than do the work themselves or try to find the resources they need. We have served nearly 3,000 authors and have more than 2,000 books currently available for sale with hundreds of books in the production process.

Q: How does the economics of self-publishing work for publishers? How can it be compared to traditional publishing?

Keith: The main differences between self-publishing and traditional publishing are who makes the investment of money, who controls the content and speed to market. In both cases, authors earn royalties, but traditional publishers have the ultimate say over the final content and how soon it is made available to readers. Self-publishing requires the author to make the financial investment, but he is in control of the content and speed-to-market decisions. Also, in most cases, the author can earn a higher royalty percentage when he self-publishes.

Q: How do you ensure availability and discoverability of self-published books?

Keith: Because we are the leader in the supported self-publishing space, we have relationships with all distributors and make sure books are pushed into the channel and available for order. We do it for the author so he doesn't have to chase all those relationships.

The key to discoverability is having a clear picture of who the audience is for your book and then reaching those people through social media to start with. If an author says the audience for his book is every man, woman, and child on the planet, he will probably never be discovered.

Q: What are the services most used? Is it publishing services or dissemination?

Keith: The services most authors use are book and cover design for both print and e-book. And we make sure those books are available in distribution. Books used to be a planned purchase, but with online purchasing and digital books, books are now a spontaneous purchase. So authors don't have to make a decision about what distribution or formats they want. We make sure their books are available for readers anywhere and in any format they want to read.

Beyond those services, a number of authors also purchase editing services to make sure their book is as good as it can be. Marketing services are not as significant for Indian authors because it is a bit more difficult to cover the market with one service.

Q: Since most of the authors don't opt for marketing services, what is the average success rate of such self-published books?

Keith: Success is defined in so many different ways for self-published authors. For traditional publishers, they have one measure, books sold through the channel, but self-published authors publish books for many more reasons. Some use it to support a business or ministry. Some use it to promote a cause. Some publish to make sure their story is preserved. Book sales are not their only motivation, so we have lots of authors who consider themselves successful even if they haven't sold a lot through traditional means. Many authors sell lots of books directly from their speaking engagements or from their websites.

Q: Many self-published books get picked up by publishers for traditional publishing. Could you tell us a bit more about how this happens and why. Please share a specific case study.

Keith: There are two primary ways books get found by traditional publishers. First, many traditional publishers operate self-publishing platforms. That gives them early visibility into books that are getting early sales momentum. A second way self-published books get discovered is by agents or editors watching lists on Amazon. If they see a book climbing, they will reach out through social media to contact the author.

A great example is the book, *The Top 5 Regrets of the Dying*, written by Bronnie Ware. Bronnie was a palliative care nurse and began to see themes among the people she was working with near the end of their lives. From that experience she wrote a book. However, she lived outside of any major city in Australia and had no hope of finding an agent or publisher so she self-published with Balboa Press, which is a division of Hay House, a traditional publisher. Her local paper wrote a story. Then the *Guardian* in the UK picked it up and it spread like wildfire on Facebook. Within a month, Hay House picked up her book and now it has been translated into 27 languages. Had it not been for self-publishing, Bronnie would have never been published and Hay House would never have seen the book and the world would not have been enriched by her writing.

Q: How do publishers remain relevant in an arena where self-publishing and purchase of bespoke services becomes easier? What is the future of traditional publishing versus self-publishing?

Keith: Publishers are like movie studios. There are some books that would benefit from the expertise and experience of a traditional publisher, just like some movies need the resources of a big studio to make the project come to life. So as long as there are books like that, traditional publishers will always have a role. As for the future, I think traditional publishers will publish fewer books, but they will be bigger books. Just like we see with movie studios. Self-publishing will continue to grow as more titles are made available in the market so readers will have more choice than ever before. That will be a good thing because more authors who can impact people with their writing will have that opportunity. Also, self-publishers will offer more resources to authors such as The Author Learning Centre (www.authorlearningcenter.com) to help authors produce better books and get to their goal.

KEITH OGOREK is President, Author Learning Centre. He has led many innovations in the self-publishing industry and is featured in the book, *Innovation – How Innovators Think, Act and Change Our World*. He has written three books and a number of white papers,and speaks at leading industry events. Keith is a regular webinar presenter for the Author Learning Centre.

60

ENGLISH AND INDIAN LANGUAGE

"A book is a product and you should be its CEO"

Naveen Valsakumar

Notion Press is a technology-based self-publishing start-up, which provides high-quality publishing services to authors, who dream of publishing their own books.

Q: What is the role of self-publishing in the publishing world today?
Naveen: Self-publishing is, like everything else in the world right now, a more accessible and fair platform to publish an aspiring author's book. It allows the author to test their content in the market and perfect it until their target readers are happy—until the book has the desired takeaway. It is like creating a Minimal Viable Product, a technique that a lot of app creaters follow. They create the app with essential features, get feedback from early adopters and then modify to cater to their target consumers.

Technology plays a huge role in every industry and the publishing industry is no different. Print on Demand is a boon for publishers and writers—mix that with self-publishing and there's no stopping writers from writing what they want to and readers from reading what they seek. Self-publishing is the future of publishing and writing. What we're doing is just taking the best of traditional publishing and creating new opportunities with modern publishing techniques.

Q: How did Notion Press come into being?
Naveen: Identifying a need is vital to any successful business. Jana, Bhargava and I, the co-founders of Notion Press, weighed that against our expertise and found this venture to be a perfect fit. Coming from a strong technology background, innovation and change were our main objectives.

Launched in January 2012, Notion Press offers various high-quality publishing, book printing and distribution options to both authors and publishers from around the world. Notion Press is a launch pad for writers from India to publish and sell paperback or hardbound books and e-books around the world. Authors are mentored by a team of publishing and book marketing experts who assist them at every step of the publishing process. Now being a published author is no longer a distant dream for anyone bitten by the literary bug and eager to narrate their stories.

Within a short span of time, we have published over 1,000 books and sold in over 100 countries, while still growing aggressively everyday. After raising funding worth US$1 million in 2016, we are currently in the process of expansion. Recently, the company has added another feather in its cap by launching India's first open access academic platform called scholarink.com. The platform has been introduced to provide academics an opportunity to collaborate with industry experts to deliver high-quality academic content. We have 110,000 community members and 85,000+ registered writers.

Q: What are the challenges you faced and how did you overcome them?

Naveen: The concept of self-publishing itself is not clear to people. A lot more awareness has to be built about how self-publishing functions. If your book has nice content, people will read it. We try to create this awareness among people. It is a continuous journey and we are constantly striving to come up with innovative ways to change the industry and make publishing fair, accessible and profitable for any aspiring writer. Our tools, packages and guided publishing programmes are fluid and constantly customized according to the needs of our authors.

We are also always analyzing our data and watching out for emerging patterns to further tailor and better the publishing process. All this, keeping in mind our vision. We are slowly seeing change for the better but we know we have a long way to go and we can't wait.

Q: How does the economics of self-publishing work?
Naveen: The author has complete control over the book. We work to guide authors and provide them the services they need to bring out the book. We have a bouquet of services and the author decides which service he wants. But the author has to be involved and be part of every step, because, like I mentioned earlier, they are the CEO. At Notion Press, we only charge for the services we provide and authors get 100 per cent royalty on their books.

Q: With self-publishing finding credibility, how has the role of publishers changed?
Naveen: Self-publishing is all about the author. We provide our expert services to guide the author. People trust us as being a repository of such knowledge and come back to us for the same. The data, feedback and expert advice, the competition, the marketing for a book which we provide is valuable. What we provide is quality to an existing product, the manuscript. By the end of the publishing process the manuscript transforms into an industry standard book. Most of our authors are repeat customers. We have published over 50 books for one author alone.

Q: Your take on e-books and print-on-demand (POD)?
Naveen: Though e-books have made inroads, book lovers still love the physical book…the smell of it, the joy of going and buying a new book. As much as the world is tech-driven, readers fondly pick up a book to get away from the virtual world. People still want to dig deep to learn about something or lose themselves in a magical universe they can be a part of for a while.

We suggest people go in for POD, as it is more feasible, logical, and convenient and saves costs. It removes the pressure of immediate sales and allows the author to build a community of followers, create a persona and reputation for themselves and sell the book whenever they want, wherever they want.

Q: What future do you foresee for self-publishing at large and for Notion Press in particular?

Naveen: By creating more awareness, more and more people will start opting for self-publishing, because authors want the publishing process to be easier and quicker. Self-publishing is growing day-by-day and is also finding credibility. Another major factor is transparency as the author always knows how their book is faring in the market. Technology is affecting the industry in ways we couldn't imagine and we have to accept, be ready and take advantage of it. Innovation is key to any industry, why shouldn't it be the same for publishing?

Apart from making the process easier and more accessible, we, at Notion Press are trying to come up with ways to help authors write better and be better informed. We are always starting new projects and experimenting with the market to come up with sustainable and practical solutions for our authors. I don't think we'll ever stop innovating. Imagine if Google did that.

NAVEEN VALSAKUMAR is Co-Founder and CEO, Notion Press, and handles business operations, marketing and sales at the company. He strongly believes in technology's ability to change lives and leverages it in his endeavour to change the way books are created and authors are launched. Naveen refers to himself as a 'humour monger' who spouts one-liners at the drop of a hat.

61

TECHNOLOGY-BASED SOLUTIONS

"Catering to a growing market"

Nitin Shah

Q: How would you define self-publishing?

Nitin: Self-Publishing will be defined differently depending on who you ask. According to people who work in traditional publishing houses, authors who pay for their editing, formatting, and cover design are self-publishing their work. The book is traditionally published only if the publishing expenses are paid by the publisher. However, this often excludes marketing services.

In the purest sense, self-publishing occurs when an author handles the entire book publication process, including printing, distribution and marketing. Author execution of all details during the self-publishing process is also commonly called independent publishing. The author either has the skills to carry out the book publishing steps, such as book formatting, or employs professionals to complete the process for him/her. The author largely creates his/her own self-publishing experience, rather than purchasing a company's services.

Then there are authors who publish with the help of a self-publishing company. This is also self-publishing as the author is financing the majority of the publishing process. There are many different self-publishing companies available to authors who want to self-publish.

Some self-publishing companies offer publishing services to authors who are unable or would rather not deal with the details of the publishing process. In this instance, the author pays the self-publishing company to handle the publishing process for her. Examples of services commonly provided include ISBN assignment, book-cover design, interior layout, editing, distribution and marketing. Some self-publishers only get the book printed, while others mimic traditional publishing houses, providing the full set of publishing and marketing services.

Some kinds of self-publishers specialize in print-on-demand (POD) and commonly work specifically with authors who need very small quantities of printed books. POD publishers don't screen submissions and primarily offer printing and design services. POD is also used by larger companies occasionally to do test marketing or while reprinting the out-of-print books.

Q: How does the economics of self-publishing work?
Nitin: Economics of self-publishing depends on various factors like author, subject and language. The normal margin that a self-publishing company would work on depends on various aspects including these. Usually a self-publishing company works on a comfortable margin.

The entire production cost like typesetting, editing and proofreading, cover design, and paper is to be borne by the author. Additional cost for arranging a release function and for marketing will also have to be borne by the author. The publisher here will help the author in all such activities.

Q: Why is self-publishing growing?
Nitin: There is positive and growing need for self-publishing, especially in a growing economy like India. There are many budding writers, young and talented, who are interested in writing and projecting their thoughts through the written world. One of the main reasons for this is increase in the reading habit in the younger generation.

Q: How is the role of traditional publishers changing?
Nitin: The regular publishers' role has not changed so far in any way; instead they are always on the lookout for good upcoming authors in the self-publishing industry to be picked up and taken into their fold.

Q: How did Sapna venture into self-publishing and how has the journey been?
Nitin: Sapna started its regular publishing in 1990 and has so far

published over 6,000 regional titles in Kannada and Tamil and over 500 books in English, including academic titles useful for college, diploma and engineering students. Sapna created its own self-publishing brand 'Sapna Ink' two years ago and has so far published more than 100 titles in English, Kannada and Tamil. Authors as young as 13 years have also self-published their books through us. We provide an equal and good platform for marketing the titles too. Our team takes care in designing of the inner pages, of the quality of paper, the cover design, the size, etc. to fulfil the needs of the author and also from the point of view of the book and its subject. We take care of fulfilling an author's ambition and arranging for release functions and marketing the product at all our 16 stores and also through our online store. A few titles have become bestsellers and have gone in for reprints.

Since Sapna has been in the book trade for 50 years and in publishing for 27 years, entering self-publishing was very smooth. Further, with the kind of brand image that Sapna has built up over half a century, authors and writers trust us.

Q: What is the future of self-publishing?

Nitin: An extremely bright future is visible for self-publishing as more and more authors are opting for it, since it gives them the freedom to market and promote the books from their end too. Moreover, all the regular publishers want to publish only the bestselling authors, making it difficult for the new upcoming authors to be published.

The book industry which has been in existence for a very long time will survive and prosper against the onslaught of the online business. This is visible in the increase in publications, increase in self-publications, increase in bookshops and walk-in customers. In short, every segment will exist and survive side-by-side.

NITIN SHAH is Managing Director of Sapna Book House. He is also President of the Bangalore Book Sellers and Publishers Association, Vice President (South) of the Federation of Publishers' and Booksellers' Association in India, and Executive Member of the Federation of Educational Publishers of India. He received the Karnataka State Rajyotsava Award in 2008 for publishing as well as the Best Publisher Award from Kannada Pustaka Pradhikara.

LIST OF CONTRIBUTORS

Aarti David is Vice President, Publishing at SAGE India. She heads marketing and leads books commissioning across all subject streams. She is also responsible for managing joint imprints with Yoda, Popular Prakashan, Stree, Samya and Vitasta.

Adil Tyabji joined Orient Longman as an editor in 1968 before moving to Oxford University Press India in 1972, where his roles included Assistant Manager of the Bombay branch and thereafter Senior Editor till 1992. He has since been working as a freelance publishing editor for a wide range of publishers, organizations and individual authors.

Aditi Maheshwari-Goyal is Director, Copyrights and Translation Department at Vani Prakashan. She is Managing Trustee at the Vani Foundation and Advisor to Jaipur BookMark, Mumbai Lit-o-Fest and Indore Literature Festival. Aditi is also Curator of India's first Hindi literary festival 'Hindi Mahotsav', and teaches publishing and editing at University of Delhi.

Ajit Kohli is Managing Director and CEO, India and South Asia, Thieme Medical and Scientific Publishers. He joined Thieme in 2007 and was responsible for setting up operations in the Indian subcontinent. He has an over 30 years of experience in managing start-ups, profit-centre operations, business expansion, foreign collaborations and equity dilutions. He has worked extensively in the advertising industry as well.

Anil Chandy is Vice President, Major Reference Works at Springer Nature, where he leads Springer Nature's global reference publishing programme including the well-known scholarly reference brands Springer Reference and Palgrave Macmillan Reference. He is based in Singapore.

Anuj Bahri heads the BAHRI Group. A third-generation bookseller and literary agent, he worked at the New Delhi's Bahrisons bookstore for more than 20 years under the tutorship of Balraj Bahri. Thereafter, he looked at other avenues in the book trade and added a small publishing division called Tara-India Research Press, and a literary agency called Red Ink, to the BAHRI business.

Aparna Sharma is Managing Director of DK India, part of the Penguin Random House Group. She began her career with DK in 1999 as Project Art Editor, and quickly rose to become Head of the General Books division in 2003, gaining valuable exposure and experience handling multi-dimensional projects and teams.

Arpit Bhargav is Director, Diamond Comics Digital. He has more than 10 years of experience working on Indian and international TV commercials, entertainment, travel and lifestyle programming, and documentary films. He has worked for production houses such as Endemol, Bunim/Murray Productions, Sony Pictures, TLC, Sun Network, Zoom TV, Star India and Zee Network.

Asoke Ghosh is Chairman and Managing Director of PHI Learning. He has been associated with the International Publishers Association (IPA) since 1974 and is currently a member of IPA's Executive Committee. He is also a founder-member and twice President of the Federation of Indian Publishers (FIP). He is currently a member of FIP's Executive Committee and Chairman of its International Relations Committee.

Atiya Zaidi is Publisher at Ratna Sagar. She has 26 years of experience in writing and preparing books for children. She specializes in ELT, and creates course material for the social sciences, maths and science as well. She is on the faculty of two major publishing courses and is a founder member of the FICCI Publishing Cell.

Baldeo Bhai Sharma, senior media personality and thinker, is Chairman of National Book Trust. He has served as Editor of dailies such as *Dainik Swadesh*, *Dainik Bhaskar*, *Amar Ujala*, *Panchjanyain* and *National Duniya*. He is known for his participation in socio-political discourse on various news channels and has long been associated with Akashvani through numerous programmes. He also works with various social institutions.

Bipin Shah is Publisher and Managing Director of Mapin Publishing, publishers of illustrated books on the art and culture of India. Mapin offers packaging services to international publishers and museums and custom publishing solutions to corporate clients in India, and has expansion plans involving the development of educational content in the art, architecture and design, and children's segments. Bipin has recently led Mapin's introduction of BooksPlus Augmented Reality for illustrated-book publishers.

Bishan Samaddar is Editor and Book Designer at Seagull Books, and Instructor in Editing at the Seagull School of Publishing. He has worked at Seagull Books for more than seven years, and has edited books by numerous authors including Gayatri Chakravorty Spivak. He is a keen traveller and a phone photographer.

Chiki Sarkar is Publisher and Co-Founder of Juggernaut Books. She started her career in publishing with Bloomsbury Publishing in London, and after seven years moved to Delhi and joined Random House in 2006. In 2011 she took over at Penguin Books India, and following the merger of Penguin Books and Random House in 2013 she was made the India head of the new company. She set up her own publication house, Juggernaut, thereafter.

Devayani Devesh Abhyankar has been Director and Partner at Marathi-language publishers Continental Prakashan since 1994. She is a member of the Federation of Indian Publishers (FIP), and has won nine national awards from FIP for excellence in book production. For her contributions to publishing, Devayani won the Parvati Bhooshan Puraskar in 2013 and was feted by Lions Club Pune in 2014.

Emma House is Deputy CEO of the Publishers Association, the trade body in the UK for books and journal publishers. Emma has worked at the PA for 9 years, having previously spent 6 years in international roles at the London Book Fair and 6 years in international magazine publishing.

Geeta Dharmarajan is Founder and Editor-in-Chief of Katha. A writer, editor and educationist, Geeta is interested in learning across boundaries. Her work has focused on education, especially for children from economically poor families, and on linking India's diverse cultures, values and traditions through translations. Her interests have shaped the inclusive and integrated work of Katha and its various activities in the fields of literature and literary translation, community activism and education.

Gulshan Rai is Managing Director of Diamond Comics, the largest comic publishing group in India. In addition to Diamond Comics, he founded Diamond Pocket Books which has published over 2,000 books in Hindi, English, Urdu, Bengali and in other regional languages.
Mr Rai has won a number of awards including International Professional of the Year by International Biographical Centre, Cambridge, UK (2005); Bharatiya Udyog Ratna Award by National Education and Human Resource Development Organisation (2005); and World Business Leader Award by World Confederation of Businesses, Houston, USA (2015).

Himanshu Giri is CEO of Pratham Books, India's largest non-profit children's book publishing house. He has 20 years of experience in publishing and has worked on many public and private educational projects for setting up libraries for underserved children in India. He was one of the key team associates that set up Scholastic in India and was associated with the company for more than a decade.

Himanshu Gupta has been Managing Director of S. Chand Publishing since 2007. He has over 15 years of experience in the knowledge products and services industry. He was Vice President (South) of the Federation of Indian Publishers in 2012-13, and received the Young Publisher Award from the Federation of Educational Publishers in India for 2011.

Indira Chandrasekhar is Publisher and Managing Editor of Tulika Books, New Delhi and has been associated with the book publishing industry in India since the early 1980s. She is a founding partner of the Independent Publishers' Distribution Alternatives, a distribution network set up by eight independent publishers to promote alternative/independent publishing in India. Indu is also a member of the Paris-based International Alliance of Independent Publishers, and a trustee of the Sher-Gil Sundaram Arts Foundation.

José Borghino is Secretary General of the International Publishers Association (IPA). He joined the IPA as Policy Director in 2013 and was appointed to his current role in 2015. He came to the IPA from the Australian Publishers Association where he served as Manager of Industry Representation. His previous professional roles include teaching journalism and creative industries at the University of Sydney, Executive Director of the Australian Society of Authors, and senior positions at the Literature Board of the Australia Council.

Kanishka Gupta, a writer and publishing commentator, is Founder of the literary agency Writer's Side. His second book is forthcoming from Speaking Tiger in 2018.

Karthika V.K. is Publisher, Westland Publications. She started her career as an editor at Penguin Books India, and thereafter moved to HarperCollins India where she was Publisher for ten years. She joined Westland Publications, an Amazon company, in January 2017 to build a list that prioritizes literary fiction and narrative non-fiction. Over the course of her twenty-one-year career, Karthika has edited and published books in different genres including fiction, non-fiction, poetry and comics, and has worked with a number of award-winning authors.

Dr. K. Sreenivasarao is Secretary of Sahitya Akademi and has worked with the organization for more than two-and-a-half decades. He is a sitting member of the Press Council of India, Rashtrapati Bhavan Literary Committee, General Assembly of the Indian Council for Cultural Relations, Raja Rammohun Roy Library Foundation, and Doordarshan's Preview Committee, and is on the Council of Sangeet Natak Akademi. He has translated a children's dictionary from English to Telugu, and received the Delhi Telugu Akademi Award for 2011.

Keith Ogorek is President, Author Learning Centre. He has led many innovations in the self-publishing industry and is featured in the book, *Innovation – How Innovators Think, Act and Change Our World*. He has written three books and a number of white papers, and speaks at leading industry events. Keith is a regular webinar presenter for the Author Learning Centre.

Kristenn Einarsson has been Chairman, IPA Freedom to Publish Committee, since 2016. His other roles include: CEO, Norwegian Publishers Association; President, Bjørnson Academy (The Norwegian Academy for Literature and Freedom to Speech); Board Member, Norwegian Literature Abroad; Chairman, RiksTV; and Chairman, Norges Televisjon. He was CEO of Norwegian Book Clubs from 1991 to 2010, Chairman of the Kunnskapsforlaget publishing house during 2000-08, and Managing Director of Kunnskapsforlaget during 2008-10.

Michael Healy is Executive Director (International Relations) at the Copyright Clearance Centre (CCC). Prior to joining CCC, he was Executive Director of the Book Rights Registry. He has also worked for more than 20 years in UK's publishing industry. Michael has been closely involved in developing standards for the international book trade and has been Chairman of the International ISBN Agency. He currently chairs the International Standard Name Identifier (ISNI) Agency and is a director of the UK Copyright Hub.

Mini Krishnan is Translations Editor at Oxford University Press India. She is involved in sourcing fiction, plays, travelogues, autobiographies and biographies from sixteen Indian languages. She consults for Thunchath Ezhuthachan Malayalam University's translation programme, and writes two monthly columns for *The Hindu*. Mini also selects short fiction in translation for *Frontline*.

Namita Gokhale is Festival Director for the Jaipur Literature Festival (JLF), and is JLF's co-Founder-Director along with William Dalrymple. Her debut novel *Paro: Dreams of Passion* was published in 1984 and she has written 14 books of which eight are fiction. Namita published the Bollywood film magazine *Super* right after dropping out of college.

Naveen Valsakumar is Co-Founder and CEO, Notion Press, and handles business operations, marketing and sales at the company. He strongly believes in technology's ability to change lives and leverages it in his endeavour to change the way books are created and authors are launched. Naveen refers to himself as a 'humour monger' who spouts one-liners at the drop of a hat.

Neeraj Jain is Managing Director of Scholastic India. Before joining the publishing industry, he worked with media and direct marketing companies and has been in the Steering Committee of 'Excellence in School Education', an initiative by IIT Delhi. He is a member of CII and the American Chamber of Commerce.

Nirmal Kanti Bhattacharjee has been Editorial Director of Niyogi Books since 2013. In his previous roles, he was Editor of Sahitya Akademi's bi-monthly journal *Indian Literature* and Director of National Book Trust. He entered the publishing industry as a member of the editorial team for the Encyclopaedia of Indian Literature Project undertaken by Sahitya Akademi, and later took charge of the Akademi's Eastern Regional Office at Kolkata. He has also been Director of K.K. Birla Foundation, a private trust devoted to the cause of art, literature and education.

Nitin Shah is Managing Director of Sapna Book House. He is also President of the Bangalore Book Sellers and Publishers Association, Vice President (South) of the Federation of Publishers' and Booksellers' Association in India, and Executive Member of the Federation of Educational Publishers of India. He received the Karnataka State Rajyotsava Award in 2008 for publishing as well as the Best Publisher Award from Kannada Pustaka Pradhikara.

N.K. Mehra is Managing Director, Narosa Publishing House and President, Federation of Indian Publishers (FIP). He started his publishing career in 1959 and set up two companies, Narosa Book Distributors and Narosa Publishing House. Nandi, as he is popularly known, has been on FIP's Executive Committee for over ten years, and has also served on the Executive Committee of the Federation of Publishers' and Booksellers' Association in India where he was President for two terms.

Pankaj Bhardwaj is General Manager, Sales Operations at Taylor & Francis India. A publishing professional with over 20 years of experience, he looks after the company's HSS publishing business across the South Asia region, and has worked with leading international publishing houses in the past.

Pranav Gupta is Director of Prints Publications, an exporter of Indian publications since 1966. He is Member, Regional Committee, Northern Region for the Books, Publications and Printing Panel of CAPEXIL; and is also on the Executive Committee of the Federation of Indian Publishers. Pranav is Director of the Afro-Asian Book Council, and regularly participates in various social welfare programmes.

Prashasti Rastogi is Director, German Book Office of the Frankfurt Book Fair in New Delhi. She works at the cross-section of publishing, technology and entertainment to create networks that will build the future of content. Her recent initiatives include the Young Publishing Professionals Programme and a translation portal to provide community orientation to German-language translators. She has previously served as Head of Communication and IT at the German Academic Exchange Service South Asia office.

Rachna Singh Davidar is a literary consultant based in New Delhi. She has worked with books and writers for 30 years in India, the UK and Canada. She started her career with The Bookshop in New Delhi, which her family owns. She is currently the Programme Director of Lit For Life, the literature festival of The Hindu.

Ramesh Chandra Jain is the founder of Manohar Publishers & Distributors. Initially selling only rare and out-of-print publications, Manohar soon branched out into local sales and export of new books published in India, and thereafter into publishing scholarly works under its own imprint.

Ramesh K. Mittal is Director of D.K. Agencies, an exporter of books and publications since 1968 and bibliographic services provider since 1973. He is also Director of LiFi Publications. He is Immediate Past President, CAPEXIL and ex-Chairman, Books, Publications and Printing Panel, CAPEXIL. He is Secretary-General of the Afro-Asian Book Council and the Indian Reprographic Rights Organization, and Advisor to Akhil Bharatiya Sanskrit Prakashak Sangh.

Ratnesh Jha is Managing Director, South Asia, Cambridge University Press, and President of the Association of Publishers in India (API). His management career spans over two decades and he is passionate about the education ecosystem. He is Co-Chair of the FICCI Publishing Committee and a member of the Higher Education Committee. He is also advises start-ups and works as a fundraiser and volunteer for NGOs.

Ravi Deecee is Managing Partner of DC Books, a leading book publisher in Malayalam. He is also Managing Director of the bookshop chain Current Books (India) Pvt. Ltd. Ravi serves as President of the All Kerala Publishers and Booksellers Association.

Ravi Singh is Publisher at Speaking Tiger, a Delhi-based independent publishing company he co-founded with Manas Saikia. In the past, Ravi has been Editor-in-Chief and Publisher at Penguin India, and Co-Publisher at Aleph Book Company. Over 23 years he has worked with most of South Asia's finest writers.

Ritu Menon is Publisher at Women Unlimited. A writer and publisher who has been active in the South Asian women's movement for over 20 years, Ritu is the Co-Founder of Kali for Women, India's first and oldest feminist press, as well as the founder of Women Unlimited, an associate of Kali for Women.

Rohit Kumar is Managing Partner of Guiding Star Digital Publishers LLP and its subsidiary Chapter Apps Inc, where he is building and leveraging mobile technology platforms to improve productivity for professionals and students. Prior to starting his entrepreneurial ventures, Rohit was Managing Director, South Asia, Health Science Division, Reed Elsevier India. He was President of the Association of Publishers in India during 2013-15, and Co-Chair of the FICCI Publishing Committee during 2013-16.

S. Anand is Publisher at Navayana. He co-founded Navayana in 2003 along with Ravikumar, and in 2007 won the International Young Publisher of the Year award instituted by the British Council and London Book Fair. He has annotated Dr B.R. Ambedkar's *Annihilation of Caste* and *Riddles in Hinduism*, and curated and co-authored *Bhimayana*, the graphic biography of Ambedkar that has been translated into nine languages.

S.K. Ghai is Chairman of Sterling Publishers and other group companies, as well as Chairman of the Institute of Book Publishing. He has been associated with the institute since its inception in 1985. He was Chairman, Books, Publications and Printing Panel, CAPEXIL during 2008-11. He is also Executive Committee Member of The Federation of Publishers' and Booksellers' Associations in India. Mr Ghai has authored many books on the publishing industry, and is Editor of the e-journal *Publishing Today*. He is on the course faculty of National Book Trust and a member of the Expert Committee (Publishing) at IGNOU.

Saikrishna Rajagopal is Managing Partner of Saikrishna & Associates, a firm in the field of intellectual property. He has worked on a variety of intellectual property disputes in the past two decades and has appeared in many landmark cases. He has appeared before a Standing Committee of Parliament deposing with respect to the 2012 amendments to the Copyright Act, 1957.

Sanjiv Gupta is Chief Operating Officer, Penguin Random House India. He manages finance and operations for the company and has over 25 years of experience across a spectrum of industries. Before joining Penguin in 2011 as Finance Director, Sanjiv was Director at Masonite Doors and was leading operations in India. He has previously worked with Hines India Real Estate, Bharti Group, Honeywell International, Honda Cars and DCM in various roles.

Sesh Seshadri is Director of Lonely Planet India. He played a key role in Lonely Planet's entry into the Indian market in 2012. In addition to over four decades of publishing experience, Sesh is an entrepreneur and consultant. He established the publishing consulting company O.V.E.R.L.E.A.F. in 1997, and is a trustee of the Neelbagh Group of Schools. He was also Founder-Director at Textech that specializes in providing content solutions to publishers.

Shalini Singh is Director, Publishing Services, SAGE India. After many years of spearheading multiple roles in advertising, she shifted gears and joined publishing at an entry level in 2005. She established the Publishing Services division at SAGE India and is now responsible for SAGE Bhasha commissioning and production. Her other core responsibilities are managing India Editorial Production (Books and Journals) and SAGE Global (Publishing Services).

Sivaramakrishnan V. is Managing Director of Oxford University Press India, with regional responsibilities including Bangladesh, Sri Lanka and Nepal. He has extensive experience in the education services, e-commerce, automobiles and FMCG domains. In his previous assignment, Siva was Executive President, Education Services at Manipal Global Education Services. He worked for nearly ten years with the Ford Motor Company and has held various consumer branding roles within Proctor & Gamble.

Sumeet Gupta is Senior Director, FICCI where he heads Publishing, Homeland Security, Private Security, and Geospatial Technologies. He has over 19 years of experience in domains including science and technology, security, media and publishing. He was instrumental in creating the first international animation awards in India, and worked a report that formed the backbone of the second phase of FM radio privatization in India.

Sushmita Das heads the Journals Peer Review team for Taylor and Francis India. Her team handles over a hundred journals and is responsible for authenticating articles, peer review and publication. She has trained journal editors and authors on peer review systems, and has led workshops on publishing ethics, plagiarism and copyright. She has 17 years of experience in knowledge management and publishing functions.

Swati Roy is Founder and Festival Director, Bookaroo. She is passionate about children's books and, through Bookaroo, makes books come alive for children. After organizing 27 editions of Bookaroo and spending 15 years in the business, she thinks there is no place better than this. She started with Eureka, an independent bookshop exclusively for children, in 2003 with her partner M.Venkatesh.

Thomas Abraham is Managing Director, Hachette India. He was CEO and President of Penguin India during 2003-07, before he started at Hachette. He joined the publishing industry in 1994 as an editor with Oxford University Press India. He thereafter moved to marketing and left OUP to join Dorling Kindersley as Marketing Director in 2000. He joined Penguin Books in the same position following the buyout of DK by Penguin.

Tridib Kumar Chatterjee is Managing Director of Patra Bharati Group of Publications, a major player in the Bengali-language publishing industry. He is also Chief Editor of *Kishore Bharati*, a children's periodical. Tridib writes regularly in various Bengali newspapers and periodicals.

Trisha De Niyogi is Business Development and Outreach Officer at Niyogi Books, where she heads business development, strategic planning and marketing. She began her career in publishing with SAGE. She has also worked in various projects in product development, marketing and advertising with multinationals including PepsiCo, Toshiba, EY and Tesco-Trent.

Vikas Gupta is Managing Director of Wiley India and Immediate Past President of the Association of Publishers in India (API). He has led innovative product and business models for technology-driven learning solutions, research and faculty development, professional certifications and skills development. He has co-founded and led ventures in IT, medical electronics and publishing. Vikas is an ardent promoter of entrepreneurship and runs his own blog and video series to share his perspective on future business models and emerging issues in the technology, education and learning industries.

Vikas Singh is Managing Director, Pearson India. He is responsible for spearheading the overall growth of the company in the Indian education sector by driving a robust business strategy and guiding excellence to strengthen the diversifying business. He has played a crucial role in making the region emerge as one of the most significant contributors to Pearson's global growth strategy.

SELECT BIBLIOGRAPHY

Altbach, Philip G. and Choi, Hyaeweol. *Bibliography on Publishing and Book Development in the Third World, 1980-1993*. Santa Barbara: Praeger. 1993

Altbach, Philip G. *Knowledge Context: Comparative Perspectives on the Distribution of Knowledge*. New York: State University of New York. 1987

Athill, Diana. *Stet: An Editor's Life*. London: Granta Publications. 2000

Bhaskar Michael. *The Content Machine: Towards a Theory of Publishing from the Printing Press to the Digital Network*. London: Anthem Press. 2013

Butcher, Judith. *Butcher's Copy-editing: The Cambridge Handbook for Editors, Copy-editors and Proofreaders*. Cambridge: Cambridge University Press. 1975

Clark, Giles and Philips, Angus (eds). *Inside Book Publishing*. Abingdon: Routledge. 2014

Cosèr, Lewis A., Kadushin, Charles and Powell, Walter W. *Books: The Culture and Commerce of Publishing*. Chicago: The University of Chicago Press. 1985

Curtis, Richard. *Mastering the Business of Writing: A Leading Literary Agent Reveals the Secrets of Success*. New York: Allworth Press. 1997

Epstein, Jason. *Book Business: Publishing: Past, Present, and Future*. New York: W. W. Norton & Company, Inc. 2001

German Book Office New Delhi. *Perspectives on Publishing in India 2014-2015*. 2015

Greco, Albert, N. *The State of Scholarly Publishing: Challenges and Opportunities*. Abingdon: Routledge. 2009

Greco, Albert, N., Milliot, Jim and Wharton, Robert. *The Book Publishing Industry*. Abingdon: Routledge. 2013

Guthrie, Richard. *Publishing: Principles and Practice*. Thousand Oaks: Sage Publications. 2011

Horowitz, Irving. *Publishing as a Vocation: Studies of an Old Occupation in a New Technological Era*. Abingdon: Routledge. 2010

Israel, Samuel. *A Career in Book Publishing*. New Delhi: National Book Trust. 2009

Jassin, Lloyd J. and Schechter, Steven C. *The Copyright Permission and Libel Handbook: A Step-by-Step Guide for Writers, Editors, and Publishers*. New York: John Wiley & Sons, Inc. 1998

Kurowski, Travis (ed.). *Literary Publishing in the Twenty-First Century.* Minneapolis: Milkweed Editions. 2016

Levine, Mark. *The Fine Print of Self-Publishing.* Minneapolis: Bascom Hill Publishing Group. 2014

Malhotra, D.N. (ed.). *50 Years of Book Publishing in India since Independence.* New Delhi: The Federation of Indian Publishers. 1998

——— (ed.). *60 Years of Book Publishing in India.* New Delhi: The Federation of Indian Publishers. 2006

McGuire, Hugh and O'Leary, Brian (eds). *Book: A Futurist's Manifesto: A Collection of Essays from the Bleeding Edge of Publishing.* Sebastopol: O'Reilly Media. 2012

Miller McCune, Sara. *Being Sage.* Thousand Oaks: SAGE Publications. 2010

National Book Trust. *Editors on Editing.* New Delhi: National Book Trust. 2014

Nielsen. *The India Book Market: Understanding the India Book Market.* Nielsen BookScan, 2015

Ramrattan, Lall, and Szenberg, Michael. *Revolutions in Book Publishing: The Effects of Digital Innovation on the Industry.* New York: Palgrave Macmillan US. 2016

Raven, James. *The Business of Books: Booksellers and the English Book Trade 1450-1850.* New Haven: Yale University Press, 2007

Schiffrin, Andre. *The Business of Books: How the International Conglomerates Took Over Publishing and Changed the Way We Read.* London and New York: Verso. 2001

——— *The Business of Words.* New Delhi: Navayana Publishing. 2011

Smith, Kelvin. *The Publishing Business: From p-books to e-books.* New York: AVA Publishing. 2012

Striphas, Ted. *The Late Age of Print: Everyday Book Culture from Consumerism to Control.* New York: Columbia University Press. 2011

Sugrue, Ciaran and Mertkan, Sefika (eds). *Publishing and the Academic World: Passion, Purpose and Possible Futures.* Abingdon: Routledge. 2016

Thompson, John B. *Merchants of Culture: The Publishing Business in the Twenty-First Century.* New York: Plume. 2012

Woll, Thomas. *Publishing for Profit: Successful Bottom-Line Management for Book Publishers.* Chicago: Chicago Review Press. 2014

ACKNOWLEDGEMENTS

This book is the outcome of the generosity of its 65 contributors. Almost all agreed to contribute and most stayed the course. For every one that didn't, there was someone else who stepped into the breach and delivered to unimaginably short deadlines. It would be no exaggeration to say that this book wouldn't have been possible, in the schedule we planned for, without their extraordinary support. A special thank you to each one of them. Their collective heft has made the book bigger than the sum of its many parts.

The *All About Book Publishing* team were equally cooperative and worked hard and long. Without their persistent and polite persuasions, we would not have had the content on time. I would especially like to thank Shweta Khurana, Varsha Verma and Smita Dwivedi, for their ever-willing and can-do attitude.

Misha Oberoi Chakravarty, seamlessly designed the layout and gave the book a striking cover. Thanks to her, to Samprati Pani for her suggestions on the Introduction and to Shalini Shekhar for editorial support. Priyanka Misra went beyond the call of duty to ensure accuracy, consistency and completion. I cannot thank her enough for her publishing support for this project. Giving the book a befitting face and frame would have been impossible to do without all of them.

My grateful thanks to the eminent individuals who gave testimonials and recommendations, ensuring strong tailwinds for the book's takeoff.

I would also like to acknowledge Cordite Publishing Inc., *Cordite Poetry Review 55,* for allowing us to use excerpts of S. Anand's interview.

My employer, Taylor & Francis, was a supportive force, that encouraged me on this journey.

NITASHA DEVASAR is Managing Director, Taylor & Francis India. In her current role, she focuses equally on business development and acquiring high quality academic content from South Asia for global markets.

An academic publisher with over two decades of experience in leading teams and managing content, she was Academic Publishing Director at Oxford University Press India from 2000-2012. In 2012 she set up PublishInc., a consulting firm that partnered with academic societies, universities and government agencies for effective outreach of quality research. She has been a publishing consultant with the Government of Sikkim, Population Foundation of India and Ambedkar University of Delhi, where she developed the concept for the first full-time teaching course in publishing.

Nitasha holds several industry positions and is currently Vice President, Association of Publishers in India (API). She sits on the FICCI Publishing Committee and the Board of the Indian Reprographic Rights Organisation. In these roles Nitasha works with peers in the industry to impact government policy on key issues relating to publishing and garners support for causes like copyright awareness.

Nitasha is Advisor to the Women Leadership Forum of Asia (WLFA) and was featured as one of Asia's Women of Substance 2017 by Channel News Asia (CNA). https://youtu.be/c3IhJp8fHrM

She is part of the Taylor and Francis Group Women Leadership Programme and its Women in Publishing group, and mentors aspiring leaders within the organization.

She writes occasionally, on life in today's India and her leadership journey, and is currently writing a book on the topic. Her articles can, most often, be found in *The Hindu*.